MW01284952

Speaking in Tongues

Speaking in Tongues

A Critical Historical Examination

Volume 1: The Modern Redefinition of Tongues

PHILIP E. BLOSSER
and
CHARLES A. SULLIVAN

Forewords by
Dale M. Coulter and *James Likoudis*

PICKWICK *Publications* · Eugene, Oregon

SPEAKING IN TONGUES: A CRITICAL HISTORICAL EXAMINATION
Volume 1: The Modern Redefinition of Tongues

Pickwick Publications
An Imprint of Wipf and Stock Publishers
199 W. 8th Ave., Suite 3
Eugene, OR 97401

www.wipfandstock.com

PAPERBACK ISBN: 978-1-6667-3777-6
HARDCOVER ISBN: 978-1-6667-9761-9
EBOOK ISBN: 978-1-6667-9762-6

Cataloguing-in-Publication data:

Names: Blosser, Philip [author]. | Sullivan, Charles A. [author] | Coulter, Dale M. (Dale
Michael), 1970– [foreword writer] | Likoudis, James [foreword writer]

Title: Speaking in tongues: a critical historical examination : volume 1: the modern
redefinition of tongues / Philip E. Blosser and Charles A. Sullivan.

Description: Eugene, OR: Pickwick Publications, 2022 | Includes bibliographical refer-
ences and index.

Identifiers: ISBN 978-1-6667-3777-6 (paperback) | ISBN 978-1-6667-9761-9 (hardcover)
| ISBN 978-1-6667-9762-6 (ebook)

Subjects: LCSH: Glossolalia | Pentecostalism | Church history | Language and languag-
es—Religious aspects—Christianity | Gifts, spiritual

Classification: BT122.5 B56 2022 (paperback) | BT122.5 (ebook)

VERSION NUMBER 092922

To the fourth-century Church Father, Cyril of Jerusalem,
whose observations on Pentecost first alerted us to the fact
that there was much more on the subject of speaking in tongues
yet to be discovered.

To those who are intellectually curious about the Christian doctrine
of tongues but have not yet found a substantive answer;
and to those experiential mystics who want to know
the history behind speaking in tongues.

To the late Thomas M. Reid, former Master of Formation
of the Community of Secular Discalced Carmelites at Assumption
Grotto Parish, Detroit, and author of *Carmelite Spirituality
and the Charismatic Renewal* (2009).

Contents

Copyright Notices

Foreword

DALE M. COULTER, DPHIL OXON.
Pentecostal Theological Seminary

FROM THE EMERGENCE OF Pentecostalism at the Azusa Street Mission, the relationship between speaking in tongues and baptism in the Spirit has been questioned. Early Pentecostals understood the charge of novelty and tried to rectify it by writing histories of tongues, the earliest of which were published in 1907 and 1908. The goal was not to find speaking in tongues under every rock in the history of Christianity, but to find enough representation to anchor their claim.

It should be no surprise that early Pentecostals sought out Luke-Acts in their quest to find a sign for the charismatic and sanctifying grace poured out through the baptism in the Spirit. They were operating within a Wesleyan framework that went back to John Wesley and John Fletcher. The association between Lukan Pentecost and baptism in the Spirit stems from Fletcher's effort to ground Wesley's notion of Christian perfection in biblical soil. Drawing on Clement of Alexandria and the Pseudo-Macarian homilies, Wesley himself sought to incorporate the idea of purity of heart and a movement from perfection to perfection into a western Protestant framework. As Wesley noted, grace is short-hand for the multiple operations of the Spirit in the heart beginning with the Spirit's prevenient work in all persons and concluding in that final movement upward and inward to glorification. In thinking about baptism in the Spirit as another work of grace or a distinct operation of the Spirit, Pentecostals were simply teasing out the implications of this Wesleyan framework through their reading of Luke-Acts.

What one discovers in Christian tradition is the regular claim that God adapts grace to the human condition as the Spirit intersects with the soul in a journey from the church's initiatory rites to its last rites. Moreover, this grace is nothing less than the Spirit's own presence as gift, poured out in love to reorder the soul's interior cognitive and affective movements. Within this framework, love as ecstatic embrace and encounter became a crucial way to talk about the adaptation of grace to the soul in and through sacramental encounters. All encounters were mediated and sacramental because the development of seven sacraments in the High Middle Ages was never divorced from sacramental practices such as anointing a church or the view that creation itself was sacramental. The early and medieval Christian worlds were charged with the grandeur of God who could be encountered in a variety of ways, including reading Cicero's *Hortensius*, as Augustine noted in his *Confessions*. The Spirit was always intersecting with the human heart to turn the affections toward God, which is the basic meaning of the Latin term *conversio*.

Given the importance of encounter, notions of sanctity and miracle-working power fused together in the Christian mystical stream. There is no clearer representative of this than Gregory the Great's portrait of Benedict of Nursia as an Italian wonder-worker. Indeed, the Catholic notion of sainthood continues to trade on the intersection of moral purity and charismatic power. Medieval theologians like Bonaventure attempted to integrate the more process-oriented journey through the seven sacraments into the encounter-driven experience of the mystic. The language of ecstasy came to the front as both a way to describe the prophetic experience of an Old Testament saint as well as the vision of a medieval saint. Ecstatic embrace was to be caught up in the grace of the Spirit poured out through the sacraments. It was a mode of spiritual encounter. There were a variety of signs for this ecstatic union such as charismatic tears, contemplative vision, affective yearning, and, yes, tongues.

In the Latin medieval imagination, there was a fluidity between speaking a known language and uttering something more mysterious and unknown. The latter normally was communicated through the Latin phrases *lingua ignota* and *lingua incognita*. Richard of St. Victor placed both phrases in the context of ecstatic encounter when he said that *lingua ignota* referred to angelic revelation while *lingua incognita* to divine *aspiratio* in which "aspiration" was more like the enunciation of a word as breath left the body. God would divinely exhale upon the person who then began to enunciate. Richard found this not only in Paul's "tongues of men and angels" but also in the Psalmist's declaration that "I heard a language I did not know" (Ps 81:5). The point for Richard was that the grace of contemplation gives rise to altered mental statements (an *alienatio mentis*) that the metaphorical expression of an unknown tongue, with its evocation of free vocalization, captures. The phenomenon Richard attempts to describe fits within a larger arena of imaginative and ecstatic speech. One could even place Hildegard of Bingen's *Ignota Lingua*, an imaginative language complete with its own alphabet, into this sphere. The Latin term *inventio* means both to find and discover, and thus language construction as well as mental imagination involves both. To engage in free vocalization is a form of *inventio* within this Latin medieval mentality, and, at least for Richard of St. Victor, one possible effect of contemplative ecstasy.

This way of interpreting "tongues speech" as ecstatic utterance is what Philip Blosser and Charles Sullivan seek to challenge in the current work. After surveying numerous writers in Christian tradition (with a strong focus on medieval Greek rather than medieval Latin writers), they find that the early Pentecostal understanding of tongues is lacking. Indeed, they go so far as to claim that it is "utterly unprecedented" and "completely unknown." Instead, most writers in Christian tradition understood tongues speech to be some human language. The debate was over whether the miracle of Pentecost was in speaking unlearned human languages or in hearing the spoken language as though it were one's own. Was the miracle in the speaking or in the hearing? Strong language indeed. Yet, the major purpose of their investigation is not to challenge the spiritual experience of ecstatic utterance, but to engage Pentecostals and Charismatics on the question of precedence. They have returned once more to the charge of novelty raised at the very beginning of the movement.

Pentecostals and Charismatic scholars should welcome the challenge that Blosser and Sullivan bring. After all, as they make clear, it is not a challenge made out of animus, but an effort to get greater historical clarity on the role of tongues within Christian tradition. If the notion of tongues as *glossolalia* or some form of ecstatic utterance is indeed an invention of nineteenth century Higher Critical thought that then filtered down to the popular level where early Pentecostals adopted it, then Pentecostals should admit the novelty of such a theory. Prior to this, Sullivan and Blosser argue that one can find only sporadic accounts of ecstatic utterance among sects such as Edward Irving's followers in England and Scotland.

Finally, Blosser and Sullivan rightly point out that the Protestant polemic against the miraculous flowed out of the Reformation debates over the status of the medieval theological synthesis. If miracles did not cease, then what does one do with all of the reports of the miraculous from medieval authors? They reinforce trends in contemporary scholarship that the doctrine of cessationism began as a weapon in the Protestant arsenal against medieval Catholicism even though Protestants never rejected the notion of ecstatic or ecstatic encounter. The emergence of the global Pentecostal-Charismatic movement has done much to disabuse Protestantism of this polemic in a way that has contributed to Protestant-Catholic relations and a kind of spiritual ecumenism that continues to bear fruit.

Good historical scholarship returns to the sources and attempts to offer fresh readings that illuminate the truth more clearly. In this sense, Blosser and Sullivan challenge the current historiography surrounding tongues while simultaneously affirming the importance of the charismatic dimension to Christianity and Christian mission. I have written this foreword to their project because I am convinced that these kinds of historical depth soundings into the great river of Christian tradition are crucial for our common mission. May iron sharpen iron as we all seek to probe more deeply into the mysteries of the faith.

—Dale M. Coulter, March 1, 2021

Foreword

JAMES LIKOUDIS, DD

President Emeritus, Catholics United for the Faith

SPEAKING IN TONGUES: A Critical Historical Examination by Dr. Philip Blosser and co-author and collaborator Charles A. Sullivan is a remarkable and ground-breaking study of the phenomenon of "tongue-speaking" familiar among Pentecostal and Charismatic religionists. Interestingly, co-author Sullivan is a Canadian Pentecostal who came to the realization that the contemporary practice and understanding of "speaking in tongues" among Pentecostals and Charismatics alike were nowhere supported in any of the primary texts of ancient Jewish and Christian Patristic and Medieval writings. This unique study by Blosser (a Catholic) and Sullivan (a Pentecostal) is a prime example of ecumenical collaboration focusing exclusively on "speaking and praying and singing in tongues." The phenomenon of "tongues" has historically fascinated theologians, religious devotees, linguists, psychologists, higher biblical critics, and outright skeptics, provoking examinations of whether the supernatural was involved in the manifestation of alleged miraculous "tongue-speaking."

There are surprising discoveries in this major study sporting an impressive lengthy Bibliography of every major work examining or investigating the subject. Sullivan initially sparked interest in the two authors collaborating on the present volume by uncovering the fact that outside a few pagan and Christian fringe groups there was no antecedent in Church history for the claim that miraculous *glossolalia* (unintelligible vocalizations) have regularly occurred among some favored initiates. This thesis was actually an innovation perpetrated by certain German Higher Critics in the 1830s. Moreover, there occurred a religious crisis among Pentecostals

1906–8, which resulted in a startling redefinition of "tongue-speaking." For official Pentecostalists, it was no longer the possessing of a miraculous gift to speak in a foreign language previously unknown to the speakers, but rather it now suffered redefinition as a "private language of the spirit" or "personal language of prayer and praise." The authors' scholarly volume is invaluable for showing that the patristic Fathers of the ancient Church, the great medieval Scholastics, and the early Protestant Reformers unanimously understood "tongue-speaking" to be speaking an ordinary human language.

With respect to the puzzling verses of St. Paul in 1 Corinthians 14, stating that the tongue-speaker of an unknown language needs have an interpreter for the congregation to understand, the authors throw much light on them with the aid of newly translated Semitic and Talmudic texts. They reveal that Jewish and early Christian liturgies used an interpreter alongside the liturgical celebrant or reader to verbally translate a foreign liturgical language (Aramaic or Hebrew) not understood by Greek hearers.

These brief comments do not do justice to the erudition of the two authors applied to unraveling the mystery of "tongue-speaking" that became widespread in the nineteenth and twentieth centuries. This work is highly recommended.

— James Likoudis, December 8, 2020

Acknowledgments

PHILIP BLOSSER: I WISH to acknowledge a debt of gratitude to the following individuals who kindly offered assistance in varying ways to our project. Many thanks to Msgr. Todd Lajiness, former Rector of Sacred Heart Major Seminary, and Fr. Timothy Laboe, Academic Dean, for their generous grant of a sabbatical in 2020 for the completion of the present project; to David M. Coulter of Pentecostal Theological Seminary, for pointing out some helpful details in D. William Faupel's *Everlasting Gospel* and Allen Anderson's *Introduction to Pentecostalism*, as well as for writing a Foreword to the present work; to the late Thomas M. Reid, former Master of Formation of the Community of Secular Discalced Carmelites at Assumption Grotto Parish, Detroit, for his monograph, *Carmelite Spirituality and the Charismatic Renewal* (2009) and cherished friendship; to Fr. Chad Ripperger, exorcist for the Diocese of Denver, for his invaluable 808-page *Introduction to the Science of Mental Health* (2013) and for a telephone consultation concerning the difference between "gratuitous grace" (*gratia gratis datae*) and "sanctifying grace" (*gratia gratum faciens*); to James Likoudis for a number of good articles and insights concerning the Charismatic movement, as well as writing a Foreword to the present work; to my colleagues at Sacred Heart Major Seminary, Ruth Lapeyre, for numerous resources on Catholic "covenant communities," including John Flaherty's website on "The Sword of the Spirit" and related Charismatic covenant communities, as well as for calling our attention to the comprehensive work edited by Stanley M. Burgess and Eduard M. van der Maas, *The New International Dictionary of Pentecostal and Charismatic Movements* (2002); to Mary Healy for calling our attention to Craig Keener's *Acts: An Exegetical Commentary*, and George T. Montague's book on the Holy Spirit; to Victor Salas for his *New Blackfriars* article on "Francisco Suárez and His Sources on the Gift of Tongues"; to Robert Fastiggi for answering numerous questions concerning Catholic doctrine and dogma; to Ralph Martin for sharing a copy of his article, "A New Pentecost?

Catholic Theology and 'Baptism in the Spirit,'" published in *Logos: A Journal of Catholic Thought and Culture*; to Elizabeth Salas for calling our attention to resources in the Carmelite tradition of Catholic spirituality in her articles, "Power Evangelization: A Catholic and Carmelite Perspective" in *Homiletic and Pastoral Review* (May 31, 2019), and "How to Personally Encounter God" in *Mosaic Magazine* (Sacred Heart Major Seminary, April, 2017); to Michael McCallion, for sharing several of his articles with us, including "Individualism and Community as Contested Rhetorics in the Catholic New Evangelization Movement," *Review of Religious Research*, 54.3 (2012) 291–310, and "New Evangelization Practices? Devotional Prayer Meetings and Christian Service," *Sociology and Anthropology*, 5.7 (2017) 503–10; and calling our attention to the work of Thomas J. Csordas in the sociology of Charismatic spiritual culture; to Fr. John Michael McDermott for valuable suggestions and his article, "Do Charismatic Healings Promote the New Evangelization? Part 1," *Antiphon*, 24.2 (2020) 85–123; and "Part 2," 24.3 (2020) 205–32; to Paco Gavriledes for lending me Patti Mansfield's *As by a New Pentecost* (1992); to Fr. Daniel Trapp, for several informative conversations and an amusing anecdote about prospective tongue-speakers "priming the pump" by repeating over-and-over phrases such as, "Bought a Toyota, should'a bought a Honda"; to Robert Fastiggi, and Victor and Elizabeth Salas for their encouragement; and numerous other family members, friends, colleagues, and pastors for their steadfast support. Finally, we owe a debt of gratitude to his Eminence Raymond Leo Cardinal Burke, who undertook to write an endorsement for the present work while recovering from his battle with the Covid virus, after it became clear that his condition would prevent him from carrying out his original generous offer to write a Foreword to the work.

CHARLES A. SULLIVAN: I, in turn, wish to also offer my special thanks to many persons and institutions that have helped further my research over the years—to Calvary Temple, one of the earliest churches in Canada to form after the great outpourings in Chicago and Azusa Street, for making available their library resources; to The Canadian Pentecostal Research Network and the many members of its Facebook group, whose level of intellectual activity and sincerity shatters many stereotypes of the Pentecostal world; to Alex Poulos who recently completed his Phd at the Catholic University of America, for his encouragement and linguistic contributions and suggestions; to Ryan Clevenger, who recently finished his doctorate at the Wheaton Center for Early Christian Studies, for his early input into the Gift of Tongues Project; to George Vasalmis (at ellopos.net) for his helpful solutions to various Greek problems; to Clif Payne, a fellow Hebrew University student from Alabama and Jewish Roots pastor and teacher; to Bruce Edminster, for his constructive communication and feedback over the years; and to my good friend and neighbor, Gary Andres, a graduate of Fuller Theological Seminary, for his ongoing friendship and support.

Abbreviations

AF *The Apostolic Faith* newspaper (Azusa Street). Published by the Apostolic Faith Mission, Azusa Street, CA, 1906–8/9. *Pentecostal Archives*: https://pentecostalarchives.org/ (September 1906–May 1908); and *Asbury Seminary*: https://place.asbury-seminary.edu/apostolicfaith/ (February/March 1907–May/June 1909).

AFP *The Apostolic Faith* newspaper (Portland). Published by the Apostolic Faith Mission, Portland, OR, 1908–29. https://archives.ifphc.org/index.cfm?fuseaction=publicationsGuide.apostolicfaithportland.

ANF *Ante-Nicene Fathers: Translations of the Writings of the Fathers Down to A.D. 325*. Edited by Alexander Roberts and James Donaldson. 10 vols. Peabody, MA: Hendrickson, 1994.

BAG *Greek-English Lexicon of the New Testament and Other Early Christian Literature*. Edited by Walter Bauer. Translated by William F. Arndt and F. Wilbur Gingrich. 4th ed. Chicago: University of Chicago Press, 1957.

CBTEL *Cyclopaedia of Biblical, Theological, and Ecclesiastical Literature*. Edited by John McClintock and James Strong. 10 vols. New York: Harper & Brothers, 1891. https://www.areopage.net/McClintock&Strong_Cyclopedia.html.

CCC *Catechism of the Catholic Church*. 2nd ed. Vatican: Libreria Editrice Vaticana, 2012.

CCR Catholic Charismatic Renewal. Catholic Charismatic Renewal National Service Committee. https://www.nsc-chariscenter.org/.

CE   *The Catholic Encyclopedia.* Edited by Charles G. Herbermann et al. New York: Appleton, 1907-1911; Encyclopedia, 1912-1922. https://www.newadvent.org/cathen/.

CEHEC   *Critical and Exegetical Handbook to the Epistles to the Corinthians*, by Heinrich August Meyer. Edited by W. P. Dickson. Translated by D. D. Bannerman. Edinburgh: T. & T. Clark, 1887.

CJPCR   *Cyberjournal for Pentecostal-Charismatic Research.* Edited by Harold D. Hunter. Pentecostal-Charismatic Theological Inquiry International. 1997–2020. http://www.pctii.org/cyberj/.

CSJ   *Cultic Studies Journal.* International Cultic Studies Association (ICSA). Founded 1979. https://www.icsahome.com/memberelibrary/csj.

DDS   *Dictionnaire de spiritualité: ascétique et mystique, doctrine et histoire.* Edited by M. Viller et al. 21 vols. Paris: Beauchesne, 1932–95. http://www.dictionnairedespiritualite.com/.

DPCM   *Dictionary of Pentecostal and Charismatic Movements.* Edited by Stanley M. Burgess and Gary B. McGee. Grand Rapids: Regency Reference Library, 1988.

EB02   *Encyclopedia Britannica.* 9th and 10th eds. Amalgamated in the free online *1902 Encyclopedia* (published 2005–19). https://www.1902encyclopedia.com/.

EB87   *Encyclopedia Britannica.* 15th ed. Chicago: Encyclopedia Britannica, 1987. https://www.britannica.com/.

GOTP   *Gift of Tongues Project.* Est. 2008, by Charles A. Sullivan. https://charlesasullivan.com/gift-tongues-project/.

HSB   *Harper Study Bible: The Holy Bible RSV.* Edited by Harold Lindsell. New York: Harper and Row, 1946, 1991.

ICCRS   International Catholic Charismatic Renewal Services. Est. 1978. http://www.iccrs-archive.org/en/homepage/

ISBE   *International Standard Bible Encyclopedia.* Edited by James Orr et al. Chicago: Howard-Severance, 1915.

ISBE2   *International Standard Bible Encyclopedia.* Fully rev. ed. 4 vols. Grand Rapids: Eerdmans, 1982–95.

JSSR   *Journal for the Scientific Study of Religion.* Society for the Scientific Study of Religion. Wiley-Blackwell, 1961–.

JTS   *Journal of Theological Studies.* New Series, 1–71. Oxford: Oxford University Press, 1950–2020.

LCL   Loeb Classical Library. London: William Heinemann, 1912–; Cambridge: Harvard University Press, 1934–; digital library, 2014–.

NCE2   *New Catholic Encyclopedia.* 2nd ed. 15 vols. Detroit: Gale Cengage Learning, Catholic University of America, 2003.

NIDCC   *The New International Dictionary of the Christian Church.* Edited by J. D. Douglas. Grand Rapids: Zondervan, 1978.

NIDNTT *The New International Dictionary of New Testament Theology.* Edited by Colin Brown. Translated, with additions and revisions, from the German *Theologisches Begriffslexikon Zum Neuen Testament.* 3 vols. Grand Rapids: Zondervan, 1975.

NIDPCM *New International Dictionary of Pentecostal and Charismatic Movements.* Edited by Stanley M. Burgess and Eduard M. van der Maas. Grand Rapids: Zondervan, 2002.

NPNF   *A Select Library of Nicene and Post-Nicene Fathers of the Christian Church.* Edited by Philip Schaff and Henry Wace. 28 vols. Peabody, MA: Hendrickson, 1996.

NSHERK *The New Schaff-Herzog Encyclopedia of Religious Knowledge.* Edited by Samuel Macauley Jackson et al. 13 vols. Grand Rapids: Baker, 1951. https://onlinebooks.library.upenn.edu/webbin/book/lookupid?key=olbp27827.

OED   *Oxford English Dictionary.* Edited by James A. H. Murray et al. 13 vols. Oxford: Clarendon Press, 1933. http://dictionary.oed.com.

PG   *Patrologia Gaeca.* Edited by Jacques Paul Migne. 162 vols. Paris, 1857–66.

PL   *Patrologia Latina.* Edited by Jacques Paul Migne. 221 vols. Paris, 1844–64.

SCG   *Summa contra Gentiles,* by Thomas Aquinas. In *Sancti Thomae Aquinatis Opera omnia,* 13–15. Editio Leonina. Rome, 1918–30.

ST   *Summa Theologiae*, by Thomas Aquinas. In *Sancti Thomae
            Aquinatis Opera omnia*, 4–12. Editio Leonina. Rome,
            1888–1906.

            Translattion by Fathers of the English Dominican Province:
            Summa Theologica, 5 vols. New York: Benziger, 1948.

TDNT   *Theological Dictionary of the New Testament*. Edited by Ger-
            hard Kittell and Gerhard Friedrich. Translated by Geoffrey W.
            Bromiley. 10 vols. Grand Rapids: Eerdmans, 1964–76, 1981.

ZPEB   *The Zondervan Pictorial Encyclopedia of the Bible*. Edited by
            Merrill C. Tenney. 5 vols. Grand Rapids: Zondervan, 1975.

An Archeological Excavation Deep into History

BY PHILIP BLOSSER

"SPEAKING IN TONGUES" IS a phenomenon that may be only on the margins of most people's awareness, if they are aware of it at all. Even where most people are familiar with the phenomenon, there is little chance of their understanding it for what it really is. For many of those involved in the explosion of Pentecostal and Charismatic movements in recent times, however, the phenomenon may be at the front-and-center of their spiritual lives. Few have doubts about what they understand it to be. Many of them make a regular practice of speaking in tongues as a personal language of the spirit, not only speaking in tongues but also praying and singing in tongues as a personal language of prayer and praise; and they understand the phenomenon as a sign that they have been baptized in the Spirit, as a kind of divine anointing.

The Apostle Luke's account of Pentecost in Acts 2 figures prominently in discussions about speaking in tongues. What happened in Jerusalem on Pentecost has been understood widely as a supernatural event in which the Apostles were miraculously given the ability to speak in foreign languages previously unknown to them. Scholars usually accept that it also could have involved a miracle of *hearing* in which the Apostles spoke in their own language, probably Aramaic, but were heard in various foreign languages by the devout Jewish pilgrims in Jerusalem "from every nation under heaven" (Acts 2:5).

What the Apostle Paul describes in 1 Corinthians 12–14, however, seems different. In his letter to the Corinthian assembly, Paul says that one who speaks in tongues speaks "not to men but to God; for no one understands him, but he utters mysteries in the spirit" (1 Cor 14:2 RSV).[1] For this reason, Paul stipulates that "if there is no one to interpret [the tongues], let each of them keep silence in the church and speak to himself and to God" (v. 28).

What were the Corinthian tongues? From the Pentecostal-Charismatic[2] perspective, the answer seems obvious: those who spoke in tongues in the Corinthian assembly were exercising the gift of tongues as a language of the spirit, a personal language of prayer and praise, a language that some scholars have called *glossolalia*, a language that isn't meant to be understood as an ordinary human language, but is a language that can only be interpreted properly "in the spirit" by someone anointed with the gift of prophetic interpretation or a word of knowledge.

With some such understanding of Corinthian tongues in mind, some Pentecostal-Charismatic scholars have gone back to Luke's account of Pentecost in Acts 2 and wondered whether this understanding could not also explain what was going on there. According to this scenario, the Apostles may have received the gift of tongues in the form of *glossolalia*, but their hearers would have understood them (or had them "interpreted") in their own native languages.[3]

Whether or not such an interpretation works with Acts 2 is debatable. On its face, however, the view that the gift of tongues in the early Church was something like a language of the spirit or *glossolalia* would seem to work in the other accounts Luke offers in the Book of Acts. For example, it would seem to work in the passage where the Holy Spirit fell on the Gentile household of Cornelius, and they were heard "speaking in tongues and extolling God" and were then baptized (Acts 10:44–48); or where Paul baptized some Ephesian believers, and "when [he] had laid his hands upon them, the Holy Spirit came on them; and they spoke with tongues and prophesied" (19:6).[4] In these cases, it would seem to make little sense to suppose that the gift of tongues involved the miracle of speaking previously unknown foreign

---

1. All Bible quotations in the Introduction are from the RSV.

2. "Pentecostal-Charismatic" is used as a hyphenated adjective to denote what these two movements share in common, without prejudice to important underlying differences between them.

3. E.g., Montague, *Holy Spirit*, 279–80; Sullivan, *Charisms*, 121–50.

4. Whether the gift of tongues should be understood as a sign of Spirit baptism, and whether it has a particular relation to water baptism, are questions that have been long debated in the Pentecostal and Charismatic movements.

languages since there is no apparent evangelistic intent on the part of those speaking in tongues.[5] Rather, the fact that they are described as "extolling God" would seem to fit more comfortably with the understanding of the gift of tongues as a personal language of prayer and praise.

The problem with this supposition—the elephant in the room, if you will—is that this interpretation of "tongues" as something other than ordinary human languages is utterly unprecedented in Church history, completely unknown in ecclesiastical writings before the nineteenth century, when a few German theologians of the Protestant school of Higher Criticism first introduced the theory of *glossolalia*.[6] Even the Pentecostal movement itself, as evidenced in notable figures like Charles Parham and William Seymour in the early twentieth century, initially held that speaking in tongues was the miraculous gift of speaking actual foreign languages previously unknown to the speaker. Pentecostal missionaries such as Alfred and Lillian Garr were sent abroad to India and China between 1906–8 without any linguistic training, in the confident expectation that their baptism in the Spirit would divinely empower them to preach the Gospel by using a miraculous gift of "missionary tongues." Their disappointing discovery that they were unable to communicate in the Bengali and Chinese languages led to a crisis in which Pentecostal leaders began to quietly accept a redefinition of the "gift of tongues" as something other than actual human languages.

5. Another view, however, is that they were speaking in previously unlearned foreign languages as a sign of the universality of the Gospel message.

6. When we say "unprecedented in Church history" and "completely unknown in ecclesiastical writings before the nineteenth century," we mean that this mystical interpretation and practice of speaking in unintelligible *glossolalic* tongues, whether ecstatic or otherwise, is found nowhere in Catholic tradition or in the mainstream of the Protestant Reformation stemming from Luther, Calvin, the Anglican divines, and their proximate successors. A reference to *glossolalia-like* vocalizations can be found in the ancient separatist sect of the Montanists, and another in the obscure ecstatics described by the anti-Christian Celsus. A very few more can be found in modern separatist sects of spiritual enthusiasts such as the Jansenist convulsionaries, Camisards, Ranters, Shakers, and Mormons, most of whom the mainstream, established churches regarded as heretical or "nonconformist." Some cases strike the reader as extreme, or accompanied by odd behavior. Charles Wesley refers to one of the French prophets (Camisards) who "fell into violent agitations and gobbled like a turkey-cock" until Wesley attempted to exorcize him; and Ronald Knox refers to a Jansenist lawyer who "barked like a dog for two hours daily," and another who "whirled round and round on the ball of his foot for an hour or two" at "nine every morning and three every afternoon." (See Southey, *Life of John Wesley*, 1:240; and Knox, *Enthusiasm*, 361, 380–81.) In most cases, those who uttered these *glossolalia-like* "tongues" nevertheless understood themselves to have received the miraculous gift of speaking foreign human languages unknown to themselves and made no attempt to redefine "tongues," as did the early Pentecostals after their early twentieth-century crisis of "missionary tongues." These issues are covered in detail throughout this 3-volume work.

In time, Pentecostal scholars found support for their new understanding of tongues in certain features of the *glossolalia* theory they adopted from the German Higher Critics, including their hypothesis linking the biblical doctrine of tongues to the unintelligible ecstatic utterances of the second-century Montanists.

Before the advent of the Higher Critical theory of *glossolalia* in the nineteenth century and the Pentecostal revision of the definition of the "gift of tongues" in the early twentieth century, there was never any discussion of "tongues" as unintelligible utterances. The universal understanding, the received tradition, was that biblical "tongues" referred to ordinary human languages. The *only* sustained debate over the nature of "tongues" in Church history before the nineteenth century was over whether the gift of tongues involved a miracle of *speaking* or *hearing*. This debate was sparked by a grammatical ambiguity in a Pentecost Oration (*Oratio* 41) by Gregory of Nazianzus (c. 329–390), which was loosely mistranslated by Tyrannius Rufinus (c. 344–411) in the late fourth century in such a way that it erroneously suggested that Nazianzus favored the theory of hearing over speaking. A few, like Gregory of Nyssa (c. 335–395), did indeed hold that the gift was a miracle of hearing, in which one voice would sound forth and subsequently divide supernaturally into diverse languages. The vast mainstream of the ecclesiastical tradition, however, stretching across the centuries from Irenaeus (c. 130–202) to Francisco Suárez (1548–1617) and more recent theologians, held that it was a gift of speaking rather than hearing; and they offered good reasons for this view.[7] Still others, like Pope Benedict XIV (1675–1758), in his four-volume treatise touching on the subject of tongues, held that it could be either a miracle of speaking or hearing.[8]

It is also true that a few Church Fathers and later ecclesiastical writers interpreted the tongues of 1 Corinthians 12–14 differently from the tongues referenced in Acts 2. Their only disagreement, however, was over whether the tongues in question were *miraculous* or not, not whether they were intelligible human languages. Some held that both Corinth and Pentecost involved a miraculous gift of tongues, while others such as Epiphanius, Cyril of Alexandria, and Ambrosiaster, understood the tongues of Corinth as involving nothing more than the *natural* problem of a foreign liturgical language requiring interpretation in the vernacular so that the whole assembly could understand it. In both cases, however, the tongues were understood to be ordinary human languages.

---

7. Salas, "Francisco Suárez," 554–76.

8. Benedict XIV, *Doctrina de Servorum*, 547–61; Benedict XIV, *De Lambertinis*, 724–38; Benedict XIV, *Heroic Virtue*, 3:217–31.

Remarkably, we find in Jewish history a tradition of employing an interpreter (called a *meturgeman*, from מתורגמן) in Hebrew religious services who stood beside the presiding speaker or reader, and verbally translated the speaker's or reader's sacred liturgical language into the local vernacular language (usually Aramaic or Greek).[9] This tradition was recognized by the seventeenth-century English theologian and rabbinic scholar, John Lightfoot, referenced by the Jewish philosopher Moses Maimonides (c. 1135–1204), identified in the Babylonian Talmud (c. AD 200–550), and described as having begun in the time of Ezra the Scribe (fl. c. 490–440 BC). After the return of the Jewish people from more than sixty years of captivity and exile in Babylon, Ezra sought to reestablish the repatriated Jews in Jerusalem based on the Hebrew Torah (Law). Nehemiah 8:1–8 dramatically describes the first public reading of the Law by Ezra in Jerusalem, and its interpretation into the vernacular common language, since many Jews returning from captivity in Babylon no longer spoke or understood ancient Hebrew.

According to records, this tradition continued for nearly a thousand years until it eventually disappeared from Jewish synagogue services around the sixth century AD. Nevertheless, the practice of verbally translating a traditional sacred liturgical language and explaining it in the vernacular sheds unprecedented light on the circumstances Paul describes in the Corinthian assembly in the first century. Paul's first letter to the Corinthians is very old, dating from possibly as early as the mid-first century AD, before the Jewish diaspora, or the scattering of the Jewish people following the cataclysmic destruction of the Temple of Jerusalem by the Romans in 70 AD. This is significant because early Jewish followers of Christ, like Paul, still considered themselves to be Jews—Jews who identified Jesus as the awaited Jewish Messiah—and were not yet "excommunicated" from Jewish assemblies as they were by Rabban Gamaliel at Yavneh, following the destruction of the Jerusalem Temple, in a decree called the *Birkat Ha-Minim* (c. AD 90). The Corinthian assembly described by Paul still preserved Jewish patterns of

---

9. Other Hebrew and Greek names used for persons performing the same or similar roles include *shaliach tzibbur* (שליח צבור); *chazzan* (חַזָּן), *skopos* (σκοπός), and *keimenos* (κείμενος). Cf. also Paul's use of *diermēneutēs* (διερμηνευτής, 1 Cor 14:28) and *anaplērōn* (ἀναπληρῶν, 1 Cor 14:16). See Bieringer et al., *New Testament and Rabbinic Literature*, 185n168; "Shaliach Tzibbur (שליח צבור)," para. 30; Wikipedia, s.v. "Precentor," https://en.wikipedia.org/wiki /Precentor, para. 3. For *skopos* ("σκοπός"), see Donnegan, *New Greek and English Lexicon*, 1130, col. 2; Lampe, *Patristic Greek Lexicon*, 1241, col. 1; Liddell and Scott, *Greek-English Lexicon*, 1361; Estienne et al., *Thesaurus* (1865), 7:431–33. For "Κείμενος" see Lampe, *Patristic Greek Lexicon*, 739–40; Estienne et al., *Thesaurus* (1865), 4:1405–6; and the verb form, κεῖμαι, in Liddell and Scott, *Greek-English Lexicon*, 746; Donnegan, *New Greek and English Lexicon*, 738, col. 2.

worship, which included the use of a sacred liturgical language, Hebrew or Aramaic, unknown to many in the assembly (such as Hellenized Jews and Greek converts), and the use of an interpreter who verbally translated this language for the laity (διερμηνευτής, 1 Cor 14:28), someone assigned to the uncatechized laity (ἀναπληρῶν, 1 Cor 14:16) so that, as Paul says, they would know when to say "Amen" (v. 16) during the liturgy. The controversy over tongues in Corinth, as described by Epiphanius, concerned which Greek dialect the interpreter should use to verbally translate the unfamiliar sacred language (the Doric, Attic, and Aeolic dialects would have been common in the Corinthian assembly of that time). Other Patristic writers, like Ambrosiaster, Cyril of Alexandria, and Chrysostom, indicate that the practice of employing an interpreter to verbally translate biblical readings, instruction, and liturgical language into the vernacular languages and to explain what was going on in the liturgy was still in use in Christian churches in the fourth and fifth centuries in areas such as Constantinople and Alexandria.

What does this mean? Should we expect these findings to "land like a bombshell exploding on the playground" of Pentecostals and Charismatics?[10] Not necessarily. The spiritual significance currently attached to the particular practice of speaking, praying, and singing in tongues as found in the Pentecostal-Charismatic movements is not necessarily discredited by these findings. The Holy Spirit works in the interiority of human hearts in ways that cannot always be easily discerned. Nor do these findings discredit all of the good Christian work of evangelism, catechesis, scholarship, or the spiritual integrity of countless Pentecostals and Charismatics striving to live faithful Christian lives and carry out the Great Commission (Matt 28:16–20). What these findings do mean, however, is that the current Pentecostal-Charismatic practice of speaking, praying, and singing in tongues is a historical novelty with no antecedents in Church history before the nineteenth century. As such, they call into question many of the common claims made by Pentecostal-Charismatic writers that these current practices are rooted in ancient Church history. For example, it severely undermines the claims of those, like Eddie Ensley, who claim that the gift of tongues went by another name and was called "jubilation" throughout most of Church history and that such phenomena as shouts of joy, tears, groanings, and other emotive expressions serve as antecedents to the Christian doctrine of "tongues."[11] Such phenomena bear no resemblance whatsoever to what the Church historically understood by "speaking in tongues." The same is even

10. The "bombshell" reference is an allusion to the appearance of Karl Barth's Commentary on the Epistle to the Romans as described by Adam, "Theologie," 276–77.

11. Ensley, Sounds, xvi–xviii, 6–10; cf. Sullivan, Charisms, 145–48. See volume 3, chapter 4 of this work for a more detailed analysis of "jubilation."

more notably true of the supposed antecedents to Christian tongues some-times presumed to exist in the ecstatic babblings of the Montanist prophet-esses or the obscure utterances of pagan oracles of the temple at Delphi in ancient Greece. Eusebius of Caesarea (c. 260–339) sought to distance the Christian practice of speaking in tongues from those of the Montanists, and Michael Psellos (c. 1018–78) did likewise with the ecstatic locutions of the Delphic priestesses by deliberately refusing any hint of a link between them and the Christian gift of tongues.

It should be clear that the authors of the present volume bear no ani-mus against their Pentecostal or Charismatic brethren. One of the authors, Charles A. Sullivan, has been involved in the Pentecostal-Charismatic movement and affiliated churches for over thirty years in Canada. I, Philip Blosser, was born in China and raised in Japan by Protestant missionary parents who, though lacking any such affiliations, briefly encountered Pen-tecostals in Japan and were led to what they described as a deeper experi-ence of the Holy Spirit, to speak in tongues, and to contribute a chapter to a book entitled *My Personal Pentecost*.[12] Sullivan and I both count individuals in the Pentecostal-Charismatic tradition among our personal friends. Sul-livan is a Protestant. I have been a Catholic since 1993. Our project is thus an ecumenical venture.

Sullivan began his exploration of the historical meaning of "tongues" because of questions that arose from personal experiences and through his interest in languages and research into the Church Fathers. He later discov-ered a trove of ecclesiastical writings on speaking in tongues, most of which have not been previously translated. Originally from a Baptist background in suburban Vancouver, British Columbia, Sullivan took a first-year inten-sive Greek course one summer in the early 1980s at Regent College in Van-couver, which whetted his appetite for biblical languages. He subsequently earned his baccalaureate degree at Providence University College and Theo-logical Seminary in Winnipeg, Manitoba, where he continued his study of Greek language and biblical studies. At Providence, he was inspired by his contact with Daniel Isaac Block, an Old Testament professor and translator with a doctorate from the School of Archaeology and Oriental Studies at the University of Liverpool, currently Gunther H. Knoedler Professor Emeritus of Old Testament at Wheaton College in metro Chicago. During his years in Winnipeg, he first encountered the Canadian Charismatic movement. In 1985, Sullivan received funding from the Jewish Foundation of Manitoba, The Canadian Friends of the Hebrew University, and the Morris M. Pulver Scholarship Fund to attend the Beth Rothberg School for Overseas Students

---

12. Koch and Koch, *My Personal Pentecost*, 177-87.

at the Hebrew University of Jerusalem, where he commenced his study of modern Hebrew and acquired his taste for biblical Hebrew, Aramaic, and Syriac studies, which became his life-long passion. His coursework included Talmudic studies with Rabbi Professor Pesach Schindler, as well as studies in comparative Semitics with Professor Stephen Pfann at the University of the Holy Land. He counts his time studying languages at the Hebrew University of Jerusalem, in the company of dynamic, intelligent, and like-minded people, as one of the highlights of his life. For personal family reasons, Sullivan was never able to complete an advanced degree that might have earned him an academic appointment in the area of his interest and expertise. However, his continuing research and interest in translating ancient religious documents from both Jewish and Christian traditions remain a consuming avocational passion, and he continues to carry on a lively correspondence with scholars in various related fields of Semitic and ecclesiastical literature, making him a consummate independent scholar and linguist.

While in Israel, he and his wife attended a church affiliated with the Pentecostal Assemblies of Canada, which he describes as having been a positive experience. The Sullivans previously attended a Canadian Baptist church that was in the process of being overtaken by a wave of Charismatic influence. Many in the congregation, however, were not as receptive to these changes as he and his wife were, and members of the congregation found themselves divided, leading the Sullivans to look for a church elsewhere. Charles first approached the tongues history to validate the Charismatic experience as a Charismatic. However, textual research unfolded a portrait that unveiled a complex history. It was a challenge that required many resources and skills. This situation initially created more questions than answers that took many years to reconcile and forced the subject into a different narrative. The meaning found in the ancient records shocked Mr. Sullivan as they will for "Spirit-led" readers. He hopes this work helps his fellow Charismatics and Pentecostals in their quest for truth and maturity in their faith.

Questions of this sort led Sullivan to delve into the writings of the Church Fathers and later ecclesiastical writers, which gave birth to his Gift of Tongues Project, with a yield of extensive research and articles based on his research. This project took full advantage of his knowledge of various Semitic and other ancient languages, such as Greek and Latin, which he continued to study throughout subsequent decades. He masterfully exploited the digitized electronic libraries increasingly available on the Internet to conduct extensive searches of such databases as Migne's *Patrologia Latina* and *Patrologia Grecae*. These powerful tools provide the possibility for high-speed word searches through vast tomes of the Church Fathers that remain untranslated in Greek and Latin. As he is fond of telling people, the most profound discovery through all of his extensive research has *not* been the fact that people have actually spoken in tongues throughout Church history. Rather, he says, the big news is the pervasive ignorance of Christians today, even with all these available resources, concerning what the Church Fathers and entire ecclesiastical tradition have consistently understood by "speaking in tongues." He attributes this ignorance to the fact that most of the *numerous* references to speaking in tongues in the Church's historical writings remain untranslated in Greek, Latin, and Syriac, and thus inaccessible to most authors today. Those works currently translated into English and other modern languages represent but a small fraction of the corpus of ecclesiastical writings, the mere tip of the proverbial iceberg. The vast majority of writings on the subject of speaking in tongues that are available from the Church's tradition, including those that are the clearest and best, thus remain largely unknown to contemporary readers and authors. The burden of the present work, therefore, is to share this discovery with readers.

In my case, I spent most of my first twenty years in Japan, where I learned Japanese, studied several modern European languages, majored in Far Eastern Studies, and minored in philosophy at the Jesuit-run Sophia University in Tokyo. Subsequently, I earned a master's degree in religion at Westminster Theological Seminary in Philadelphia, where I studied Greek and Hebrew as well as theology; another master's degree in philosophy at Villanova University; and a doctorate in philosophy at Duquesne University. While teaching at the Lenoir-Rhyne University, a Lutheran school in North Carolina, I was received into the Catholic Church in 1993 by an African-American priest with ancestral roots in Madagascar. The first time I heard Charismatics "singing in tongues" was at Franciscan University in Steubenville, Ohio, where I attended several conferences. The experience was not unpleasant. The subject of "tongues" remained on the margins of my experience, however, until I moved to Detroit in 2007 and began teaching at Sacred Heart Major Seminary. The growing number of Charismatic members on the faculty awakened my interest in the subject. Although many students welcomed these Charismatic professors, others expressed concerns about being pressured to join the movement, both by Charismatic faculty and student members. Because of these concerns, the rector appointed a commission to study the proper role of the Charismatic movement within the seminary. Although I was not a member of this commission, I submitted several written opinions to the commission and decided to devote a sabbatical to an in-depth study of the phenomenon of speaking in tongues more carefully on my own. Like other members of the faculty, I also had questions about healing and deliverance practices, as well as about "tongues," within the Catholic Charismatic Renewal, and participated in a published exchange of ideas with fellow faculty members.[13]

The more I investigated the roots of the Catholic Charismatic movement and the phenomenon of speaking in tongues, the more I came to realize that there were very few, if any, objective or detailed historical or systematic studies by Catholic scholars on this phenomenon. Instead, there were only apologetic works by Catholic Charismatics already convinced of the spiritual importance and supernatural source of speaking in tongues as practiced and understood in their own circles. Furthermore, I noticed that most of the scholarly Charismatic studies tended to focus on the Catholic Church's magisterial documents from the Second Vatican Council (1962–65) onward; and even those devoted to Patristic studies usually interpreted them through the lens of contemporary Charismatic experience, overlooking the vast resources of the Church's ecclesiastical tradition.[14] Hence, the need for a critical historical study such as the present one became clear; and when I discovered the extensive pioneering work by Sullivan on the topic in his Gift of Tongues Project, it took little time for us to recognize the mutual benefit to be derived from partnering in the joint venture to produce the present work.

The present study is structured after the model of an archeological excavation or "dig." Starting at the surface level with the current state of affairs in Pentecostal and Charismatic circles, we begin digging down into deeper and deeper levels of history—all the way down through Church history to the New Testament; then even deeper, down into the intertestamental period and Old Testament times. Just as the work as a whole is structured after an archeological dig, so most of the chapters are also structured similarly, beginning with a more recent figure or movement and then delving back

13. These include Salas, "Francisco Suárez"; Blosser, "Questions"; Healy, "Answers"; Salas, "How to Personally Encounter God"; Salas, "Power Evangelization"; Thelen (not a faculty member but a graduate), "John of the Cross"; McDermott, "Do Charismatic Healings Promote the New Evangelization?" (Parts I and II) followed by various responses.

14. For example, we have yet to see a Pentecostal-Charismatic scholar refer to Lapide's *Great Commentary*, authored by the great seventeenth-century Flemish Jesuit exegete, let alone any of the numerous *earlier* commentaries and resources he sites. For example, on 1 Cor 12–14 alone, Lapide cites not only well-known Patristics and Scholastics but works by Aquila of Sinope, Cassianus, Clarius, Forterius, Franciscus Albertinus, Galatinus, Haymo, D. Jordanes, Juan de Salas, Maldonatus, Oecumenius, Possidonius, Primasius, Prudentius, Rabbi Abraham, Rabbi David, Severian, Symmachus, Theodoret of Cyrus, Theophylact, Vatablus, Viguerius, and many others whom most scholars have never heard of today. Lapide's level of historical scholarship is virtually unmatched by any biblical commentator today. See Lapide, *Commentaria*; and W. F. Cobb's English translation, Lapide, *The Great Commentary*.

into antecedent thinkers or movements preceding them. As such, most of the chapters in the work are structured like miniature archeological "digs."

Volume 1, subtitled *The Modern Redefinition of Tongues*, comprises the first five chapters of the work:

Chapter 1, "The Current State of the Question," surveys the current discussion about speaking in tongues in both Protestant and Catholic circles, distinguishing between (a) the widespread understanding of the Pentecost account in Acts 2 as involving a miraculous gift of speaking ordinary human languages previously unknown to the speaker and (b) the contemporary Pentecostal and Charismatic understanding and practice of "tongues" as an unintelligible "language of the Spirit."

Chapter 2, "Contemporary Charismatic Culture" focuses more generally on the current culture of charismatic gifts in two significant contemporary movements, (a) the Toronto Blessing and (b) the Catholic Charismatic Renewal, tracking these back to common roots and noting common patterns exhibited in both movements.

Chapter 3, "The Pentecostal Crisis and Its Background," delves back into the historical beginnings of the Pentecostal movement with the revivals of Charles Parham in Topeka, Kansas, and of William Seymour in the Azusa Street mission in Los Angeles in the early 1900s. The origins of these revivals are then traced back through proximate historical antecedents, such as the Latter Rain movement, and the Holiness movements of the post-Civil War Wesleyan realignment associated with the Second Great Awakening, to the British Irvingite revivals of the 1830s. Against this background, the Pentecostal redefinition of "tongues" following the Pentecostal crisis of "Missionary Tongues" is analyzed in detail.

Chapter 4, "Who Coined the Word, *Glossolalia*, and Why?" traces the origins of this neologism back to a theory developed by German theologians in the Higher Criticism movement of the 1830s, and the introduction of the term *glossolalia* into the English language by Frederick Farrar in his book, *The Life and Work of St. Paul*, in 1879. The attempt of Higher Critics to link their understanding of the Christian doctrine of "tongues" to the ecstatic utterances of the ancient Greek Delphic Oracles and the unintelligible ecstatic vocalizations of the Montanist prophetesses is then analyzed in detail.

Chapter 5, "Cessationism and the 'Unknown Tongues' Construct," considers two developments rooted in the anti-Catholicism of the Protestant Reformation period. The first is the Cessationist doctrine, which did not change the traditional understanding of "tongues," but emerged as a reaction against the profusion of medieval Catholic accounts of miracles and led to the Protestant claim that miraculous gifts—including the miraculous gift of speaking in foreign languages previously unknown to the speaker—had completely ceased by the close of the apostolic age or shortly thereafter. The second is the "Unknown Tongues" construct that made its way into English Bible translations in the fourteenth century, which was subsequently exploited by Reformation-era Protestants as a device for attacking the Catholic Church's use of Latin by relating it to the "unknown tongues," "other tongues," or "strange tongues" criticized by the Apostle in 1 Corinthians 14 as unprofitable in the absence of an interpreter.

The discussion in chapter 5 of Cessationism and tongues is long and detailed. Some readers may find this section irrelevant to their outlook. Yet this subject has a significant place with many conservative Protestants and requires respectful attention within the history of the Christian doctrine of tongues.

Volume 2, entitled *Tongues through Church History*, covers the next five chapters of the work, which are devoted to an archaeological excavation of how "speaking in tongues" was understood through Church history:

Chapter 1, "The Francis Xavier Controversy and Pope Benedict XIV," delves into Protestant skepticism about the Catholic Church's claims that Xavier manifested the miraculous gift of speaking in foreign languages previously unknown to him. Protestant Cessationist criticisms of these claims are weighed against Catholic responses, including Pope Benedict XIV's four-volume treatise on the beatification and canonization process, which touches on the subject of Xavier's gift of tongues, offering careful criteria for evaluating such claims.

Chapter 2, "A Miracle of Hearing or Speaking?" considers the single solitary debate concerning "tongues" in Church history before the nineteenth century, a debate that lasted upwards of a millennium: the debate over whether the gift of tongues is a gift of *speaking* or *hearing*—that is, whether it is a gift of *speaking* foreign languages previously unknown to the speaker, or a gift of listeners miraculously *hearing* in their own language what was spoken in another. This debate, which is found also among contemporary Charismatics, is traced back through Nicetas of Heraclea in the twelfth century, Michael Psellos, the Venerable Bede, Maximus the Confessor, and Gregory of Nyssa, to Gregory of Nazianzus in the fourth century, with whom the debate began, sparked by a misunderstanding of his Easter Oration. Finally, this debate is related to a minor concurrent theory found among some ecclesiastical writers, which suggests that the tongues of Pentecost involved "one sound" that was heard in many distinct languages.

Chapter 3, "Two Major Scholastics: Suárez and Aquinas," explores the views of two theological giants, separated by a span of four hundred years, both of whom offer clear rationales for why the gift of tongues should be considered a gift of speaking rather than hearing and both of whom underscore the consistent ecclesiastical tradition that the gift of tongues involves ordinary human languages, as opposed to anything mystical.

Chapter 4, "Two Later Patristics: Augustine and Chrysostom," considers two beloved Fathers of the Church, correcting later Cessationist misinterpretations of their writings. It notes the remarkable claim of Augustine that the individual role of speaking in foreign tongues has been taken over by the corporate Church, since the Church, now being universal, "speaks in all the languages of the world." It also examines Chrysostom's notable observation that in 1 Corinthians 14, Paul was describing a situation in which untranslated foreign sacred languages were not understood by the Corinthian assembly and required someone skilled in these languages to interpret them.

Chapter 5, "Eight Early Patristics: Didymus to Irenaeus," begins in the fourth century with Didymus and tracks the early Patristic view of tongues back through Cyril of Jerusalem, Ephrem the Syrian, Pachomius, Eusebius of Caesarea, Origen, and Tertullian, to Irenaeus in the second century, revealing a consistent adherence to the interpretation of "tongues" as ordinary "languages."

Volume 3, entitled *The Tongues of Corinth*, covers the final four chapters of the work, which develop a cultural and historical framework for understanding the Apostle Paul's meaning in 1 Corinthians 12–14, as well as offering a general Conclusion of the work:

Chapter 1, "Key Patristics on Corinth: Cyril of Alexandria, Epiphanius, and Ambrosiaster," takes up the remarkable revelation from these writers that the tongues of Corinth did not involve a miraculous and mysterious gift of tongues in the sense usually understood by contemporary Pentecostal or Charismatic interpreters, but rather an ordinary problem of a human language—in this case, a sacred liturgical language—that could not be understood by most of the assembly without the service of an interpreter to verbally translate what was being spoken and read.

Chapter 2, "The Tongues of Corinth: Part 1," excavates the sources of the claim that the tongues of Corinth involved the use of Hebrew as a sacred liturgical language that had to be interpreted for the sake of the laity. Starting with the support for this claim found in the seventeenth-century English divine and rabbinical scholar, John Lightfoot, the chapter delves back through earlier attestations found in Moses Maimonides (c. 1135–1204) and the Babylonian Talmud (c. AD 200–500), to Nehemiah's account of the origins of this tradition in Ezra's first public reading of the Law (Torah) in Hebrew to the Jews in the fifth century BC, after their return from captivity in Babylon when many of the younger generations no longer understood Hebrew. In this chapter, we also explore the Jewish cultural background of the Corinthian assembly as described in Paul in 1 Corinthians and evidence for the claim that the earliest Messianic assemblies did not lose their Jewish identity before the destruction of the Jerusalem temple in AD 70 and, therefore, continued to retain Jewish liturgical traditions and conventions.

Chapter 3, "The Tongues of Corinth: Part 2," considers the role of the Hebrew language in the Aramaic-speaking and Greek-speaking Jewish communities. It then explores the liturgical language of the Corinthian assembly, the mysterious *anaplērōn* of 1 Corinthians 14:16, and the meaning of *charisma* in Church History, which often turns out to mean something closer to a "talent" than a miraculous endowment.

Chapter 4, "Praying in Tongues," addresses the alternate ways in which the "tongues of Corinth" have been interpreted, beginning with a consideration of "angelic tongues," then delving into the Book of Enoch and Testament of Job, and concluding with a brief critical analysis of the claim that "tongues" in earlier Church history went under another name and was called "jubilation."

A few remarks are in order about the text. First, while contemporary movements that have descended from the earlier Pentecostal and Charismatic movements are sometimes referred to as belonging to the "Third-Wave" or "Spirit-empowered Christianity," we have decided, for the sake of broader recognition, to continue referring to "Pentecostal" and "Charismatic" movements, even if these terms may be technically anachronistic in certain cases. Second, we have opted to drop canonical religious titles (such as "St." or "Saint," "Rev." or "Reverend," "Fr." or "Father," "Msgr." or "Monsignor," "S.J." for "Society of Jesus," "O.P." for "Order of Preachers," etc.), except where needed for purposes of identification or easily recognized because of widely established conventions (such as the "Venerable Bede," or "Pope John Paul II"). Third, we have chosen to use the conventional English names for Patristic and medieval authors even where the cited sources use Latin (thus "The Venerable Bede" over "Bedae Venerabilis," for example). Fourth, we have opted to capitalize "Charismatic," "Pentecostal," "Higher Critical," "Cessationist," "Scholastic," and "Patristic" in their adjectival as well as nominal forms to underscore their reference to specific historical developments, although most other adjectival appellations (e.g., "biblical," "apostolic") are left uncapitalized. Fifth, books of the Bible are abbreviated according to widespread usage in the Protestant world (e.g., "Matt" for "Matthew," "Rom" for "Romans," etc.). Sixth, while we draw a technical distinction between *xenolalia* (speaking in intelligible foreign human languages) and *glossolalia* (speaking in unintelligible language-like vocalizations) in chapters 1 and 2, we generally try to avoid language that is overly technical where possible. Seventh, we follow the diacritical conventions of the Society for Biblical Literature wherever we transliterate Greek words in definitions, but we omit diacritical marks in the case of widely used words like *glossolalia* that have made their way into the English language. Eighth, as previously indicated (n6 above), when we refer to the literature of "Church history" or "ecclesiastical writings," we are referencing what is common to the Catholic tradition and the mainstream of the Protestant Reformation stemming from Luther, Calvin, the Anglican divines, and their proximate successors, and not to the anomalous beliefs and practices of those lying outside of this common tradition, including such nonconformist or separatist sects such as the Montanists, Ranters, Jansenists, Camisards (French Prophets), Shakers, or Mormons.

CHAPTER 1

The Current State of the Question

Introduction

WHAT DOES IT MEAN for a Christian to "speak in tongues"? Is there an established Christian doctrine of tongues? Amidst the many ready answers to such questions we may expect to hear today, the burden of this chapter is the relatively modest one of finding the right questions with which to begin our inquiry. Do Christians "tongues" properly refer to actual human languages? A mystical language of heaven? A language of angels? A private language of prayer? All of the above? Does the meaning of "tongues" vary from one historical context to another? Has it changed over time? We must make our beginning by considering those large bodies of Christians today who believe the gift of tongues to be a private or personal language of prayer and praise. This is, after all, where we find ourselves today. We shall consider whether the uttered sounds of such tongues have any definable meaning or are mere gibberish with an overlaid patina of spiritual significance. We shall explore the discrepancies involved in the buzzwords involved in gift-of-tongues discussions. We shall examine whether the gift of tongues is something generated naturally or preternaturally (unnaturally or inexplicably); whether it is a naturally learned and acquired skill, or an extraordinary gift miraculously imparted to the recipient in some mysterious way. We shall also make an initial foray into the mechanics behind speaking in tongues, inquiring whether speakers are always in control of what they are saying or whether their vocalizations simply come spontaneously of their own accord. Another question concerns the origins of tongues, whether they are divinely inspired, imparted quasi-hypnotically by the power of suggestion, or, perhaps in rare cases, of diabolical origin. All of these questions are not only legitimate but important and call for clear answers.

Here it may help to relate an anecdotal account of speaking in tongues that casts into high relief many of the questions surrounding the issue. The account is one related by Gerry Matatics. Like his well-known former seminary classmate Scott Hahn, Matatics was a Presbyterian pastor before being received into the Catholic Church in 1986. During one period of his earlier life, he frequented Pentecostal prayer meetings and worship services when he began having doubts about the manifestations he was witnessing, especially the phenomenon of speaking in tongues.[1] The practice of "tongues" in those meetings was similar to that described by Ronald Knox in his classic study, *Enthusiasm* (1950): a person would stand and announce something in an "unknown tongue," and then somebody else with a presumed gift of prophecy would stand up and interpret what had been said.[2] So Matatics, in response to the doubts he was having, quietly decided to conduct some personal tests. He would stand up in meetings and speak some unintelligible gibberish in his own improvised version of an "unknown tongue," memorizing exactly what he had said. Then at another meeting, he would say exactly the same thing. He noted, however, that whenever he did this, although he would say the same exact "words" (i.e., make the same sounds), the interpreter would interpret his "tongues" differently each time.

Then he took things one step further. At this point, Matatics had been teaching himself Greek and Hebrew so that he could read Scripture in the original languages. He had memorized Psalm 23 in Hebrew (Ps 22 in some Catholic Bibles): "The Lord is my shepherd, I shall not want . . ." (KJV). Then, during a Charismatic meeting, he stood and recited the Psalm in Hebrew. When he did this, the interpreter did not translate for the others in the room what Matatics had said in Hebrew, namely "The Lord is my shepherd, I shall not want . . ." Instead, the interpreter claimed that Matatics' "tongue" was a message from Heaven saying, "Oh my children, don't hold back, oh ye of little faith. *Build that extra wing onto the pastor's house* and I will bless you and open the flood gates of Heaven and pour out abundance upon you if you make this financial commitment." Not surprisingly, the interpreter turned out to be one of the pastor's best friends. So, after a few incidents

---

1. The word "tongues" when originally used to translate the New Testament Greek word *glōsses* (γλῶσσες) simply meant "languages," but readers should bear in mind the equivocality of the term as used in Pentecostal and Charismatic history, where the it is used with more than one meaning.

2. Knox, *Enthusiasm*, 554, 557.

of this sort, Matatics became quite disillusioned with the phenomenon of "tongues" he was witnessing.[3]

Such accounts, although they are far from universal, raise many questions. Before delving precipitously into a quest for answers, however, let us step back for a moment and ask ourselves some even more basic questions: Why should we concern ourselves with tongues at all? Why should anyone care what tongues are? Why should it matter whether tongues are authentic or delusional, as long as they don't hurt anybody and perhaps even bring joy to those who believe in them and practice speaking in tongues? Do they hurt anyone? Does anyone claim that speaking in tongues is necessary for salvation? Why should it matter what anyone thinks about "tongues" as long as the tongues-speaker is a faithful Bible-believing Christian? Why should anyone consider "tongues" anything more than a phenomenon of marginal importance to the Christian life?

For one thing, a growing number of Christians consider tongues to be very important indeed. Christians involved in the Neo-Pentecostal or Charismatic movement (sometimes called the "Third Wave" or "Neo-Charismatic" movement, often identified with "Signs and Wonders," "Power Evangelism," or the "New Apostolic Reformation"),[4] speak of a "Tsunami of the Spirit" sweeping the world in these "end times" in fulfillment of the prophecy of the prophet Joel in which God declares: "I will pour out my Spirit on all flesh; your sons and your daughters shall prophesy, your old men shall dream dreams, and your young men shall see visions" (Joel 2:28 RSV).[5] The phenomenon of tongues is regarded, thus, as one of these special gifts poured out by the Holy Spirit, as one of the gifts or charisms received through baptism in the Spirit.[6] No less importantly, it is considered a foundational or "gateway" gift that opens up the recipient to still other gifts of the Spirit (like those mentioned in Rom 12; 1 Cor 12; Eph 4; 1 Pet 4); and in that sense, the gift of tongues is considered one of the most important charisms

3. Matatics' account is related by Vennari, *Close-ups*, 65–67.

4. The term "Third Wave" was coined by Fuller Seminary professor, Peter C. Wagner, *Third Wave of the Holy Spirit* (1988), to distinguish three phases of these modern renewalist movements: (1) the birth of Pentecostalism in the Azusa Street Revival of 1906, (2) the Charismatic movement in the 1960s, and (3) the Signs and Wonders movement associated with Wagner and John Wimbur. The "New Apostolic Reformation" is also identified with Wagner and the "Third Wave." An earlier more critical Lutheran assessment is Hollenweger, *Pentecostals*, esp. chs. 1–2.

5. References to "Tsunami of the Spirit" can be found in Clark and Healy, *Spiritual Gifts*, 105; and Healy, *Healing*, 9.

6. The expression "baptism in the Spirit" is perfectly biblical, but its interpretation involves an unsettled and controverted doctrine. It will be considered briefly in the next chapter, though an adequate analysis is beyond the scope of the present study.

or gifts. The phenomenon of tongues has become so commonplace among Christian groups over recent decades as to be considered nearly normative in certain Christian communities, Catholic as well as Protestant. It is no longer a phenomenon confined predominantly to Pentecostal denominations, as it was in the past. Numerous books have appeared promoting the phenomenon of tongues—from the early 1964 classic, *They Speak with Other Tongues*, by the Episcopalian John Sherrill, to the more recent 2019 study, *The Language of Heaven*, by the evangelical Calvinist Sam Storms. On January 21, 2014, at its annual Ministers' Conference, Kenneth Copeland Ministries received a widely publicized personal video message from Pope Francis reaching out to Protestant Pentecostals and calling for Christian unity, to which Copeland and his assembly responded with a collective volley of praying in tongues for Pope Francis. Charismatic mass rallies with thousands of raised arms and people praying or singing in tongues are no longer an exclusively Pentecostal Protestant thing. On June 1, 2014, Pope Francis met with more than fifty thousand Catholic Charismatics in Rome's Olympic Stadium, inviting them to come to St. Peter's Square for Pentecost in 2017 to celebrate the fiftieth anniversary of the Catholic Charismatic Renewal, which traces its origins to a retreat held in 1967 with students and staff at Duquesne University in Pittsburgh. Two books that helped ignite the Catholic Charismatic Renewal are *They Speak with Other Tongues* (1964) by John Sherrill, and *The Cross and The Switchblade* by the Pentecostal preacher David Wilkerson, originally published in 1963 and reissued in 2018 with John and Elizabeth Sherrill as contributing authors.

Furthermore, the phenomenon of tongues represents the most prevalent and consistent distinctive characteristic of the Pentecostal and Charismatic movements, which, in recent decades, have represented the fastest growing sectors of Christianity throughout the world. If one were to ask what explains the explosive growth of these movements, the answer is not likely to lie in those areas where their beliefs and practices are held in common with other Christians. *Most* of their beliefs and practices are not particularly unusual. Like other evangelical Christians and practicing Catholics, they generally believe in the divine authority of Scripture, the divinity of Christ, original sin, the indispensable necessity of Christ's atonement for salvation; and they evangelize, catechize, baptize, celebrate the Lord's Supper, and so forth. For example, a book by the Catholic Charismatic, Patti Mansfield, *As by a New Pentecost*, lists the following as effects of baptism in the Spirit: a deeper awareness of the presence and love of God, a new understanding of Christ's Lordship, a growth of intimacy with God in prayer, a hunger for God's word and the sacraments, a love for the Church, a new desire to witness, growth in the fruit of the Spirit (peace, joy, love), an experience of the promptings and guidance of the Holy Spirit, awareness of the reality of spiritual warfare, a call to purification and holiness, a desire for Christian unity, a call to serve the needs of others, etc. None of these things is unique to those involved in Pentecostal and Charismatic movements or the least bit controversial. Christian believers, preachers, theologians, bishops, and popes throughout Church history have stressed the importance of the very same things. Indeed, *any* devout Christians, from a Catholic traditionalist to a Calvinist Cessationist, could readily affirm as much. Thus, we find here *nothing* more than the expected virtues that God desires to see flourish in all his sons and daughters as they grow in grace, sanctity, and discipleship in their Christian lives.

Yet everyone familiar with Pentecostal and Charismatic movements knows that this does not begin to define what is distinctive about them. Whether Pentecostal or Charismatic, Protestant or Catholic, there is invariably "something more" that colors everything in these movements, from their preferred style of worship and prayer to their taste in music, and their assumptions about things like prophecy, faith healing, and "tongues."[7] For many Catholics, this "something more" signals a distinctive set of assumptions and practices widely recognized as having been imported into the Catholic Charismatic circles from Protestant Pentecostalism; something that stands out as a novel obtrusion within the Catholic tradition and confirms Cardinal Newman's observation that "to be deep into history is to cease to be Protestant."[8] Something similar would likely be claimed by some Protestants, like the Calvinist evangelical John F. MacArthur, whose books, *Charismatic Chaos* (1993) and *Strange Fire: The Danger of Offending the Holy Spirit with Counterfeit Worship* (2013), signal a similar view of Pentecostal distinctives as alien to Calvinism and even to the mainstream evangelical tradition. Yet since this "something more" often occupies such a low profile in the inventory of concerns publicly expressed by Charismatics, it may often easily pass unnoticed; and one may miss the disproportionate importance it has acquired in the daily practice of Charismatic spirituality.

---

7. Their preferred style of worship is sometimes described as "contemporary" and "freewheeling"; their preferred style of prayer as "extemporaneous," "intimately personal," and often in "tongues"; and their preferred style of music as "praise and worship music," typically led by a "worship band" or "praise team" and characterized by "metaphorical interpersonal language" ("I give you my heart," "Draw me close," etc.) with a "subjective," and "emotional" cast. See Csordas, *Language*, 108–11, and the summary of his thesis in Csordas, "Phenomenology"; Wikipedia, s.v. "Contemporary Worship Music," https://en.wikipedia.org/wiki/Contemporary_worship_music, para. 7–11; Wikipedia, s.v. "Catholic Charismatic Renewal," https://en.wikipedia.org/wiki/Catholic_charismatic_renewal, para. 3–6.

8. Newman, *Essay*, Introduction, pt. 5.

Let us illustrate. In Mansfield's above-cited list of effects of baptism in the Spirit, there is one entry that we left out. We did so because that entry alone in her list uniquely signals the "something more" that gives the Catholic Charismatic movement its unique "Charismatic" identity, gives rise to controversy, and casts into doubt its claims that its distinctive beliefs and practices are deeply rooted in Catholic history and tradition rather than idiosyncratic.[9] Ironically, it is precisely this "something more" that also gives the movement its massive appeal. So, what is the entry in question in Mansfield's list? Those in the Charismatic movement typically expect that one of the effects of baptism in the Spirit will inevitably be "a Manifestation of the Charismatic gifts such as the gift of tongues."[10]

This expectation that baptism in the Spirit will manifest itself in spiritually powerful Charismatic gifts, most notably in "tongues," is replete throughout Charismatic literature and constitutes the powerful appeal of Pentecostal-Charismatic movements. Though there is some debate about whether the gift of "tongues" necessarily *always* follows baptism in the Spirit, it is generally considered nearly normative. For example, in the *Life in the Spirit Team Manual* (1979), which is used to lead Charismatic "Life in the Spirit" seminars, we read that a team member "should have yielded to the gift of tongues himself"; that "when the Holy Spirit comes to a person . . . he discovers that he can pray in tongues"; that "tongues come when a person is baptized in the Holy Spirit"; that "everyone should want the gift of tongues."[11] Hence, speaking in "tongues" is treated as a normal expectation: "There are some people . . . who say that they do not want to have the gift of tongues. This is a wrong attitude. The person is placing limits on God's working. . . . Everyone should want to have tongues."[12] In the book, *Baptized in the Spirit and Spiritual Gifts*, by Steve Clark—an early leader in the Catholic

---

9. For example, Francis Martin's *Baptism in the Holy Spirit* (1998), despite its subtitle, *Reflections on a Contemporary Grace in the Light of Catholic Tradition*, fails to furnish any evidence of the kind readers might expect to find for the claim that the distinctive experiences of contemporary Charismatics are clearly grounded in *Catholic tradition*, as his subtitle claims. Virtually all of his references, instead, are to the documents of Vatican Council II (1962–65) and more recent articles mentioning the Holy Spirit.

10. Mansfield, *As by a New Pentecost*, 280 (The "M" in "manifestation" is capitalized in the original); cf. also Martin, "A New Pentecost?," 18, 22.

11. *Life in the Spirit Team Manual*, 20, 114, 147. Described as "Developed by the Word of God" [i.e., the Word of God Charismatic community in Ann Arbor, Michigan], the volume expresses the expectation that speaking in tongues will follow upon being baptized in the Spirit, a belief that is described as a fundamental doctrinal tenant among Pentecostals. Cf. Hoekema, *What About?*, 38–39.

12. *Life in the Spirit Team Manual*, 143.

Charismatic Renewal (unrelated to Randy Clark) whose works are repeatedly recommended by the *Life in the Spirit Team Manual*—we read that a person is "not fully in the Spirit unless he has yielded to this kind of prayer [in 'tongues']."[13] Again, in a book published by the Doctrinal Commission of the Catholic Charismatic Renewal, *Baptism in the Holy Spirit*, authors Mary Healy and Peter Hocken state that wherever the Catholic Charismatic movement is "healthy and the exercise of the charisms is mature . . . the gift of tongues has become quite common, and in this sense ordinary, primarily as a gift of prayer and praise."[14]

Given the exceptionally prominent role of tongues as a uniquely prized effect of baptism in the Spirit in both Catholic and Protestant Charismatic movements, the phenomenon begs for further scrutiny. The question of tongues, thus, will be subjected to critical scrutiny from many angles in the present inquiry. It should not be supposed, however, that the authors entertain an attitude of skepticism about the power of God to perform miracles or about the documented miraculous gifts He has granted to various believers throughout history—gifts of speaking unlearned foreign languages, healing, prophecy, exorcism, and even raising the dead. The Old and New Testaments and the lives of various Christian saints throughout the ages offer some compelling examples of such gifts. This does not mean, however, that these gifts are necessarily common or that they are quite what they are claimed to be in Pentecostal-Charismatic movements.

In the opening paragraphs of this chapter, we saw how Gerry Matatics became disillusioned with the phenomenon of "tongues" after conducting some personal tests to check their authenticity in several Pentecostal services. This incident calls us back to the key questions raised at the beginning of this chapter. If "tongues" are not always actual human languages, what are they? Are they a private "language" of prayer and praise, as many claim today? If so, do the uttered sounds have any definable, translatable meaning, or are they no more than vocalized gibberish with an overlaid patina of spiritual significance?

Considerable confusion surrounds the question of tongues, or *glossolalia*, as they are sometimes called. Authors who purport to address the subject often simply assume that the reader knows what the term means; or, if they attempt to define it, they may do so in ways that evade an unequivocal definition and instead embrace a maddening variety of unrelated meanings.

13. Clark, *Baptized in the Spirit*, 38.

14. ICCRS, *Baptism in the Holy Spirit*, 22. The authorship of Mary Healy and Peter Hocken is indicated on p. 6, although the authority behind the publication is shown as the International Catholic Charismatic Renewal Services (ICCRS) Doctrinal Commission.

In the course of a single essay or book, an author may unaccountably shift from one meaning to another without in any way signaling the difference linguistically—all the while using the same term. In one instance "tongues" may refer to the supernatural gift of speaking (or hearing and understanding) a previously unlearned human language as in the Pentecost narrative in Acts 2. In another instance, it may refer to the mysterious experience of uttering sounds in a heightened state of spiritual consciousness that corresponds to no known human language. Sometimes one wonders whether authors addressing the topic even know exactly what they mean by "tongues."

Typical is the Wikipedia article, "Speaking in tongues," which, citing various authorities, states: "*Glossolalia* or *speaking in tongues* is a phenomenon in which people speak words that are apparently in languages unknown to the speaker. One definition used by linguists is the fluid vocalizing of speech-like syllables that lack any readily comprehended meaning, in some cases as part of religious practice in which it is believed to be a divine language unknown to the speaker."[15] The article goes on to apply the terms "glossolalia" and "tongues" interchangeably to biblical, historical, and pagan examples, often without indicating whether the "language" spoken or heard is a natural human language or something humanly incomprehensible and alien.[16] One exception is where the article observes that "sometimes a distinction is made between 'glossolalia' and 'xenolalia' or 'xenoglossy' which specifically designates when the language being spoken is a natural language previously unknown to the speaker."[17] The same equivocity can be found in Russell P. Spittler's article, "Glossolalia," in the *International Dictionary of Pentecostal and Charismatic Movements* (2002), which indiscriminately uses *glossolalia* for references to "tongues" both as ordinary human languages and as unintelligible vocalizations.[18]

Given this confusing semantic range of different meanings associated with the "tongues," it may be helpful at this point to draw a clear distinction between two basic definitions of "tongues"—(1) *"tongues" as ordinary human languages* and (2) *"tongues" as an unintelligible "language" of the spirit.*

---

15. Wikipedia, s.v. "Speaking in Tongues," https://en.wikipedia.org/wiki/Speaking_in_tongues, para 1, cites Colman, *Dictionary*, s.v. "Glossolalia." (An internet search for "Glossolalia" notably leads to the same Wikipedia article.)

16. Another example is Johnson, *Speaking in Tongues*, 7–10.

17. Fahlbusch et al., *Encyclopedia*, 415; Lum and Harvey, *Oxford Handbook*, 801.

18. Spittler, "Glossolalia," 670–76.

"Tongues" as Ordinary Human Languages

The greatest unanimity in the debate over tongues is found in connection with what "tongues" means in the Pentecost narrative in Acts 2. In that account, the Apostles were "filled with the Holy Spirit and began to speak in other tongues, as the Spirit gave them utterance." There were present in Jerusalem devout Jews "from every nation under heaven" who were "bewildered because each one heard them speaking in his own language." They were amazed and wondered, saying "Are not all these who are speaking Galileans? And how is it that we hear, each of us in his own native language? Parthians and Medes and Elamites and residents of Mesopotamia, Judea and Cappadocia, Pontus and Asia, Phrygia and Pamphylia, Egypt and the parts of Libya belonging to Cyrene, and visitors from Rome, Jews, and proselytes, Cretans and Arabians, we hear them telling in our own tongues the mighty works of God" (Acts 2:4–11 RSV).

The unanimous testimony of Church history[19] before the Pentecostal redefinition of tongues in the twentieth century is that the tongues of Pentecost were actual human languages and that this miraculous gift was intended for the purpose of propagating the Gospel. As indicated in the Wikipedia article, sometimes the term *xenolalia* or *xenoglossy* is used (instead of *glossolalia*) for "tongues" in this sense, to specifically designate that the language being spoken is a natural human language.[20] There was never any serious debate about this in Church history until modern times. The only sustained debate about "tongues" concerned whether the gift involves a miracle of *speaking* or *hearing* (and understanding) a previously unlearned foreign language. Whether or not the gift of tongues in this sense is always a miraculous supernatural gift, or whether it could also reference a natural "gift for languages" in the common, mundane sense of the expression, is a question that remains to be addressed.

There has been no significant dissent, however, from the consensus view that the "tongues" of Pentecost were actual human languages, even among the vast majority of Pentecostals and Charismatics.[21] The few

19. As mentioned in our Introduction, when we refer to "Church history" or "ecclesiastical writings," we are referencing what is common to the Catholic tradition and the mainstream of the Protestant Reformation stemming from Luther, Calvin, the Anglican divines, and their proximate successors.

20. Wikipedia, s.v. "Speaking in Tongues," https://en.wikipedia.org/wiki/Speaking_in_tongues, para. 2, cites Johns and Macchia, "Glossolalia," *Encyclopedia*, 413. The term *xenoglossy* was coined, reportedly, by French parapsychologist Charles Richet in 1905 (Wikipedia, s.v. "Xenoglossy," https://en.wikipedia.org/wiki/Xenoglossy, para. 1).

21. In his massive study of Acts 1–2, Keener, *Acts*, 780–836, marshals an immense amount of evidence in support of the thesis that the tongues of the New Testament

dissenting opinions seem to be confined to two groups. On the one hand are modern proto-Pentecostal sectarians such as the Irvingite minister, John S. Davenport, who in 1878 denied that the "tongues" of Pentecost were actual languages or were intended for evangelism and who, like other followers of the English mystic, Edward Irving (1792–1834), first began to allow that "tongues" might also include unintelligible spiritual utterances.[22] On the other hand are modern theologians of the more liberal type found among the disciples of the great "demythologizer" of Scripture, Rudolph Bultmann. One example is Hans Conzelmann, who in his widely-acclaimed *Commentary on the Acts of the Apostles* (1987) takes a subtly skeptical view of the literal historicity of the Pentecost account. On the one hand, he denies that Luke's account is based on mere "naïve legend"; but on other hand, he describes Luke as fashioning his account into "an episode with a burlesque impact" and as having lost the original, ecstatic, *glossolalic* sense of "tongues."[23] Conzelmann has been roundly criticized by some evangelicals.[24]

Few Pentecostals and Charismatics today would accept the view that the gift of "tongues" refers exclusively to ordinary human languages. One exception is the Catholic Charismatic, Steve Clark, who apparently holds this view, although he also heightens the level of mystery surrounding such "tongues" by insisting that the speaker does not understand what he is saying. He says that speaking in tongues is just "speaking in languages," by which he means speaking ordinary human languages that the speaker himself does not happen to understand.[25] The rationale he offers for this curious miraculous gift is that speaking in a foreign language one does not understand makes it easier for people to "yield to the Spirit than it is in English."[26] Why? Because most Americans (ostensibly he has English-speaking Americans in mind) can overcome their inhibitions about exercising this gift, he says, only by "bypassing their mind."[27] "Tongues" in Clark's sense could be interpreted easily by those who know the foreign language being spoken; but as far as the one speaking in tongues is concerned, they remain unintelligible, suggesting a view effectively no different from the second view discussed below.

---

always represent actual languages, no less in 1 Corinthians 12–14 than in Acts 2.

22. M. H. W., "Gift of Tongues," 14.

23. Conzelmann, *Acts of the Apostles*, 15.

24. Bruce, "Commentaries on Acts," 84; Cullmann, *Salvation in History*, s.v. "Conzelmann"; Dockery, "Theology of Acts," 44; cf. Conzelmann, *Theology of St. Luke*, 14–17; Conzelmann, *Acts of the Apostles*, 15; cf. 244.

25. Clark, *Baptized in the Spirit*, 127.

26. Clark, *Baptized in the Spirit*, 38.

27. Clark, *Baptized in the Spirit*, 38.

"Tongues" as an Unintelligible "Language of the Spirit"

The other major division within the currently-accepted meanings of "tongues," although far from being uncontroversial, is most often identified with what the Apostle Paul appears to be describing in the Church of Corinth, especially in the 1 Corinthians 14 (although some dissent from this view).[28] In Paul's account, he describes what seems like an altogether exceptional, mysterious otherworldly language: "For one who speaks in a tongue speaks not to men but to God; for no one understands him, but he utters mysteries in the Spirit" (v. 2). He continues, "If you in a tongue utter speech that is not intelligible, how will anyone know what is said? For you will be speaking into the air" (v. 9). A little later, he adds: "For if I pray in a tongue, my spirit prays but my mind is unfruitful" (v. 14). Further on, he adds this caveat: "If, therefore, the whole church assembles and all speak in tongues, and outsiders or unbelievers enter, will they not say that you are mad?" (v. 23). Given, this prospect, he offers the following instruction: "If any speak in a tongue, let there be only two or at most three, and each in turn; and let one interpret. But if there is no one to interpret, let each of them keep silence in church and speak to himself and to God" (vv. 27–28 RSV).

"Tongues" in this second sense is often given the more technical name, *glossolalia* (in contrast to *xenolalia* or *xenoglossy*). The word "tongues" in this sense does not refer to ordinary human languages, but to utterances that are unintelligible to both the speaker and hearer, unless the hearer is ostensibly given the miraculous gift of understanding and able to "interpret" what is said. While disagreement persists over whether such "tongues" are natural or preternatural, ordinary or extraordinary, routine or ecstatic, a learned behavior or supernaturally inspired, a growing consensus seems to have emerged over the last century as to their general import. Most often, such "tongues" are described as a "private language of prayer and praise," in which case, whether they are expressed as "praying in tongues" or "singing in tongues," they are spontaneously manifested and no "interpretation" is necessary or provided, whether they are presumed to have any communicable meaning at all. Less frequently, such "tongues" are presumed to bear a divinely-inspired message requiring an interpretation by another individual with a gift of prophecy, as in the Pentecostal services attended by Matatics as described at the beginning of this chapter. Even some Charismatics, however, doubt the claim of "prophetic interpretation" of *glossolalia*. The late

---

28. Examples of scholars who argue that the "tongues" of Corinth involved natural human languages include Davies, "Pentecost and Glossolalia," 228–31; Gundry, "Ecstatic Utterance," 299–307; Ford, "Toward a Theology," 3–29.

Notre Dame theology professor Josephine Massyngberde Ford, who was an active member of the Catholic Charismatic movement, states that her own involvement in Pentecostal prayer meetings led her to doubt that such "interpretations" should be identified with the supernatural gift of prophecy, and should rather be classed as a word of "knowledge" or "wisdom."[29]

The existence of disagreements within Pentecostal-Charismatic circles over the meaning of "tongues" in this second sense demonstrates the need for caution and circumspection in our analysis. For this reason, we must extend our investigation into this second sense of "tongues" a little further. This confusion, especially that surrounding this second sense, is the special focus of the present study, whose animating purpose is to help bring clarity to the issue. At this point let us begin by introducing a linguistic clarification suggested by the sources we have consulted. As we have already seen, many of the available discussions of "tongues" apply the term *glossolalia* indiscriminately to "tongues" both in the first sense of actual human languages and in the second sense of an unintelligible language of the spirit. Spittler, in his article on "*Glossolalia*," goes so far as to confusingly classify *xenolalia* as a "variety" of *glossolalia*.[30] Thus it may be helpful for practical purposes to distinguish between the first and second sense of "tongues" above by calling the first *xenolalia* and restricting the term *glossolalia* exclusively to the second. It should be kept in mind, however, that Pentecostal and Charismatic writers do not always make this distinction; and we will not employ it generally beyond this chapter, because we prefer using Biblical language over abstract technical terms.

In 1972 University of Toronto linguist William J. Samarin published the results of a major international study of *glossolalia* based on participant observation in diverse Charismatic Christian communities, and concluded his extensive study by stating that *glossolalia* is "only a façade of language"; that it "consists of strings of syllables, made up of sounds taken from all those that the speaker knows, put together more or less haphazardly but emerging nevertheless as word-like and sentence-like units because of realistic, language-like rhythm and melody"; that it is "language-like because the speaker unconsciously wants it to be language-like" but "fundamentally is not language."[31] Thus, although *glossolalia* is frequently described as a personal or private "language" of prayer and praise, it is debatable whether it can be properly called a "language" in any credible sense of the word since

29. Ford, "Charismatic Gifts," 118.

30. Spittler, "Glossolalia," 675.

31. Samarin, *Tongues of Men*, 120, 128; Samarin, "Sociolinguistic vs. Neurophysiological Explanations," 293–96; cf. Nickell, *Looking for a Miracle*, 108.

languages always involve a communal element in which meaning is developed in a socio-historical setting. As the well-known philosopher of language Ludwig Wittgenstein famously asserted, there can be no such thing as a private language.[32]

Despite the growing acceptance over the last two centuries of this second, *glossolalic* view as a legitimate interpretation of "tongues," its basic claim regarding the existence of this unintelligible form of "tongues" in Scripture and Church history remains hotly contested by some. On the one hand are *Cessationists* like the aforementioned Calvinist evangelical John MacArthur, who deny that such "tongues" are anything more than fatuous delusional gibberish, and who insist that genuine tongues (in the first sense above) have now *ceased*. On the other hand are *Continuationists* like the Catholic scholar Victor Salas, who acknowledge that the miraculous gift of tongues in the first sense above has *continued*, but appeal to the great theologians of the past like Francisco Suárez (1548–1617), whose exhaustive knowledge of the entire theological tradition that preceded him proves, as Salas argues, that the understanding and practice of speaking in "tongues" as it currently exists in contemporary Charismatic circles cannot be reconciled with what is found in the long history of the Catholic theological tradition's understanding of this gift.[33]

There is also some question whether speaking in *glossolalic* tongues is a natural, learned skill, or a supernaturally bestowed gift. As we have seen, the Catholic Charismatic authors, Healy and Hocken, claim that wherever their movement is "healthy and the exercise of the charisms is mature . . . the gift of tongues has become quite common, and in this sense ordinary, primarily as a gift of prayer and praise"; but they also state later that charisms (spiritual gifts, such as tongues) are "not merely natural endowments or acquired skills," but "supernatural gifts that either enable what is humanly impossible (such as healings or miracles) or enhance a natural gift, such as teaching or service, to a level of supernatural efficacy."[34] This raises the question of whether tongues as a personal language of prayer and praise should be understood as a supernatural gift that is truly miraculous (as fluently speaking a foreign language one does not know would be) or a gift that merely enhances a natural skill (such as uttering strings of word-like syllables in a way that sounds language-like) "to a level of supernatural efficacy," whatever that might mean. This view was also articulated by Léon Joseph Cardinal

---

32. Wittgenstein, *Philosophical Investigations*, §§244–71, cited by Salas, "Francisco Suárez," 558.

33. See Salas, "Francisco Suárez," 554–76.

34. ICCRS, *Baptism in the Holy Spirit*, 49.

Suenens, who writes: "The importance of speaking in tongues is not mini-mized if we situate it on a natural plane, which can assume a supernatural character through the intention which animates it."[35]

Opinion seems to be divided on this question. Some, like Ford, seem to agree with Healy and Hocken's claim that *glossolalic* "tongues" are not merely natural acquired skills, but supernatural gifts. Ford writes: "Genuine speaking in tongues is a prayer gift which comes without human interven-tion. Suddenly the recipient finds that he or she can speak, and very often sing, in a language which has not been learned through any human art."[36] On the other hand, John P. Kildahl, former professor at New York Theologi-cal Seminary and author of a ten-year study of "tongue-speaking" financed by the National Institute of Mental Health and American Lutheran Church, entitled *The Psychology of Speaking in Tongues* (1972), advances the hypoth-esis that *glossolalia* is a learned experience: "My glossolalia research has con-vinced me that it is a learned behavior," which can bring "a sense of power and well-being," as well as lead "to excesses resulting in community disrup-tion"; and he adds: "The capacity of being hypnotized and the capability of speaking in tongues are closely related."[37] Some have doubtless witnessed or heard of the semi-comic attempts of some *glossolalists* to instruct inquirers in techniques for learning to speak in "tongues" by repeating phrases such as "Tie a bow tie, untie a bow tie" or "Bought a Toyota, shoulda bought a Honda," over and over, in an attempt to circumvent the intellect and kick-start *glossolalia*, sometimes presenting "humility" and "receptivity" toward the Spirit as the rationale for what at first may appear completely silly. As Suenens writes: "If at the outset, a person accepts this act of humility—the risk of appearing foolish or childish—he soon discovers the joy of pray-ing in a way that transcends words and human reasoning, bringing great peace and an openness to spiritual communication with others."[38] Healy and Hocking seem to straddle the fence, somewhat like Suenens, suggesting that "tongues" could be perhaps both natural in one sense and supernatural in another—perhaps a naturally cultivated skill that could be miraculously "elevated to a supernatural level of efficacy," and thus used by God to al-low the user to grow in grace. Similarly, Francis Sullivan views *glossolalia* as a "latent capacity" activated in the subconscious, though distinct from

---

35. Suenens, *A New Pentecost?*, 101.

36. Ford, "The Charismatic Gifts," 114.

37. Kildahl, "Psychological Observations," 142; cf. 131; cf. Hopkins, "Glossolalia," 676–77, which also offers a sociopsychological analysis.

38. Suenens, *A New Pentecost?*, 102.

a deliberately-produced "pseudo-language" because of its spontaneity and capacity to be used by God as a means of "deeper surrender" to the Lord."[39]

The one thing about which there seems to be no disagreement is that this "gift of tongues" (in the second sense of *glossolalia*) has a profound spiritual significance to the practitioner. In his study entitled *Tongue Speaking* (1981), the Episcopal priest, Jungian psychologist, and former Notre Dame professor, Morton Kellsey observes: "All who have written of their first experience of speaking in tongues call it one of the most valuable and transforming experiences of their lives. To many of them it was the most important event they had known. . . . They had been seeking, knocking, asking, and now they had found what they were looking for, and it was even more wonderful than they had hoped."[40] Kildahl also acknowledges this, citing an article, "Glossolalia and Mental Health," sponsored by the National Institute of Mental Health and co-authored with Paul A. Qualben, in which they mention that *glossolalists* are "less depressed than non-glossolalists" and "continued their sense of well-being following a year's interval as they continued the practice of glossolalia."[41] Kildahl also states that the positive effects of "tongue-speaking" reported by *glossolalists* include personal happiness, a sense of greater personal power, more firmly held religious convictions, and warm fellowship with other "tongue-speakers."[42] There seems to be little reason for doubting the profoundly precious spiritual significance that *glossolalic* "tongues" have for those who manifest them. There seems to be just as little reason for believing, however, that they have any objectively verifiable meaning, apart from this subjectively perceived personal spiritual significance.

Some less-positive characteristics associated with *glossolalia* have also been noted. Kildahl details the psychological profile of the *glossolalist*, noting that "tongue-speaking" of this kind is often preceded by "a great sense of personal distress" or "existential crisis" in which the subject "is generally drawn to a person who is a leader whom he trusts" who inducts him into the practice of "tongue-speaking." The feelings of well-being experienced by the new "tongue-speaker," he says, are not caused by the actual making of the sounds in *glossolalia* itself, but by "feelings of acceptance by the leader and group of fellow tongue-speakers," as well as the belief, reinforced by the group, that *glossolalia* is "an act of God's intervention" in their speech. Thus, *glossolalists* as a group tend to be "more submissive, suggestible, and

39. Sullivan, *Charisms*, 140–43.
40. Kelsey, *Tongue Speaking*, 219.
41. Cited by Kildahl, "Psychological Observations," 142n1.
42. Kildahl, "Psychological Observations," 138–39.

dependent in the presence of authority figures" and more susceptible to the hypnotic power of suggestion than non-tongue-speakers, he says. "Hypnotizability constitutes the *sine qua non* of a glossolalia experience," he writes, adding that the phenomenon can also prove divisive and alienating in many communities.[43] Kelsey, who ultimately defends *glossolalia*, also expresses concern about the issue of divisiveness, citing St. Mark's Episcopal parish in Van Nuys, California, which split over the issue of tongues and baptism in the Spirit introduced by its pastor, Dennis Bennett, ultimately leading to his resignation. Episcopal Bishop James Pike, says Kelsey, warned about the same danger, stemming from "overzealous claims for power." Pike went so far as to intimate that "tongues" may well represent a "heresy in embryo," given the tendency of some *glossolalists* to maintain that unless there is a conscious experience of contact with God in some manifestation such as "tongues," sacraments and church services have no value or validity. Kelsey further suggests that "tongue-speaking" can become a "shortcut to religious and psychological growth which stunts it instead of giving full measure."[44]

What criteria should govern the evaluation of *glossolalia*? Kildahl points out that *glossolalists* themselves sometimes claim that anyone who has not *experienced* the phenomenon is in no position to evaluate it. He comments: "It may be said with equal validity that the person who has experienced the phenomenon may tend to place undue significance on the feelings of well-being that accompany speaking in tongues," adding that "subjective experience cannot alone determine the value of any phenomenon."[45] What criteria, then, would be fair? Kildahl writes: "A minor criterion is whether it has an upbuilding and uplifting effect on oneself. The major criterion is whether it edifies the community as a whole."[46] Many Christians—Protestants and Catholics, clergy and laity—have personally testified that their experience in the Charismatic Renewal has been a source of grace and spiritual growth in their lives. For some, it seems to be the first time in their lives that their faith has come alive and become "real," engaging them personally and emotionally, not only doctrinally and intellectually. For others, it seems to be the source of a deepening of existing faith, with a sense of renewal and reawakening. Yet, for all this, it would be disingenuous to ignore the uncomfortably large number of negative experiences others have also reported, in some cases even resulting in individuals

43. Kildahl, "Psychological Observations," 128–29, 139–40, 142n1.

44. Kelsey, *Tongue Speaking*, 222–26.

45. Kildahl, "Psychological Observations," 135.

46. Kildahl, "Psychological Observations," 141.

leaving the Church and losing their faith entirely.[47] Since such reports are not uncommon, it is hard to give an unqualified endorsement of everything in Pentecostal-Charismatic movements or to recommend that anyone without prior experience of them should become actively involved in them. As with all things spiritual, what one needs before embarking on any particular spiritual journey is discernment; and one thing this unavoidably requires is careful study and evaluation of beliefs and doctrine.

Different Types of Glossolalia

What are the possible sources, the causal agencies, that give rise to *glossolalia*? Ford distinguishes three possible sources in her article on *glossolalia* in the second edition of the *New Catholic Encyclopedia* (2003): (1) God, (2) hypnotism, and (3) diabolical influence.[48]

The first, authentic, type of *glossolalia*, she says, comes from God and can be seen in the tongues of saints such as the great Carmelite mystic, Teresa of Avila, and the pioneering missionary to India and the Far East, Francis Xavier. This suggests some lack of clarity: does Ford means "tongues" in the sense of *glossolalia* or *xenolalia*, since Teresa of Avila is widely-and-mistakenly thought by Catholic Charismatics to have experienced speaking in an unintelligible language (*glossolalia*), while Francis Xavier is believed to have evangelized native peoples of Asia by miraculously speaking to them in their own language (*xenolalia*).[49] In any case, Ford's article seems primarily concerned with *glossolalia*, which she identifies with what Paul describes as occurring in Corinth and defines as an "individual prayer gift to be used in private devotion for personal edification (1 Cor 14:2–4), or, if there is an interpreter, in the public assembly"; and it is clear that she believes that *glossolalia*, not only *xenolalia*, can be "genuine" and inspired by the Holy Spirit. She also concedes that "according to Samarin even the genuine gift of tongues [*glossolalia*] does not appear to be a language in the technical sense of the term but it is a 'non-cerebral' means of communicating with God akin to silent prayer, well-known liturgy, the Jesus Prayer or the Rosary (Baer)."[50]

---

47. Crumm, "Rise and Fall," 1–17; Tydings, "Shipwrecked in the Spirit," 83–179; Reimers, "Charismatic," 28–42. For these and related articles, see *Charismatic Movement and Catholic Tradition*, s.v. "History."

48. Ford, "Glossolalia," 249–50.

49. On Teresa of Avila, see Reid, *Carmelite Spirituality*, chs. 3–4; McDermott, "Do Charismatic Healings Promote the New Evangelization? Part II," 236–37.

50. Ford, "Glossolalia," 249–50; cf. Baer, "Quaker Silence," 150–64.

The second, "hypnotically-induced" type, she says, is exemplified by the "tongues" of the second-century heretical sect, the Montanists, and similar to ecstatic utterances in many religious traditions. In her 1975 essay, "The Charismatic Gifts in Worship," she distinguishes Montanist "tongues" from genuine *glossolalia* by calling them *xenophoneo* ("strange sounds") and states that their utterances were made in a state of ecstatic trance, in which they were "seized by a power beyond them" and "not in control of themselves," whereas in genuine *glossolalia*, the subject remains in control and "knows what is happening."[51] In her 2003 encyclopedia article, however, Ford states that hypnotically-induced "tongues" are found alongside genuine *glossolalia* in the "neo-pentecostal movement" today, Catholic as well as Protestant. In a striking passage, she catalogs a list of dangers associated with this hypnotically-induced type of "tongues":

> The hypnotic type produces the characteristics of divisiveness, projection of anger, group camaraderie, histrionic display, preoccupation with glossolalia, and, most importantly, a regression of the ego which results in subordination to the authority figure who introduces the recipient to "tongues." In light of this danger, it would seem advisable to refrain from the imposition of hands and repetition of syllables after leaders in order to help in yielding to tongues lest the hypnotic element be inadvertently introduced.[52]

The third, diabolical type is associated by Ford with demonic activity. Ford says little about this species of "tongues," or how it might apply to *glossolalia* or *xenolalia*. There is, however, a great deal on the subject in Catholic circles. For example, there is a relevant passage in a chapter on exorcism in the *Roman Ritual*—a work containing all of the official rituals of the Roman Rite that may be performed by a priest or deacon but are not contained either in the *Roman Missal* or *Breviary*. After recommending prudence and discretion before making a judgment about demonic influence, the passage indicates certain signs that allow for a diagnosis of authentic diabolical possession, which include the ability to speak in a strange and unknown language or to understand perfectly one who speaks in an unknown language.[53] Here it seems to apply only to *xenolalia*—the ability, under demonic influence in this case, to speak or understand a foreign language one has not learned.

---

51. Ford, "Charismatic Gifts," 115.

52. Ford, "Glossolalia," 259–50; Ford, "Charismatic Gifts," 117.

53. Marin, *Theology of Christian Perfection*, 253–54.

Other cases of demonic influence have been identified, however, with the practice of seeking the gift of *glossolalic* "tongues" in Charismatic circles. Fr. Chad Ripperger, an exorcist currently serving the Diocese of Denver, stated in a lecture in 2018: "The worst case of possession I have ever had was a woman who asked for the gift of tongues"; and he adds: "I cannot tell you—when I was in the Diocese of Omaha, the first place I was an exorcist. . . . I cannot tell you how many people I've had to clean up from the Charismatic Renewal, [despite] . . . the highest estimations I have of some of these people."[54] Adam Blai, a *peritus* or advisor on religious demonology and exorcism for the Catholic Diocese of Pittsburgh and auxiliary member of the International Association of Exorcists, stated in a lecture in Raleigh in 2015: "We have a real full-blown possession going on fifteen years now in this country from a [lay] person who prayed over somebody else who had a demonic problem."[55]

The imposition of hands is used in Charismatic circles sometimes not only for receiving and imparting the gift of "tongues," but for imparting the antecedent gift of baptism in the Spirit. It is important to understand, however, that "impartation" generally has a unique meaning in Pentecostal and Charismatic circles. It does not refer to the ordinary, mundane, and indirect means (such as evangelizing or preaching) by which the Holy Spirit may come to enter a person's heart. Rather it refers to a mystical supernatural "anointing," typically performed by the laying on of hands, whereby the Holy Spirit is thought to be directly transmitted to another individual and evidenced in "manifestations" such as the supernatural gifts of speaking in tongues or healing—or, in venues such as the "Toronto Blessing," even in gifts such as uncontrollable laughter, tears, shaking, fainting, or barking like a dog.[56] In fact, Rodney Howard-Browne, the controversial advocate of "spiritual drunkenness" and self-styled "bartender of the Holy Spirit," is reported to have transmitted his "anointing" to Randy Clark (unrelated to Steve Clark), who brought these sorts of extraordinary manifestations to Toronto, giving birth to the "Toronto Blessing" movement.[57] Ford's counsel that "it would seem advisable to refrain from the imposition of hands and repetition of syllables after leaders in order to help in yielding to tongues" could be prudently extended well beyond the dangers of inadvertently

---

54. Ripperger, "Speaking in Tongues," 2:24, 6:8.

55. Blai, "Exorcism in the Modern Church," 43:13.

56. See Rogers, *Power of Impartation*; Johnson and Miskov, *Defining Moments*; Beverley, *Holy Laughter*; Randles, *Weighed*, 135–83.

57. Randles, *Weighed*, 132.

introducing the "hypnotically-induced" variety of "tongues" here, given the far more dangerous threat of possible diabolical influence.[58]

Non-Christian varieties of *glossolalia* have also been reported. Some of these are detailed by Spittler in his extensive article on "Glossolalia."[59] In an important 1956 study that predates the rise of the Charismatic movement, anthropologist L. Carlyle May shows the widespread occurrence of contemporary non-Christian or *pagan glossolalia* among twentieth-century cultures. He employs a taxonomy of *glossolalia* ranging from mumbles and grunts and imitations of animal sounds to the locutions of esoteric priestly languages and widely related instances of *xenolalia* in the Far East, Southeast Asia, Siberia, Arctic regions, Africa, and the Middle East.[60] Some have claimed, on debatable grounds as we shall see, that an ancient parallel to modern *glossolalia* may be found in the Delphic Oracle of classical Greece, and the strange ecstatic utterances of the Pythian priestess, which were subsequently translated by the attending priest.[61] *Spiritualistic glossolalia* and related phenomena among spiritual mediums were initially investigated, according to Spittler, by psychologists at the beginning of the twentieth century: "Pentecostals have attributed a satanic origin to such cases," he writes, "even though proof lies outside scientific methods of socio-psychological inquiry."[62] More susceptible to scientific analysis is the category of *pathological glossolalia*, which has been for some decades the subject of medical and psychiatric investigation, particularly in cases resulting from neurological damage, effects of drugs, and psychotic disorders such as schizophrenia. A 1985 study by H. Malony and A. Lovekin reviewing the past century of social science research disputes earlier contentions that all *glossolalia*, including its Christian varieties, arises from mental or social disorders.[63] The aforementioned studies by Kelsey and Kildahl nevertheless underscore the importance of certain psychological considerations such as personal traumas and crises, authority relationships, the power of suggestion, hypnotic effect, and the potency of emotionally charged group dynamics.

In Christian Charismatic circles, *glossolalia* is typically limited to several types. Some of these can seem a trifle exotic, such as the gift of writing in unknown languages, called *xenography*, or the form mentioned by J. L. Smith as occurring in hand gestures among the deaf, which is admitted to

---

58. Ford, "Glossolalia," 259–50.

59. Spittler, "Glossolalia," 670–76.

60. May, "Survey," 75–96.

61. Parke and Wormell, *History*; cf. Spittler, "Glossolalia," 670–71.

62. Spittler, "Glossolalia," 670.

63. Malony and Lovekin, *Glossolalia*.

be very rare and called *manual glossolalia*.[64] Other accounts may prove improbable, such as Eddie Ensley's attempt to link glossolalia with the equivocal term *"jubilation."*[65] More typical are the varieties listed in *The Spiritual Gifts Handbook* (2018), co-authored by Healy, a Catholic Charismatic, and Randy Clark, a Pentecostal Vineyard revivalist associated with the controversial "Toronto Blessing" movement. Their classification of genuine *glossolalia* includes: (1) *Tongues as a personal language, or gift for prayer, praise, and worship*, which "by-passes the mind and comes directly from the heart"; (2) *Tongues as a public message* for a congregation, which is "more rare" and a "form of prophecy" (instead of a word of "knowledge" or "wisdom," as J. M. Ford argues); (3) *Tongues as a gift of intercession* based on the "inexpressible groanings of the spirit" (cited by Paul in Rom 8:26–27), in addition to *xenolalia*, which they call the "more obviously supernatural" gift: *"the miraculous gift of tongues."*[66] If we group together the first three varieties of "tongues" listed above, excluding *xenolalia*, it seems clear that they all may be classified as species of *glossolalia*, and that the most common and popular among them is that identified as "a personal language, or gift for prayer, praise, and worship." This suggests that the most common form of what is generally considered to be *authentic glossolalia* is here acknowledged to be a non-miraculous, acquired skill, even if, as Healy and Hocken suggest, it may be somehow "elevated to a supernatural level of efficacy."[67]

This raises an interesting question, particularly (but not only) for Catholics. The official teaching office of the Catholic Church, called the *magisterium*, historically nowhere explicitly references an authentic gift of "tongues" in any other sense than the miraculous gift of *xenolalia*. Some suggest that magisterial approval of *glossolalia* was indicated in Pope Francis' 2014 public endorsement of the Malines Documents (1974–86), six documents authored by Léon Jozef Cardinal Suenens aimed at providing theological and pastoral guidelines for the Catholic Charismatic movement.[68] In these documents, however, Suenens seems to be writing as a private theologian, so that the magisterial authority of these documents does not extend

---

64. Smith, "Glossolalia, Manual," 677–78.

65. Ensley, *Sounds*; cf. Healy, *Healing*, 204–5; Clark and Healy, *Spiritual Gifts*, 91–92; ICCRS, *Baptism in the Holy Spirit*, 62. But see Solignac, "Jubilation," 8:1472–78; Wikipedia s.v. "Jubilus," https://en.wikipedia.org/wiki/Jubilus, para. 1–2; Baumann, "Jodeln," 1488–1504; Salas, "Francisco Suárez," 554–76; McDermott, "Do Charismatic Healings Promote the New Evangelization? Part II," 236–37.

66. Clark and Healy, *Spiritual Gifts*, 178–84.

67. ICCRS, *Baptism in the Holy Spirit*, 49.

68. Suenens, *Malines Documents*. These documents emerged from a conference hosted by Suenens in Malines, Belgium, in 1974.

beyond the personal reflections of one particular cardinal archbishop. As helpful as some of these Maline Documents may be, they also reflect similar confusions to those found in many Pentecostal-Charismatic references to "tongues," and they fail to make critical distinctions between *xenolalia* and *glossolalia* where they are needed. Whatever the Malines Documents and Suenens may have said about "tongues" in the 1970s, the Church's doctrinal stance becomes crystal clear when we turn to its official magisterial documents. Even in its most recent reference to the gifts of the Spirit, the Congregation for the Doctrine of the Faith, in its Letter to the Bishops of the Catholic Church entitled *Iuvenescit Ecclesia* (May 15, 2015), classifies the gift of "tongues" in the same way that the gift of *xenolalia* at Pentecost has always been classified: as a miraculous, supernatural gift. Specifically, in its discussion of the gifts mentioned in the Pauline Epistles (Rom 12:6–8; 1 Cor 12:8–10, 28–30; Eph 4:11), it classifies "tongues" as one of the "exceptional gifts" alongside other supernatural charisms such as the miraculous gift of healing, in explicit contrast to "ordinary gifts" such as teaching and service.[69] This should come as no surprise. Charismatics typically also recognize *xenolalic* "tongues" such as those at Pentecost as miraculous, while conceding that *glossolalic* "tongues" may not always be miraculous. Clark and Healy, for example, refer to *xenolalia* as "the gift of tongues in a *more obviously supernatural way*, where the person is able to speak in a human language that he or she has never learned" [emphasis added].[70] The Catholic magisterium likewise consistently refers to the gift of tongues as "exceptional" and "extraordinary" and has never questioned the traditional view that this miraculous and supernatural gift is *xenolalic* (speaking foreign human languages).

This poses a special difficulty for those involved in the Catholic Charismatic movement. On the one hand, like many other Pentecostals and Charismatics, they accept non-*xenolalic* forms of "tongues" such as a "personal language of prayer and praise," which they often identify with *glossolalia*. "Tongues" in this sense they sometimes treat as a teachable skill to be learned through prayer and practice, by laying hands on a person's head and having him repeat a string of unintelligible word-like utterances. *Glossolalia* in this sense is treated as belonging to that class of spiritual gifts that one should "strive eagerly" to acquire (1 Cor 12:31; 14:1) because of their "powerful capacity to edify others."[71] The difficulty here is not merely that unintelligible word-like utterances have little capacity to "edify others,"

---

69. Congregation for the Doctrine of the Faith, *Iuvenescit Ecclesia*, 6.

70. Clark and Healy, *Spiritual Gifts*, 181.

71. Clark and Healy, *Spiritual Gifts*, 116; ICCRS, *Baptism in the Holy Spirit*, 50.

but that such "tongues" don't seem to meet the magisterium's criteria for such gifts as "extraordinary" and miraculous. On the other hand, therefore, Catholic Charismatics also seem eager to classify *glossolalia* as a supernatural gift, as we have seen in Ford's description of it as a "gift which comes without human intervention," and Healy and Hocken's insistence that such charisms are "not merely natural endowments or acquired skills" but "supernatural gifts," even if the supernatural element is achieved by enhancing a natural talent "to a level of supernatural efficacy." The difficulty here is that *glossolalia* as a "personal language of prayer and praise" doesn't rise to the level of what is obviously recognizable as miraculous or supernatural, even when it is perceived by the subject as having deep spiritual significance. Thus, it does not fall among those gifts that the magisterium declares to be "extraordinary" or "exceptional."

Another problem is that Catholic Charismatics, like others, generally view *glossolalia* as a virtually normative effect of baptism in the Spirit, as something inevitable, expected, and in that sense common, for which believers should "strive eagerly." This is not, however, how the magisterium views the gift of "tongues." In the Catholic tradition, gifts in the category of *xenolalic* "tongues" belong to the category of a "gratuitous grace" (*gratia gratis data*), which is freely bestowed by God for the purpose of edifying and helping *others* attain salvation, not like "sanctifying grace" (*gratia gratum faciens*) whose purpose is the sanctification of the recipient. As such, this gratuitous grace and the gifts that belong to it cannot be acquired, according to Catholic teaching, by any natural means.[72] For example, Ripperger, the aforementioned exorcist for the Diocese of Denver, in his 808-page *Introduction to the Science of Mental Health*, explicitly rejects the widespread assumption that supernatural charismatic gifts (*gratia gratis data*) "can actually be prayed for and merited, i.e., obtained by virtue of one's prayer," adding: "This is contrary to the very nature of gratuitous gifts and it manifests a lack of theological understanding."[73] The great Dominican scholar, Jordan Aumann, also observes: "Since [graces *gratis data*] do not form part of the supernatural organism [of the Christian life], they are not contained in the virtualities of sanctifying grace, and hence *the normal development of the life of grace could never produce or demand them*" (emphasis added).[74] For this reason, the Catholic magisterium insists that *extraordinary* gifts "are not to be sought after rashly, nor are the fruits of apostolic labor to be

72. See Marin, *Theology of Christian Perfection*, 74, 639–45.

73. Ripperger, *Science of Mental Health*, 442–43. See Aumann, *Spiritual Theology*, 237, 303–18.

74. Aumann, *Spiritual Theology*, 300; see also Salas, "Francisco Suárez," 564.

presumptuously expected from their use; but judgment as to their genuinity and proper use belongs to those who are appointed leaders in the Church, to whose special competence it belongs, not indeed to extinguish the Spirit, but to test all things and hold fast to that which is good."[75]

This may be why some Catholic Charismatics, like other Charismatics but for different reasons, seem to equivocate between a definition of "tongues" that is obviously *supernatural* (like *xenolalia*), which would place it under the magisterium's description of it as "extraordinary," and a definition of it that is more evidently *natural* (like *glossolalia* understood as a "personal language of prayer and praise"), which would allow it to escape the magisterium's definition of the gift as "extraordinary," uncommon, unexpected, and incapable of being sought by any natural means, and its prohibition against seeking it "rashly" by any means. The latter definition, by contrast, would also permit one to classify "tongues" among those gifts that Paul says we should "strive eagerly." In other words, as Victor Salas notes, "wittingly or not, the [Catholic Charismatic Renewal] is content to trade upon an ambiguity in language when it proposes 'speaking in tongues' But this is precisely the sort of ambiguity that [Francisco] Suárez had in mind, when he authored [his treatise on grace,] *De gratia*, 'to avoid the deceptions of the heretics, who under the ambiguities of various words attempt to introduce their errors.'"[76] Although Salas himself makes no accusation of heresy here, the ambiguities in question are clearly problematic.

In this chapter, we have seen many provocative questions raised about the "gift of tongues" and various phenomena associated with it. We have also seen that most of the controversy surrounding this gift is associated with *glossolalic* tongues, or tongues in the sense of unintelligible vocalizations most often called a personal or private "language of prayer and praise." Hence, our focus in chapters 2–4 will be on *glossolalic* tongues. Where do we find *glossolalia* being promoted today? Why are there so many confusing interpretations of the phenomenon? How did the idea of *glossolalia* arise as an interpretation of "tongues" distinct from *xenolalia*, and where did it originate, and why? Our investigations will begin with the present and take us back in time, tracking various clues and seeing where they lead. As such, our journey will involve a good bit of detective work and linguistic and cultural "archeology." In our next chapter, we shall examine the broader contemporary Pentecostal-Charismatic culture in which the phenomenon of *glossolalic* tongues is found today.

75. Paul VI, *Lumen gentium*, no. 12.
76. Salas, "Francisco Suárez," 576.

CHAPTER 2

Contemporary Charismatic Culture

From 1994 (Toronto Blessing launched)
back to 1967 (Catholic Charismatic Renewal begins)

IN TODAY'S CHARISMATIC CULTURE, especially in certain quarters, one finds a profusion of exceptional manifestations of spiritual gifts. Sometimes these are greeted by newcomers and observers with infectious eagerness and openness. At other times they are met with some hesitation or even perceived as off-putting and frightening. It is often only amidst such profusions of extraordinary enthusiasms, sometimes nearly obscured, that we find expressed the gift of tongues. It is understandable why people are attracted by the presumption of directly experiencing God, and, as it were, "channeling" the very power of the Holy Spirit. Who would not wish for such a grace, were it readily available? Since the Holy Spirit and his graces belong not to the natural order but the supernatural order, however, it must be asked whether they, unlike their *effects*, do not escape our direct experience and whether they are capable of being known in any other way than by faith.[1] Another question that must be asked is whether this proliferation of strange manifestations, along with the manner in which the gift of tongues is usually expressed today, do not arise less from the direct guidance of the Spirit than from ignorance of what the Church has taught throughout its history about charisms, and particularly about the gift of tongues. What has led to this new, strangely mysterious understanding of how God works through us?

---

1. *CCC*, # 2005; cf. Margerie, "Gifts."

In 1995 Metro Vineyard Fellowship in Kansas City published a thirty-page document in its *Renewal Series* intended to help participants in their ministry in interpreting what their church leaders consider to be "manifestations" of the Holy Spirit. Entitled "God's Manifest Presence: Understanding the Phenomena That Accompany the Spirit's Ministry," the document has a section entitled "Catalogue of Manifestations" in which the authors, Mike Bickle and Michael Sullivant, write:

> The Hebrew and Biblical model of the unity of personality implies that the Spirit affects the body. At times, the human spirit is so affected by the glory of God, the body is not capable of containing the intensity of these spiritual encounters, and strange physical behavior results. . . . However, this does not imply that they are therefore carnal and should be forbidden. The following are phenomena that have been observed in contemporary experience: shaking, jerking, loss of bodily strength, heavy breathing, eyes fluttering, lips trembling, oil on the body, changes in skin color, weeping, laughing, "drunkenness," staggering, travailing, dancing, falling, visions, hearing audibly into the spirit realm, inspired utterances—i.e., prophecy, tongues, interpretations, angelic visitations, and manifestations, jumping, violent rolling, screaming, wind, heat, electricity, coldness, nausea as discernment of evil, smelling or tasting good and evil presence, tingling, pain in the body as discerning of illness, feeling heavy weight or lightness, trances, altered physical states while seeing into the spiritual world, inability to speak normally, disruption of the natural realm, e.g., electrical circuits blown.[2]

Surely one of the more stunning and extensive inventories of "manifestations" understood by certain Charismatics today to be the work of the Holy Spirit, this list includes examples that many Christians would likely consider extreme. Not everyone who "speaks in tongues" experiences all these other "manifestations"; nevertheless, the listed phenomena collectively provide a much-needed larger framework for understanding something important about the contemporary context in which *glossolalic* "tongues" are experienced today as a "gift of the Spirit," even where some of these more bizarre "manifestations" are absent. Whatever we think of such "manifestations," this must be the point of departure for our investigation of the mystery and origins of *glossolalia*.[3]

2. Mike Bickle and Michael Sullivant, "God's Manifest Presence," cited in Randles, *Weighed*, 13–14, 19.

3. As noted in chapter 1, we shall generally avoid technical terms where possible, but in the present work we use the term *glossolalia* generally for unintelligible

In 1988, C. Peter Wagner, then a professor at Fuller Theological Seminary's School of World Missions and a key leader in the Church Growth Movement, published a book of some historical significance, entitled *The Third Wave of the Holy Spirit: Encountering the Power of Signs and Wonders Today*. In his scenario, there were three "waves" in the outpouring of the Holy Spirit in these "latter days." The "First Wave" was the movement of classic Pentecostalism, sparked by William Seymour's Azusa Street revival in Los Angeles in 1906, which included healing, prophecy, and of course speaking in tongues. The "Second Wave" was the Charismatic movement, which spilled out of Pentecostal denominations into mainline Protestant denominations, independent churches, and parts of the Catholic Church in the 1960s. Wagner coined the term "Third Wave" to represent the major shift in the 1980s, as one commentator writes, among "evangelicals from reformed [Calvinist] and dispensational backgrounds who . . . experienced a paradigm shift and now believe that the miraculous or sign gifts portrayed in the Gospels and Book of Acts continue to the present."[4]

This "Third Wave," sometimes also called the "Signs and Wonders" movement, involves what has been, initially at least, primarily an American phenomenon. Peter Wagner, who spent time as a missionary in Bolivia, promoted the principle of "spiritual warfare" against demons in his book, *Spiritual Power and Church Growth* (1986). John Wimber, a colleague of Wagner in church growth studies at Fuller Theological Seminary from 1974–78 and founder of the Association of Vineyard Churches in 1982, promoted the principle of "miraculous healing" through his preaching and books such as *Power Evangelism* (1986) and *Power Healing* (1987). George Otis Jr., an advocate of trans-denominational "Transformational Christianity," also promoted the idea of "spiritual mapping," a process of identifying locations from which demons must be dislodged, based on the work of the Kenyan evangelist Thomas Muthee.[5] Kenneth E. Hagin, a "prosperity gospel" preacher in the Word of Faith movement, promoted the principle of "power evangelism," by which believers and evangelists could directly tap into the Holy Spirit's miraculous and powerful gifts. Wagner coined the title "New Apostolic Reformation" to underscore the "post-denominational" nature of the movement, which recruits pastors from independent congregations and individual members from other churches through cell group meetings, and advocates the restoration of the "lost offices" of church governance, notably

---

non-linguistic vocalizations, and *xenolalia* for ordinary human speech, intelligible to those who know the language.

4. Sarles, "Appraisal," 57–82. This is significant because Calvinists are traditionally Cessationists.

5. Lampman, "Targeting Cities," para. 1–2, 8–11.

the offices of "prophet" and "apostle."[6] In 2011, according to the Pew Research Center, the movement, combined with the Charismatic movement (the "Second Wave"), numbered 305 million people worldwide; and combined with the world's Pentecostal Christians (the "First Wave"), numbered over half a billion adherents.[7]

These vast numbers represented by Pentecostal and Charismatic movements throughout the world have their roots, generally speaking, in the restorationist impulses of the Protestant Reformation, which aimed to restore what was presumed to have been lost over the centuries of Church history by retrieving a purer and more potent form of Christianity from the early apostolic Church.[8] These movements today, however, present a dizzying and seemingly endless variety of subdivisions and sub-movements which defy easy categorization. The most that we can aim for in this chapter, therefore, is to sketch a rough outline of two of the most prominent of these movements—one representing the "Third Wave," and another originating in the "Second Wave" but merging with the "Third"—to get a sense of the cultural milieu in which *glossolalic* "tongues" are experienced today as one of a variety of "manifestations of the Spirit." This will set the stage for the next chapter, in which we begin identifying the clues that will lead us back along the historical trajectory by which the current "tongues" doctrines have developed. It should prove helpful and illuminating to consider here the wider context in which contemporary "tongues" are exhibited alongside other "manifestations," as well as the pattern of motives and dispositions that the principal leaders and actors exhibit in these movements.

The Toronto Blessing

One of the most notable recent examples of the "Signs and Wonders" movement is the "Toronto Blessing," a name apparently coined by the British news media for the unusual manifestations appearing at the revivals of the Toronto Airport Vineyard Church, launched in 1994 by John and Carol Arnott in affiliation with the thousands of churches worldwide linked to the Vineyard movement started by John and Carol Wimber. The story of how

---

6. Newman, *Loss and Gain*, 200–201, 307, 348–50, illustrates Newman's response to similar nineteenth-century Irvingite claims to have restored the office of "prophet" and "apostle" by appealing to the Catholic doctrine of apostolic succession.

7. Pew Research Center, "Global Christianity," last two paragraphs.

8. The nineteenth-century American Restoration Movement (Stone-Campbell Movement) is merely one among many specific examples of this restorationist impulse. See Wikipedia, s.v. "Restoration Movement," https://en.wikipedia.org /wiki/Restoration_Movement, para. 1.

the church began is fascinating. After years of ministering in an evangelical church in Stratford, Ontario, and another in Toronto, Arnott and his wife reportedly found themselves in a period of spiritual dryness and discouragement. Witnessing other "powerfully anointed ministries" in action, they began praying that their ministry might be similarly empowered by God. Their search took them to Argentina, where they witnessed the lively revival meetings of the American evangelist, Benny Hinn, as well as various Argentinean evangelists. At one meeting, Claudio Freidzon, an Assembly of God evangelist, singled John out from the crowd and asked him "Do you want the anointing?" "Oh, yes!" he replied. "Take it!" said the evangelist, and Arnott reported something "clicking" in his heart.[9]

Meanwhile, a Vineyard pastor from St. Louis, Missouri, named Randy Clark reported having experienced a similar period of spiritual dryness. As he told *Charisma* magazine, "I felt empty, powerless, and so little anointed. Emotionally, spiritually, and physically, I knew I was burning out."[10] Clark had pastored a Baptist church in Kentucky since 1978, then resigned in order to found Vineyard churches in Illinois and St. Louis, Missouri in the 1980s; but by 1986 he reported that Vineyard churches themselves had succumbed to spiritual "dryness," leaving him discouraged and disillusioned. In the summer of 1993, a friend named Jeff McClusky related how he had been saved from suicide and through the revival ministry of Rodney Howard-Browne. Brown himself, though born into a Pentecostal home, had also been restless in his earlier life for "something more." In 1979, he had "cried out to God in sheer desperation" and received what he called a "baptism of fire."[11] By 1987, however, searching again for something more, he left his native South Africa and came to the United States where, by 1993, he had established himself as a revivalist internationally known for holding revivals bursting with manifestations of intoxicating uncontrollable laughter, crying, rolling on the floor, and "spiritual drunkenness." Styling himself "God's bartender," he would invite people to "have a drink at Joel's Place" (a reference to Joel 2:28) and "party with the Lord."[12]

---

9. Poloma, "Toronto Blessing," 1149–50; McHale and Haykin, *Toronto*, 245, quotes Arnott as admitting to having been a friend of Benny Hinn's for twenty years and to his being a leading figure in shaping Arnott's view of divine healing and anointing; Chevreau, *Catch the Fire*, 22–23, admits that Arnott "longed for a similar kind of empowerment" as Hinn demonstrated; Randles, *Weighed*, 7–8; Riss, "History," sec. on "John Arnott."

10. Doucet, "Renewal Excites Canadian Churches," 52–53.

11. Howard-Browne, *The Touch of God*, 73–74.

12. Poloma, "Toronto Blessing," 1150; Randles, *Weighed*, 111–33; cf. Riss, "History," secs. on Howard-Browne.

When Clark's friend related the powerful spiritual "manifestations" he had experienced at Howard-Browne's revivals, Clark said, "What my friend was describing—people shaking, falling, laughing—was what I had seen many years earlier in the Vineyard revivals. I knew this was what I needed."[13] So Clark decided to attend Howard-Browne's meeting, was "prayed over" and received the "impartation" of Howard-Browne's "anointing" and experienced a powerful encounter with the Holy Spirit; and after he returned home, he witnessed similar "powerful manifestations" beginning to occur in his own church. When Arnott heard about the effect of Howard-Browne's "anointing" on Clark's ministry, he invited Clark to come and preach four revival meetings at their Toronto Airport church. Clark came on January 20, 1994, and the unexpected happened. Clark reportedly gave his testimony on how he got "drunk" in the Spirit; and in response, "the congregation erupted in pandemonium with people laughing, growling, dancing, shaking, barking like dogs, and even being stuck in positions of paralysis."[14] In Arnott's words, "It hadn't occurred to us that God would throw a massive party where people would laugh, roll, cry and become so empowered that emotional hurts from childhood would just lift off. Some people were so overcome physically by God's power that they had to be carried out."[15] Clark's visit to Toronto was supposed to last less than a week, but instead, his involvement in the Toronto Blessing has continued to this day.

One visitor to Toronto witnessed the preaching of Marc DuPont, an associate pastor at the Toronto Airport Vineyard Church. In his sermon, DuPont declared that "God is bored with the church," quipping that the "angels appointed to watch over us are so bored they went back to heaven and are now in counseling!" The visitor then observed:

> After the sermon, the chairs were stacked and removed for ministry time. You could feel the sense of expectation, something was about to happen. . . . The ground rules were announced: "You are here to receive, so when you are getting prayed for, don't pray in tongues or in English, for you are here to receive and that can hinder your reception." [Then] DuPont calmly invoked the Holy Spirit, "Come Holy Spirit," and immediately people all over began to twitch, tremble, compulsively bend over face forward and straighten up, over and over. Knees would give, arms would thrash, and some people would violently shake and quake. A few would become intensely cold and others feverishly hot! I saw a

13. Randles, *Weighed*, 8; Riss, "History"; Poloma, "Toronto Blessing," 1150.

14. "What Is the Toronto Blessing?," para. 1–3.

15. Arnott, "Toronto Blessing," 5, cited in Poloma, "Toronto Blessing," 1152; cf. doubts raised by Jackson, "What in the World?," secs. 1–4.

woman in her 50s laying on her back, suddenly convulse into a form of a sit-up, rapidly and repetitively. Each time she would come up, out of her mouth would come the word "cuckoo!" . . . Laughter, screams, moans, and roars mingled together into an otherworldly cacophony.[16]

What attracts people to the events like the Toronto Blessing? Some may be drawn by simple curiosity, but most seem to be seeking "something more" spiritually, just as many of their spiritual leaders did after periods of spiritual "dryness" or spiritual "boredom" of the kind mentioned by Du-Pont. This would seem to accord with findings like those of John P. Kildahl's *The Psychology of Speaking in Tongues* (1972), cited in the previous chapter, which showed that those who became *glossolalists* tended to do so after periods of personal distress or existential crisis in which, being more "submissive, suggestible and dependent in the presence of authority figures," they seek and find fulfillment in the belief, reinforced by their leader and group, that *glossolalia* is an "act of God's intervention" in their speech. Similarly, participants in the Toronto Blessing are often reportedly drawn by the spiritual and emotional catharsis of the "soaking prayer" meetings offered there, as well as by the expectation that God is actively involved in effecting the "manifestations" evoked in these revivals, some of which go far beyond *glossolalia* and are reminiscent of those in Howard-Browne's revivals, if not even more dramatic and shocking in effect. In many cases, people reportedly do seem to experience spiritually positive effects, though this is not always the case. Paul Gowdy, a former pastor associated with the Toronto Airport Christian Fellowship (or TACF, as the ministry was renamed in 1996), became so disillusioned by his experiences that he left that ministry, writing: "In hindsight, I look back and think how could I have been so blind? I laughed at people acting like dogs and pretending to urinate on the columns of the TACF building. I watched people pretend to be animals, bark, roar, cluck, pretend to fly as if they had wings, perpetually act drunk and sing silly songs. How I thought that any of this was from the Holy Spirit of God amazes me today."[17]

In 1995 the Toronto Vineyard Church was ousted from the Association of Vineyard Churches, largely as a result of its more controversial, extreme "manifestations" and Arnott's attempt to defend them in his book, *The Father's Blessing* (1995).[18] The following year, Arnott's church was re-

16. Randles, *Weighed*, 139–40.

17. Gowdy, "Toronto Pastor Repents," para. 7; cf. "Interview with Pastor Paul Gowdy."

18. Beverley, "Vineyard Severs Ties," para. 1–4.

named the Toronto Airport Christian Fellowship; and in 2010 it was again renamed "Catch the Fire Toronto." Toronto's influence has been felt around the world. Thousands of churches have experienced similar revivals and "manifestations," from Holy Trinity Brompton in London and Holy Trinity Cheltenham in Gloucestershire, to Cagayan de Oro in the Philippines and Brownsville Assembly of God in Pensacola, Florida. *Charisma* magazine reported in 2014 that an estimated four thousand churches in England and another seven thousand churches in North America had been impacted by the Toronto revival.[19] The Brownsville Revival, inspired by Toronto in 1995, reportedly led to almost a quarter of a million people being converted to the Christian faith, though criteria for determining "conversions" were not indicated.[20] The October 21, 2000 issue of *The Guardian* reported that 250,000 agnostics in the United Kingdom turned to a belief in Jesus through the *Alpha* course, a simplified introduction to post-denominational Christianity with Charismatic overtones designed by Nicky Gumbel, who attended and was impacted by the Toronto Blessing meetings—though, again, criteria for this judgment were not indicated.[21] In 2014, twenty years after he was invited by Arnott to Toronto, Clark founded *Global Awakening* as an outgrowth of his involvement with the Toronto revival, which he regards as the greatest revival in the second half of the twentieth century.

One recurrent theme among critics of the movement is a notable shift in focus—from doctrine to experience, from mind to heart, from received denominational traditions to something new and exciting and nondenominational, from mundane discipleship to extraordinary "manifestations," from "head knowledge" of the truths of the Christian faith to dramatic tangible "signs," like tingling, physical sensations of warmth, electrical hot flashes, tears, laughter, shaking, and "tongues."[22] This pattern is far from unique to the Toronto Blessing and has also been witnessed in related movements, such as the Kansas City Prophets, the Manifest Sons of God, and the Latter Rain movement. A greater emphasis on experiential bonding and community-building than on doctrine can be seen also in Gumbel's *Alpha* course, although it has been successful in introducing people to the basics of the Christian faith.

19. Strang, "More, Lord!," quoted in Steingard and Arnott, *From Here*, 94.

20. Poloma, "The 'Toronto Blessing,'" 257–71; Poloma, "Inspecting the Fruit," *Pneuma*, 43–70.

21. Ronson, "Catch Me If You Can," para. 2–3; and Dueck, "Enduring Revival," para. 5 to end.

22. These types of concerns are voiced by Randles, *Weighed*, 92, 96, 105, 124, 126–30, 139–40, 161, 165–83.

Many questions occur at this point. Where did these ideas come from? Furthermore, as to "tongues," where did the idea come from that people should utter a cacophony of unintelligible vocalizations and that this should be considered a gift of the Holy Spirit, let alone all the accompanying "manifestations" evident in events like the Toronto Blessing? According to the common tradition of the Church, Pentecost has always been seen as an event promoting *comprehension* and *unity*, in which God miraculously allowed people from many foreign nations of the world to hear and understand the apostolic message *intelligibly* in their own languages, a reversal of the *confusion* of languages and *division* of peoples represented by the Tower of Babel in the Old Testament. The note to Acts 2:7 in *The Jerusalem Bible* says that one characteristic of the Pentecost miracle of the Apostles speaking "a universal language" is that "the unity lost at Babel is restored"; and it adds: "This symbolizes and anticipates the apostles' worldwide mission."[23] Before turning our attention in the next chapter to the question of how our modern *glossolalic* conception of "tongues" developed, however, there is another example of a contemporary Charismatic movement and culture that illustrates the powerful influence that the earlier Charismatic movement, as well as the more recent "Third Wave" movement, have had within a conservative religious tradition with a historical reputation for being something like an immovable colossus of steel and bronze—namely, the Catholic Charismatic Renewal. A survey of this movement will help to further define the current Charismatic culture that serves as the point of departure for our investigation of "tongues" in the rest of the present "archeological" work.

The Catholic Charismatic Renewal

Randy Clark was among the prominently featured speakers at *Encounter 2020*, a conference of more than three thousand people hosted by Encounter Ministries at the Seagate Convention Center, in Toledo, Ohio from January 2–4, 2020. Along with Charismatic speakers like Randy Clark of *Global Awakening* and Jim Baker of Zion Christian Fellowship, the conference advertised "spirit-filled worship," a "healing service," and featured trademark "praise and worship" music. What was different about this conference, however, was that it also included the Catholic Mass, "Eucharistic Adoration," seventy Catholic priests, a bishop from Green Bay, Wisconsin, and numerous Catholic Charismatic speakers, including three priests associated with the sponsoring organization, Encounter Ministries: Brian Gross (an

23. JB, 203n"f"; cf. Soal and Desmond, "The Reversal of Babel," 1–10; Ford, "Toward a Theology," 25–29.

Associate), Patrick Gonyeau (Healing Evangelist for Encounter Ministries), and Mathias Thelen (President of Encounter Ministries). Encounter Ministries describes itself as a canonically-approved association whose stated purpose is "to train and disciple Catholics to demonstrate the power and love of God in their sphere of influence through the gifts of the Holy Spirit."[24] Their website (accessed in January, 2020) adds: "Evangelization cannot be reduced to words and persuasion only. Our vision is to see a Church truly empowered by the Holy Spirit where disciples are confident to proclaim the Gospel and then demonstrate it through signs, wonders, and miracles."[25]

Another speaker at *Encounter 2020* was Mary Healy, professor of Scripture at Sacred Heart Major Seminary, who recently co-authored *The Spiritual Gifts Handbook* (2018) with Randy Clark.[26] Healy previously published *Healing: Bringing the Gift of God's Mercy to the World* (2015), after spending part of her 2013 sabbatical performing healings with Randy Clark and his team in Brazil.[27] Yet another speaker at *Encounter 2020* was Sarah Kaczmarek, Associate Director of *Alpha Catholic*, a Catholic version of the *Alpha* course designed by Nicky Gumble, of "Toronto Blessing" connections. This *Alpha* course was implemented recently in the Archdiocese of Detroit as part of its "New Evangelization" initiative following Archbishop Allen H. Vigneron's Pastoral Letter, "Unleash the Gospel," aimed at re-evangelizing lapsed Catholics and stemming the tide of hemorrhaging Catholic church membership. Fr. John Riccardo, popular preacher and former pastor of Our Lady of Good Counsel Church in Plymouth, Michigan, was tapped for the position of Director of Evangelization for the Archbishop of Detroit, which makes wide use of the *Alpha* course.[28]

The "think tank" behind the New Evangelization initiative in Detroit, however, is Sacred Heart Major Seminary, nearly half of whose present faculty are active members of the Catholic Charismatic Renewal (CCR) and some of whom have international celebrity status. Ralph Martin, for instance, is not only director of graduate programs in the New Evangelization

24. *Encounter Ministries*, s.v ."Home."

25. *Encounter Ministries*, s.v. "About Us," accessed January 6, 2020; subsequently removed from website.

26. Healy and I are amicable colleagues at Sacred Heart Major Seminary, though we have serious unreconciled differences concerning a number of issues related to the Charismatic movement. This is also true of other members of the faculty, which is divided (as of 2021) roughly in half in terms of its disposition toward the Charismatic movement, though all share a common commitment to the basics of the Christian faith.

27. The expression "healing impartation" is used for such healings by Clark, "How to Move," para. 1.

28. Alpha USA, "Catholic Context," prominently features clergy and laity of the Archdiocese of Detroit among members of the Catholic Board for *Alpha USA*.

at Sacred Heart, but an internationally known speaker and televangelist, a Consultor to the Pontifical Council for the New Evangelization, and president of Renewal Ministries, which hosts his own TV show, *The Choices We Face*, as well as books and CDs by Martin and other Catholic Charismatics.[29] Another bright star is Healy herself, who in addition to teaching Scripture at Sacred Heart, is also an internationally-known speaker, a member of the Pontifical Biblical Commission, and Encounter School Curriculum Coordinator for Encounter Ministries, the nerve center of the CCR's Signs and Wonders movement in the North American Midwest. It is rumored, in fact, that the Pastoral Letter "Unleash the Gospel" was ghostwritten by Healy— a rumor supported, some say, by reliable sources and by key Charismatic phrases employed in the document. If this is true, it shows just how deeply the Archdiocese is invested in the CCR.

How far has the Signs and Wonders movement penetrated the CCR? Peter Hocken cites Henri Lemay of Quebec, a member of the International Catholic Charismatic Renewal Services (ICCRS), as "a major promoter" of the Toronto movement, as well as Msgr. Vincent Walsh of Philadelphia, "a veteran leader in the CCR."[30] According to T. Paul Thigpen, "The more extreme manifestations of Protestant Pentecostalism, such as the "holy laughter" of the Toronto Blessing movement, have easily crossed over into some charismatic Catholic circles."[31] Some of these phenomena are not unique to Toronto but common to the older Pentecostal traditions. For example, the phenomenon of being "slain in the Spirit," or, as some prefer, "resting in the Spirit," is defended by contemporary members of the CCR such as Healy, who says that it is a common occurrence in healing ministries and wherever "people are prayed over," and that it is "a human response to the overwhelming presence and power of the Holy Spirit."[32]

How did this all happen? How did the "Signs and Wonders" movement promoted by Wagner, Wimber, and Hagin, with its "power evangelism," "tongues," "miraculous healings," and other "manifestations" find its way into the Catholic Church? According to most accounts, the CCR began in 1967 at Duquesne University in Pittsburgh, Pennsylvania. "More than any other development," says Hocken, "the spread of the [Charismatic movement] to the Roman Catholic Church decisively affected the shape of the wider movement."[33] Of course, the Charismatic movement as a whole

---

29. See https://www.renewalministries.net/, esp. the "Resources" tab.
30. Hocken, "Charismatic Movement," 507.
31. Thigpen, "Catholic Charismatic Renewal," 466.
32. Healy, *Healing*, 139–40.
33. Hocken, "Charismatic Movement," 481.

had antecedents well before this in the American healing evangelists of the 1940s such as William Branham, Oral Roberts, Gordon Lindsay, and T. L. Osborn, who were instrumental in spreading "Spirit-baptized" Christianity beyond the confines of Pentecostal denominations. Also instrumental was the Full Gospel Business Men's Fellowship International, the ecumenical outreach of David du Plessis, and the watershed event sparked by Episcopal priest Dennis Bennett, when he announced from his pulpit at St. Mark's Church in Van Nuys, California on April 3, 1960, that he had been baptized in the Spirit and had spoken in tongues. While individual Catholics had been exposed to Pentecostalist influences before the mid-sixties, it was only in 1967 that the CCR emerged decisively from the watershed events of the "Duquesne Weekend," as it is sometimes called, at which about 25 students and several faculty members from Duquesne University received "baptism in the Spirit" and "spoke in tongues." From there, it rapidly spread to the University of Notre Dame in South Bend, Indiana, and quickly became a well-organized movement. According to Hocken, the origins of the CCR differed in significant ways from those of the Neo-Pentecostal movement among Protestants, because it (1) developed in a university setting and had well-educated leaders, (2) was led by members of the laity, (3) acquired a unique cohesion from the common background previously shared by its leaders at Notre Dame, and (4) was "renewal-minded" because of the influence of the Second Vatican Council (1962–65) and its emphasis on the renewing power of the gifts of the Spirit.[34]

The influence of popular Protestant Pentecostalism was nevertheless decidedly evident in the beginnings of the CCR, which should come as no surprise given the spiritual and ecclesiastical crisis undergone by Catholics during the Second Vatican Council and its aftermath. Catholics lost their centuries-old traditional liturgy, lectionary, liturgical calendar of popular saints' days and feast days, and a wealth of popular devotions. Many seminaries and religious orders were emptied and closed, foreign missions collapsed, and many Catholics ceased going to church or defected to Protestant congregations.[35] Many Catholics experienced severe disorientation and loss of their spiritual footing. Thus, it is not surprising that in February of 1967 Ralph Keifer, Patrick Bourgeois, William Storey, and some other lay faculty and students at Duquesne found themselves reading popular Protestant

34. Hocken, "Charismatic Movement," 481; cf. Thigpen, "Catholic Charismatic Renewal," 460.

35. The relevant statistics are detailed in Jones, *Index*, 5–17, 30–40. The traditional Latin Mass was restored to Catholics who desired it by Benedict XVI in his apostolic letter, *Summorum Pontificum* (2007), until Francis attempted to suppress it again in *Traditionis Custodes* (2021).

Pentecostal books, such as David Wilkerson's *The Cross and the Switchblade* (1963), later made into a movie, and John Sherrill's *They Speak with Other Tongues* (1964), or that they desired to be empowered by the "baptism in the Spirit" they had read about, or that they sought out a Protestant Charismatic prayer group in their area, where they subsequently had hands laid on them and received "Spirit baptism." In March of 1967, two recent graduates of Notre Dame who were to become major leaders of the CCR, Ralph Martin and Stephen (Steve) Clark, heard about these events from a visitor from Duquesne. Together with Gerry Rauch and Jim Cavnar from Notre Dame, they organized the Word of God Community in Ann Arbor, Michigan, in 1967, which became a major hub of CCR influence with its own publishing house, Servant Publications. The other center of early influence was Notre Dame, where the news media first took note of the CCR in April of 1967 when about one hundred students and some faculty held a weekend meeting. By 1973, more than twenty thousand were assembling in Notre Dame's football stadium to accommodate the crowds.[36]

In 1972, Léon Jozef Suenens, a cardinal who was active as an initiator and leader of the progressive reform movement that dominated the Second Vatican Council, first came into contact with the CCR in the United States, where he visited Notre Dame. Despite holding dissident progressive views on contraception, marriage, liturgy, and mode of reception of the Eucharist, which were at odds with Catholic tradition, he was warmly embraced by CCR leaders when his support for them became apparent. In 1974 he hosted a conference at Malines, Belgium, at which an attempt was made to evaluate the CCR and provide theological and pastoral guidelines for the movement. Suenens authored several monographs from 1974–86 that came to be known as the Malines Documents.[37] He also invited Martin and Clark to develop an International CCR Information Office in Belgium, which was eventually moved to Rome and became the International Catholic Charismatic Renewal Services (ICCRS).[38] Suenens later expressed concerns about certain trends in the CCR, particularly its tendency to act independently of the Church. As a result, in 1976 he decreed that in Belgium, only priests could lead prayer groups, stressing the importance of integrating the CCR into the ecclesial structure of the Church.[39] A decade later, after extensive international consultations, he published the sixth of the Malines Documents on the phenomenon of being "slain in the Spirit" or "resting in the

---

36. Thigpen, "Catholic Charismatic Renewal," 461.

37. Suenens, *Malines Documents*.

38. Bundy, "Suenens," 1108–9.

39. Bundy, "Suenens," 1109.

Spirit" in *A Controversial Phenomenon* (1987), reporting his conclusion that not only is the phenomenon *not* a manifestation of the Holy Spirit, but it threatens the authenticity and credibility of the CCR.[40]

Particularly controversial was the CCR's establishment of "covenant communities," such as the Word of God Community in Ann Arbor and its umbrella organization, the Sword of the Spirit; True House, and People of God in South Bend, Indiana; the Mother of God Community in Gaithersburg, Maryland; Servants of Christ the King in Steubenville, Ohio; and the Alleluia Community in Augusta, Georgia.[41] The "covenant" aspect of these communities typically involved, as in the popular counter-cultural "commune" movement of the 1970s, divisions into "households" composed of families and/or individuals, with some level of commitment to sharing financial resources, participation in regular community gatherings, submission to the direction of the group's authoritative patriarchal leaders. In some cases, these arrangements led to problems of excessive control and overstepping of boundaries, and even egregious abuse. At the True House community in South Bend, for example, a Notre Dame student in 1972 was taken in the middle of the night to the head of the community and ordered to make a general confession and reveal all his most painful memories in front of this lay community leader, as well as his secretary and the person who had brought him there. The next night the same lay leader attempted to perform an "exorcism" on him, using the traditional Ritual for the "Exorcism of Satan and the Fallen Angels," forbidden to the laity. One of the early CCR leaders, Notre Dame theology professor William Storey, intervened and wrote a letter on April 2, 1975, notifying the local bishop, Leo Pursley, of his concerns. Several communities were investigated by Church authorities. Examples include the Word of God community, where charges of "cult-like abuse" and ecclesial confusion had been made in the 1980s; the Servants of Christ the King, investigated by Bishop Albert Ottenweller of Steubenville in 1991 not only for practical abuses but "errors in teaching" related to "fundamentalism," "perfectionism," and a pessimistic "gnostic" worldview; the Mother of God community in Gaithersburg, Maryland (where Healy served as a coordinator after its reorganization), investigated in 1995 by James Cardinal Hickey, Archbishop of Washington, DC, for practices such as "resting in the spirit" and unequal treatment of spouses in marriage, a deficient view of the Church, and a failure to integrate the concept of "baptism in the Spirit" into the Catholic understanding of the sacraments of baptism

---

40. Suenens, *Controversial Phenomenon*, 79–80.

41. Detailed documentation on many of these covenant communities is provided in Flaherty's "Index."

and confirmation. These interventions led to restructuring, divisions, defections, or dissolution.[42]

By 1982 Steve Clark was asking publicly whether the charismatic renewal had peaked, and leaders recognized the need for redirection. Four years later, in response to Pope John Paul II's call for a "New Evangelization," the CCR began redirecting its primary focus toward adopting this call as its major agenda.[43] As a result, wherever the CCR has become involved, the "New Evangelization" inevitably has taken on Charismatic distinctives, such as "baptism in the Spirit," "speaking in tongues," and other "signs and wonders."

Given the Protestant Pentecostal roots of the CCR, it is not surprising that "Spirit-baptized" Protestants and Catholics hold much in common. Nevertheless, several distinctions of theology and practice may be noted within the development of CCR spirituality.[44] First, in contrast to Protestant Pentecostals, who tend to view the Church as having lost the power of the Holy Spirit for most of its history, Catholics are more disposed to look for evidence throughout the centuries for some continuity of the Spirit's work since Pentecost, as argued in Kilian McDonnell and George T. Montague's *Christian Initiation and Baptism in the Holy Spirit: Evidence from the First Eight Centuries* (1991). Second, Catholics generally attempt to fit "Spirit baptism" into their traditional framework of sacramental theology and their teaching that the Holy Spirit is already given in baptism and confirmation, rather than subsequently, preferring to speak of a later "release of the Spirit" or "activation" of latent spiritual gifts, which may occur once or more in a believer's life. Third, although Catholic Charismatics in practice often expect the gift of *glossolalia* to follow "Spirit baptism," in principle they generally reject the Protestant Pentecostal claim that authentic "Spirit baptism" is *always* "initially evidenced" by *glossolalia*. Rather, they argue that the Spirit sovereignly bestows a variety of gifts. As Paul Thigpen writes: "Catholics reading the lives of the saints find not only evidence of tongues, prophecy, healing, and other charisms noted in the Pauline epistles; they read about gifts that most Protestant Pentecostals have never even heard of: St. Thomas' levitation in prayer; St. Joseph Cupertino's flights to the treetops; Padre Pio's bilocations."[45] Fourth, Catholics believe in a special divine presence in the Eucharist and sometimes speak of receiving gifts of physical

---

42. See Thigpen, "Catholic Charismatic Renewal," 462–63. For additional details, see *Charismatic Movement and Catholic Tradition*, s.v. "Magisterium," parts 3 and 4. Also see the remarkable photos in Crumm, "Rise and Fall."

43. Thigpen, "Catholic Charismatic Renewal," 463.

44. Thigpen, "Catholic Charismatic Renewal," 465–66 is followed here.

45. Thigpen, "Catholic Charismatic Renewal," 466.

and emotional healing through the reception of Holy Communion; and they often hold gatherings of prayer and praise apart from Mass in order to preserve the centrality of the Eucharist in worship. Finally, the Blessed Virgin Mary, though not typically the focus of CCR meetings, is part of the Catholic experience and her intercession may be invoked sometimes in hymns or prayers.

How was the phenomenon of "tongues" itself received in the CCR? Though we touched on this question in the previous chapter, it will be of interest to return to Cardinal Suenens and examine briefly his impressions when he first encountered Catholic Charismatics. What is surprising is how quickly he absorbed the equivocal way of discussing "tongues" typical of Pentecostals and Charismatics. In the first of the Malines Documents, *Theological and Pastoral Orientations on the Catholic Charismatic Renewal* (1974), Suenens notes that "praying in tongues" is "very common" in the CCR and suggests that polemics against this practice are not always well-grounded, pointing out that "praying in tongues was very common in the early Church."[46] This observation, which makes no distinction between *glossolalia* and *xenolalia*, is followed by a footnote that reads: "Cf. note in *The Jerusalem Bible* to Acts 2:4." The note states: "One element, vv. 4, 11, 13, of the Pentecostal miracle is the gift of *glossolalia* common in the early Church," and cites various biblical passages, as well as "early prophecy in Israel."[47] The relationship between *glossolalic* and *xenolalic* "tongues" and prophecy is left unclarified. In the second Malines Document, *Ecumenism and Renewal: Theological and Pastoral Orientations* (1978), Suenens refers to *glossolalia*, which he identifies with "praying in tongues," and writes: "This form of prayer, which is more free and spontaneous than formulated prayer, has its own place and significance. In a previous study, I have described the spiritual benefit that can be derived from it and why, having experienced it at first hand, I do not hesitate to class it among the fruits of the grace of renewal."[48] As he indicates in a footnote, the "previous study" to which he refers is his book, *A New Pentecost?* (1975). In the latter work, Suenens denies that *glossolalia* is either miraculous or pathological. Concerning the former claim, he writes:

> Charismatics of many denominations, but especially classic Pentecostals, consider glossolalia as the indisputable sign that one has received the "baptism of the Holy Spirit." And they hold that it is an infused gift enabling someone to pray in a real language

46. Suenens, *Theological and Pastoral Orientations*, 41.

47. Suenens, *Theological and Pastoral Orientations*, 41, 67n26; JB, 203n"d."

48. Suenens, *Ecumenism and Renewal*, 61, 68n; cf. 32.

he himself does not understand. This we cannot accept. But we do not exclude the possibility that in certain rare cases it has happened, for we believe in miracles, and such a phenomenon would pertain to the order of miracle.[49]

In response to the question, "*What then is glossolalia?*" Suenens then says, "We should first recognize that we are dealing with something that is referred to in the Scriptures: there are, indeed, about thirty allusions to praying in tongues." Making no distinction here between *xenolalic* and *glossolalic* forms of "tongues," he obliquely states: "There are undoubtedly exegetical problems, but this should not blind us to the simple fact that the New Testament speaks of this phenomenon as real and relatively frequent." What phenomenon? "This form of non-discursive prayer . . . that is within reach of everybody," he says, "a verbal expression independent of any specific linguistic structure."[50] While stressing that such "tongues" should not be over-emphasized, he says that they can be spiritually enriching.

There is some notable ambiguity in Suenens' statements about "tongues." There is also some ambiguity as to whether the Malines Documents are "magisterial," meaning doctrinally authoritative and binding for Catholics. Charismatics in the CCR usually treat them as though they were. Suenens, however, even though he was an archbishop and cardinal, seems to be writing as a private theologian. The magisterial authority of these Malines Documents, therefore, seems to be limited to the personal reflections of one particular archbishop and cardinal, much as Pope Benedict XVI's three-volume *Jesus of Nazareth* (2007–12) was the reflection of a private theologian rather than a magisterial document.

Strangely, Suenens does not reference the "tongues" of Pentecost (Acts 2) as *xenolalic*, that is, as involving genuine languages, as most contemporary Charismatics do.[51] Some Catholic Charismatic scholars, influenced by certain modern Scripture scholars, seem to doubt that the Pentecost account described in Acts 2 was actually *xenolalic* and argue that all biblical "tongues" should be interpreted in light of the more "mystical" Corinthian account. For example, Francis Sullivan, in *Charisms and Charismatic Renewal* (1982), questions "how literally we should take Luke's description of the tongues of Pentecost as a miraculous speaking of real foreign languages," assuring us that "we are surely on safe ground when we follow the lead of modern exegetes in basing our understanding of the gifts of tongues on 1 Corinthians, rather than on Acts 2"; and thus he promotes the prevailing

49. Suenens, *A New Pentecost?*, 99–100.

50. Suenens, *A New Pentecost?*, 99–104.

51. Spittler, "Glossolalia," 671–72.

Charismatic view of *glossolalia* as a private language of prayer, which he explains as non-miraculous, extending this interpretation indifferently to all "tongues," whether apostolic or contemporary.[52] A slightly more cautious view is taken by Healy, who writes: "Of the many instances where the gift of tongues is mentioned in the New Testament (Mark 16:17; Acts 2:4–11; 10:46; 19:6; 1 Cor 12:10, 28; 13:1, 8; 14:2–39), only *one*, the account of Pentecost, clearly refers to tongues as speaking in known human languages"; and she adds: "It is not clear whether Luke was referring to a miracle of *speech* or of *hearing* (i.e., the disciples may have been speaking in non-intelligible speech, but the listeners heard it as a proclamation of the Gospel). In favor of the latter interpretation is the emphasis on 'hearing' (Acts 2:6, 8, 11) and the fact that they were accused of being drunk."[53] (Gregory of Nazianzus, however, saw the accusation of drunkenness as attesting to a miracle of speaking rather than hearing.)[54] Other CCR writers, like most Protestant Charismatics, accept that other New Testament references to "tongues" outside of 1 Corinthians were most likely *xenolalic.*

Most CCR writers deny that "speaking in tongues" occurs in a state of ecstasy or trance-like state, insisting that vocalizations are entirely voluntary, conscious, and effortless, unlike the deliberate attempt to produce a pseudo-language. Sullivan suggests that participants in the CCR are often induced to speak in "tongues" by the way it is stressed in the preparation of newcomers for the reception of "baptism in the Spirit." He writes: "Probably the most commonly used method for such preparation, at least in the Catholic charismatic renewal in English-speaking countries," he says, "is called the Life in the Spirit Seminars."[55] One has only to read the *Team Manual for the Life in the Spirit Seminars*, he says, to see how much stress is laid on the importance of speaking in "tongues." For many, this involves a first significant experience of "letting go"; and one purpose of these seminars is to create the *desire* to "take the plunge." The motive which the *Manual* presents is that speaking in tongues will give the person "a clear experience of what it means to have the Holy Spirit work through him."[56] Another factor, says Sullivan, is "the role which speaking in tongues plays in many prayer groups, as the tangible sign of full commitment to the charismatic renewal."[57] Despite his focus on natural and human factors in *glossolalia*, Sullivan says

---

52. Sullivan, *Charisms*, 122; see 121–50.

53. Healy, "Answers," n19, cites Montague, *Holy Spirit*, 279–80.

54. Gregory of Nazianzus, *Oratio* 41.15 (*PG* 36:450).

55. Sullivan, *Charisms*, 140–41.

56. *Life in the Spirit Team Manual*, 147, 146–52.

57. Sullivan, *Charisms*, 142.

he is also convinced that a genuine work of divine grace can also play a role in the experience of speaking in "tongues."

Common Roots, Common Patterns

In summary, we have seen that the CCR shares many ideas in common with other Pentecostals and Charismatics. Many of them share with their Protestant counterparts the idea of a special "end-times" outpouring of the Holy Spirit in fulfillment of the prophecy of Joel 2:28 with charismatic "manifestations," as we saw in the previous chapter. While the CCR generally does not share in the most extreme sorts of "manifestation" one finds in the Toronto Blessing, there remain undeniable connections, especially with groups such as Encounter Ministries that have connections with Toronto Blessing veterans such as Randy Clark. We have seen that certain practices, such as "resting in the spirit" (though censured by Cardinal Suenens), are approved by some in the CCR, such as Healy. Despite leadership disclaimers, we also have seen that those in the CCR usually expect those "baptized in the Spirit" to speak in *glossolalic* "tongues," and may even pressure newcomers to do so. We have also seen in the last chapter that in Catholic magisterial documents, the gift of "tongues" is always classed among the miraculous "extraordinary" gifts that are bestowed by God purely gratuitously (*gratia gratis data*) so that, as the Dominican scholar Jordan Aumann says, "the normal development of the life of grace could never produce or demand them"; yet we also have seen how, despite this, the CCR continues to treat them, in the words of Kilian McDonnell and George Montague, "as among the ordinary manifestations of the Christian life."[58] Even though Suenens and Sullivan, like Hocken and Healy in the last chapter, regard the "tongues" experienced in the CCR as capable of mediating divine grace, they also regard them originally as a decidedly natural and human phenomenon, which would not likely rise to the level of the magisterial criterion of "extraordinary" (miraculous) gift as understood in Catholic magisterial tradition. Thus, it may be inferred that there is a bit of equivocation or "waffling" by the CCR on some of these issues.

Another such issue is the role of *glossolalia* as "evidence" of "Spirit baptism." In classic Protestant Pentecostalism, "tongues" were viewed as "initial evidence" of Spirit baptism, which was seen as a normative and universally-available second work of grace that empowered believers for ministry after the Spirit's work of regeneration. The doctrine was controversial,

---

58. Aumann, *Spiritual Theology*, 300; McDonnell and Montague, *Christian Initiation*, 88.

complicated by debates over whether the gift of "tongues" was simultaneous with or subsequent to sanctification, and repeatedly challenged from within Holiness and Pentecostal circles, especially by leaders of the Assemblies of God denomination. Later Charismatic groups also held conflicting positions, many holding "tongues" as only one of several possible evidences of "Spirit baptism," as found in the Toronto Blessing group and the CCR. We have seen that the CCR in principle denies the necessity of "tongues" as a sign of "Spirit baptism," but in practice tends to expect it and sometimes even insist on it. A few Catholic Charismatics deny that "Spirit baptism" is necessary for salvation, while others take a position in practice closer to Wimber's identification of it with spiritual conversion. Still others insist that "Spirit baptism" is a one-time event, while others accept the possibility of it occurring several times in one's life.[59]

Finally, as we have seen, Charismatic leaders often seem to be motivated by a desire to be delivered from a sense of spiritual poverty—a "dryness," "dissatisfaction," or even "boredom" with the status quo in institutional churches—and by a yearning for "something new," "something more," "a new thing," "renewal," "a new Pentecost" or, as Catholics said after the Second Vatican Council, "a new springtime" and a "New Evangelization." This often seems to have gone hand-in-hand with a shift in emphasis from doctrine to experience, from mind to heart, from received denominational traditions to something new and exciting and nondenominational, and from mundane discipleship to extraordinary "manifestations." This pattern can be seen not only in the dissatisfaction of Arnott and Clark that led to the Toronto Blessing movement but in the dissatisfaction of the students and faculty members from Duquesne and Notre Dame that led to the CCR movement. It can be seen in the attempt to restore the "lost offices" of "prophet" and "apostle," a rapidly growing presumption that is found as readily in the CCR as in other groups like the "Kansas City Prophets."[60] Similar patterns can also be seen in more self-serving varieties of "healing ministries" such as those of William Branham and Oral Roberts, or E. W. Kenyon and Kenneth Hagin's "Word of Faith" movement, which renounces poverty, suffering, and defeat as unnecessary to the Christian life, emphasizing instead health and prosperity in a message sometimes called "the health and wealth gospel." It may be seen in the desire to garner spiritual power and renown even at the

59. McGee, "Initial Evidence," 784–91; ICCRS, *Baptism in the Holy Spirit*; Clark and Healy, *Spiritual Gifts*, ch. 4; Wimber, *Power Evangelism*, 142, concedes that "conversion and the initial filling of the Holy Spirit can happen simultaneously."

60. E.g., Bruce Yocum, of the Servants of the Word community (CCR), claims to rival the Old Testament prophet Jeremiah in his gift of prophecy. Yocum, "Surviving a Tsunami," 0:24–0:35.

cost of making outlandish claims and overlooking moral compromise and heresy, did as did Paul Cain, one of the Kansas City Prophets, who claimed that he made trips to heaven, declared that President Bill Clinton was God's anointed despite his record of philandering and support for abortion, and claimed that William Branham was the "greatest prophet that ever lived" despite Branham's rejection of the doctrine of the Trinity as diabolic.[61] It may be seen also in the desire simply to succeed, which may serve just as easily as a motive for being drawn to things like the Church Growth Movement as a desire for the salvation of souls. While such motives cannot be always easily discerned, it is not impossible to infer their likely existence where extraordinary gifts and powers are constantly promoted, and where "signs and wonders" are emphatically embraced, as in the Toronto Blessing movement and CCR organizations like Encounter Ministries. In some cases, leaders readily state their motives. Healy, for instance, envisions how much more successful the Church might be in evangelistic outreach if it could unleash an army of "joyful missionary disciples" who could perform miraculous healings: "The New Evangelization would be propelled," she writes, "to a whole new level of dynamism."[62]

Where did the CCR acquire these ideas? CCR Scripture scholars sometimes give the impression that they have derived their theology of charisms directly from Scripture or even from Catholic tradition, but this claim is debatable. Others point to the fact that in 1962, on the eve of the Second Vatican Council, Pope John XXIII prayed that the Council might produce a "New Pentecost," and they view the birth of the CCR as an answer to that prayer.[63] Yet this still does not explain what led Catholic faculty and students at Duquesne University to read Wilkerson's *The Cross and the Switchblade* and Sherrill's *They Speak with Other Tongues* or to seek out Protestant Pentecostal prayer meetings in 1967. It also does not explain what role may have been played by the profound crisis of spiritual disorientation that followed the Second Vatican Council for many Catholics, instead of a "New Pentecost." Others point back still farther in history to Pope Leo XIII, who—allegedly in response to the urgings of Sister Elena Guerra (1835–1914), an Italian nun who insisted that "Pentecost is not over"—wrote an encyclical on the Holy Spirit, *Divinum Illud Menus* (1897), and on January 1, 1901, invoked the Holy Spirit by singing the hymn *Veni*

---

61. Alnor, *Heaven Can't Wait*, 9–14, 101–38; Dager, *Vengeance*, 55; Randles, *Weighed*, 33–34; Oppenheimer, "Prophet," para. 6–14, 19.

62. Healy, *Healing*, 166–67.

63. Thigpen, "Catholic Charismatic Renewal," 460.

Creator Spiritus on behalf of the entire Church.[64] Catholic Charismatics sometimes point out that Leo's invocation occurred on the very night that a group of Protestant Holiness students at Bethel Bible College in Topeka, Kansas, prayed for and reportedly began receiving the gifts of "baptism in the Spirit" and "speaking in tongues," starting that very night with a young Bible student named Agnes Ozman. According to a common CCR conjecture promoted by Mary Healy at an ecumenical conference in Kansas City called *Kairos 2017*, Leo's initiative was met with only a "tepid response" by Catholic bishops since the Catholic Church at the time was "not prepared to welcome a new outpouring of the Holy Spirit," and the Church had to wait for the advent of Protestant Pentecostalism for the torch of revival to be passed under divine inspiration to the Catholic faculty members and students at Duquesne who were spiritually aroused by reading Pentecostal authors Wilkerson and Sherrill in 1967, thus rekindling life in the Spirit in the Catholic Church.[65]

Regardless of the details of how the CCR acquired its ideas, it's clear that they were largely imported, with minor modifications, from the Protestant Pentecostal tradition. In this respect, their movement exhibits a striking disregard, if not ignorance, of Church tradition, as we shall see. This is true not only of the CCR but for Protestant Charismatic and "Third Wave" movements as well. Now that we have briefly examined the contemporary Charismatic culture through the examples of the Toronto Blessing and CCR, we are ready to dig our way down into the meaning of "tongues" in the Pentecostal tradition.

64. Burgess, "Guerra, Elena," 682.

65. Burgess, "Guerra, Elena," 682; Naumann, "Make 'Missionary Disciples,'" relates Healy's message at *Kairos 2017*. See also Goff, "Parham," 956; Thigpen, "Catholic Charismatic Renewal," 460; Goff, "Topeka Revival," 1148.

CHAPTER 3

The Pentecostal Crisis
and Its Background

From 1906 (Pentecostal crisis) back to 1830 (Irvingite revival)

*So Balaam rose in the morning, and saddled his ass . . . [and he] was
riding on the ass. . . . And the ass saw the angel of the LORD standing in the
road, with a drawn sword in his hand. . . . And when the ass saw the angel of
the LORD, she pushed against the wall, and pressed Balaam's foot against the
wall . . . and Balaam's anger was kindled, and he struck the ass with his staff.
Then the LORD opened the mouth of the ass, and she said to Balaam, "What
have I done to you, that you have struck me these three times?"*

~ NUMBERS 22:21–30 (RSV) ~

*If Balaam's mule could stop in the middle of the road and give the first
preacher that went out for money a "bawling out" in Arabic, anybody today
ought to be able to preach in any language of the world if they had horse sense
enough to let God use their tongue and throat.*

~ CHARLES F. PARHAM, "THE LATTER RAIN" ~

THERE IS NOT A little irony in the fact that "Spirit-baptized," "tongue-
speaking" Pentecostal and Charismatic leaders today should attribute the

62

beginnings of their movements to an early twentieth-century revival that involved a significant embarrassment concerning the gift of "tongues"—an embarrassment which, if they are even aware of it, they seem content to ignore. Even the leaders of the Catholic Charismatic Renewal, as we saw in the previous chapter, point to the student revival at Bethel Bible College in Topeka, Kansas, as the divine answer to Pope Leo XIII's invocation of the Holy Spirit and as the spark that led to the outpouring of the Holy Spirit in the Catholic Church at Duquesne University in 1967; and, as proof, they stress that the Topeka Revival began with Agnes Ozman receiving "Spirit baptism" and "speaking in tongues" on the same night that Pope Leo sang the *Veni Creator Spiritus* in Rome on January 1, 1901. Both Protestant Pentecostals and Catholic Charismatics recognize that the Topeka Revival, together with the Azusa Street revival in Los Angeles in 1906, as important antecedents in the development of the Pentecostal movement. These two revivals are representative of a much larger phenomenon of revivals in the Holiness tradition spreading to other parts of the country such as the North Avenue Mission in Chicago, and similar developments in Atlanta, New York, and even Toronto.[1] Yet they substantially reflect what was happening throughout many churches in the United States. The Topeka revival, under the leadership of Charles Parham, synthesized many elements of the Holiness movement and other mystical ideas of his age, as attested by the legacy of numerous documents from his career. The Azusa Street revival represents the coming of age of the Holiness movement, where the movement and its practices first came to national and international attention.

What is hardly ever mentioned, however, is the major crisis in the development of their *glossolalic* "tongues" movement that was precipitated by those revivals. The fact is, the term *glossolalia* was hardly even known among most Pentecostals much before the 1960s; and those who received the gift of "tongues," both in the Topeka and Azusa Street revivals, initially believed that they were miraculously speaking actual foreign languages that they did not previously know. This was also the belief of Charles F. Parham, the Holiness evangelist who founded the Topeka Bible College and imparted "Spirit baptism" and the gift of "tongues" to Agnes Ozman by the laying on of hands. It was also the initial belief of William Seymour, the former student of Parham who preached the Azusa Street revival, where the gift of "tongues" went viral. To top matters off, when Pentecostal missionaries who had received "Spirit baptism" and the gift of "tongues" in Seymour's church were sent to Asia with the understanding that their gift of "tongues" was intended for the propagation of the Gospel in foreign languages and would

---

1. See Anderson, *Introduction to Pentecostalism*; Faupel, *Everlasting Gospel*.

miraculously enable them to communicate without the benefit of prior language training, they found to their embarrassment that they could not make themselves understood. What had happened? Had they been misinformed about "tongues"? Had they been mistaken? What should they do? Should they admit they had been wrong? Should they simply ignore the problem? Should they attempt to redefine "tongues"? For the most part, Pentecostal leaders initially opted to ignore the problem, though an eventual change in how the gift of "tongues" was experienced among their members led to a quiet rethinking of their theology of "tongues." This, in a nutshell, is the crisis that precipitated the Pentecostal redefinition of the gift of "tongues"— a crisis that provides a major clue in our "archeological excavations."

This chapter, therefore, covers how the historically-received, traditional definition of "tongues" as the speaking or hearing and understanding of actual foreign languages all but died out and was replaced by a wider set of expressions—such as "language of adoration," "singing and writing in tongues," and "private language of prayer." Our journey will start with the Pentecostal revivals of Topeka and Azusa Street in the early 1900s, then take us back into history to examine the antecedents of Pentecostal "tongues" in the Irvingite movement of the 1830s in Great Britain, and finally, bring us to the great crisis of "missionary tongues" in early Pentecostalism, and to the subsequent redefinition of "tongues" that was carried forward into the Neo-Pentecostal, Charismatic movements of the 1960s, which we examined in the last chapter. We must begin our journey, however, during the Second Great Awakening and Methodist revivals of the late-eighteenth and nineteenth centuries, and particularly with the Holiness movement and its expectations of "Spirit baptism" and an "end-times" restoration of miraculous gifts of healing, prophecy, and "tongues," accompanied by growing anticipation of the imminent return of Christ and a pressing missionary conviction that the Gospel must be preached to the ends of the earth. Our primary purpose at this point is not so much to verify or falsify the perceptions of those involved in these movements—as participants or as observers—but to ascertain exactly what they subjectively believed "tongues" to be.

Charles Parham and the Topeka Revival

Charles Fox Parham (1873–1929) is ranked as a milestone figure in the history of the Holiness movements anticipating the birth of Pentecostalism. Yet, as we shall see, his understanding of "tongues" was quite different from the common view of today. Parham left the Methodist church in 1895, chafing under hierarchical restrictions and complaining that Methodist ministers "were not left to preach by direct inspiration."[2] Rejecting denominations, he established his own itinerant evangelistic ministry within the less constrained framework of the broad Holiness movement, establishing his "faith-based" mission in Topeka, Kansas, in 1898. In this respect, Parham differed little from the disaffected Methodists and Baptists of the Piedmont region of western North Carolina and eastern Tennessee, such as Richard G. Spurling Sr., who broke with their erstwhile denominations to form Holiness revivals that came to be identified as the Latter Rain movement of the 1880s, elements of which would later merge with and contribute to the rise of modern Pentecostalism.[3] It was Parham's teaching and mission emphasis that inspired some of his followers—particularly his children's African-American nanny, Lucy Farrow, and William Seymour—to go to California as major patrons of the Azusa Street Revival. Parham remains a controversial and complex figure whose significance goes far beyond his view of "tongues." The many contributions of his *Apostolic Faith Movement* are already well documented and lie beyond the scope of the present investigation. Our initial purpose here is limited to documenting what Parham believed the miracle of "tongues" to be—whether he thought they were a foreign language, a heavenly one, ecstatic utterances, or some combination of these—and what happened to his view of "tongues" in the years following the missionary crisis.

Parham's views on the gift of tongues, both experientially and theologically, are not hard to find. His perspective is quite traditional. He believed tongues to be, as in the Book of Acts, the miraculous gift of speaking in a foreign language unknown beforehand by the speaker, to be used for evangelistic and missionary outreach. His opinions on the matter are indicated in several sources, including his wife's biography of him, as well as first-hand accounts published in *The Apostolic Faith* newspaper, which he established in 1899—not to be confused with the paper by the same name established by William Seymour in 1906.

Sarah Parham's *The Life of Charles F. Parham: The Founder of the Apostolic Faith Movement* (1930) attests to his views on tongues, as well as those of other participants in the Topeka Revival.[4] Chapter 7 of the book—entitled "The Latter Rain: The Story of the Origin of the Original Apostolic or Pentecostal Movements"—was written by Charles Parham himself, who describes the beginning of his work in Topeka:

---

2. Goff, *Fields White unto Harvest*, 36.

3. Mayer and Piepkorn, *Religious Bodies of America*, 308.

4. Parham, *Life of Charles F. Parham*; cf. Frodsham, *With Signs Following*, ch. 2.

We opened the Bible School at Topeka, Kansas in October 1900. . . . In December of 1900, we had had our examination upon the subject of repentance, conversion, consecration, sanctification, healing, and the soon coming of the Lord. We had reached in our studies a problem. What about the 2nd Chapter of Acts? I had felt for years that any missionary going to the foreign field should preach in the language of the natives. That if God had ever equipped His ministers in that way, He could do it today. That if Balaam's mule could stop in the middle of the road and give the first preacher that went out for money a "bawling out" in Arabic, that anybody today ought to be able to preach in any language of the world if they had horse sense enough to let God use their tongue and throat.[5]

Chapter 8 of the biography includes a firsthand account by Miss Lilian Thistlethwaite, the sister-in-law of Charles Parham, entitled "The Wonderful History of the Latter Rain" (later reprinted in *Apostolic Faith*), which relates the incipient connection between the gift of tongues and the emerging doctrine of "Spirit baptism" as these were interpreted in the Topeka Revival. Because she sets the stage for what happened in the Topeka Revival in such illuminating detail, we quote her at length:

It was just before the Christmas holidays that we took up the study of the Holy Ghost. Mr. Parham was going to Kansas City to conduct meetings there and to bring some friends back with him to spend Christmas and be present for the watch night meeting. Before leaving, the following is the substance of what he said:

"Students, as I have studied the teachings of the various Bible Schools and full gospel movements, conviction, conversion, healing, and sanctification are taught virtually the same, but on the baptism ['Spirit baptism'] there is a difference among them. Some accept Stephan Merritt's teaching of baptism at sanctification, while others say this is a baptism received through the "laying on of hands" or the gift of the Holy Ghost, yet they agree on no definite evidence. Some claim this fulfillment of promise "by faith" without any special witness, while others, because of wonderful blessings or demonstrations, such as shouting or jumping. Though I honor the Holy Ghost in anointing power, both in conversion and in sanctification, yet I believe there is a greater revelation of His power. The gifts are in the Holy Spirit

---

5. Parham, *Life of Charles F. Parham*, 51–52. Some have noted discrepancies between the details of Parham's account and those of others such as Ozman's. Cf. Hayford and Moore, *Charismatic Century*, 38.

and with the baptism of the Holy Spirit the gifts, as well as the graces, should be manifested. Now students, while I am gone, see if there is not some evidence given of the baptism so there may be no doubt on the subject.

"We see the signs already being fulfilled that mark the soon coming of the Lord and I believe with John Wesley that at Christ's second coming the Church will be found with the same power that the apostles and the early Church possessed."

Thus closed the regular Bible lessons, for a time, but there was individual and collective prayer and study of the Bible continuously.

On Mr. Parham's return to the school with his friends, he asked the students whether they had found any Bible evidence of the baptism of the Holy Spirit. The answer was, unanimous, "speaking in other tongues."

Services were held daily and each night. There was a hallowed hush over the entire building. All felt the influence of a mighty presence in our midst. Without any special direction, all moved in harmony. I remember Mrs. Parham saying, "Such a spirit of unity prevails that even the children are at peace, while the very air filled with expectancy. Truly He is with us, and has something more wonderful for us than we have known before."

The service on New Year's night was especially spiritual and each heart was filled with the hunger for the will of God to be done in them. One of the students, a lady who had been in several other Bible Schools, asked Mr. Parham, to lay hands upon her that she might receive the Holy Spirit. As he prayed, her face lighted up with the glory of God and she began to speak with "other tongues." She afterward told us she had received a few words while in the Prayer Tower, but now her English was taken from her, and with floods of joy and laughter she praised God in other languages.

There was very little sleeping among any of us that night. The next day still being unable to speak English, she wrote on a piece of paper, "Pray that I may interpret."[6]

One of the students at Charles Parham's Bethel Bible College in Topeka was Agnes N. Ozman (1870–1937). She is considered by Pentecostal-Holiness historians to have been the first person to speak in tongues in the Topeka Revival of 1901 that sparked the Pentecostal movement. She came from a Methodist-Holiness background and, before coming to Topeka, had attended the Bible schools of T. C. Horton in St. Paul, Minnesota, and of

---

6. Parham, *Life of Charles F. Parham*, 59; cf. Thistlethwaite, "Wonderful History."

A. B. Simpson, the founder of the Christian and Missionary Alliance, in New York. She was introduced to the concepts of divine healing, sanctification, and "Spirit baptism" through them, and to the idea of "tongues" as the initial evidence of "Spirit baptism" by Parham in Topeka. In her personal testimony, she writes that she came to Parham's school in October of 1900, where, with other students, she studied the Bible and prayed night and day in a special prayer tower in Stone's Folly, where she had "many blessed hours of prayer in this upper room during the night watches."[7] She says that she "tasted the joy of leading some souls to Christ" and was "blessed with the presence of the Lord, who, in response to my prayer, healed some who were sick."[8] Notably, she then adds: "Like some others, I thought that I received the baptism of the Holy Ghost at the time of consecration, but when I learned that the Holy Ghost was yet to be poured out in greater fullness, my heart became hungry for the promised comforter and I began to cry out for an enduement with power from on high."[9] Her words reflect Parham's teaching that "Spirit baptism" is a second work of grace subsequent to conversion and water baptism, and, according to her own belief, subsequent even to the personal "consecration" she references here.

As we saw earlier, Parham invited his students to take an inductive approach to the question of the "initial evidence" doctrine, for which the gift of tongues would serve as a subsequent attestation to Spirit baptism: he gave them three days, while he was away, to ponder the meaning of the Bible verse "receive the gift of the Holy Spirit" in Acts 2:38 and whether any evidence specifically related to this gift could be found.[10] By the time he returned, his students collectively agreed that if the Holy Spirit had descended upon an individual, then "speaking in tongues" would follow as sufficient proof of the fact.[11] Ozman then describes her version of what happened:

> As the end of the year drew near some friends came from Kansas City to spend the holidays with us. On watch night we had a blessed service, praying that God's blessing might rest upon us as the New Year came in. During the first day of 1901, the presence of the Lord was with us in a marked way, stilling our

7. Ozman, "Personal Testimony," para. 3. "Stone's Folly" refers to a three-story eighteen-room mansion rented by Parham in 1900–1901 and built by Erastus R. Stone in 1887 but left uncompleted due to economic depression. See the photo in Goff, "Topeka Revival," 1148; "Stone's Folly," 1.

8. Ozman, "Personal Testimony," para. 4.

9. Ozman, "Personal Testimony," para. 4.

10. Hayford and Moore, *Charismatic Century*, 38, notes some discrepancies in details between such accounts.

11. Frodsham, *With Signs Following*, 19.

hearts to wait upon Him for greater things. The spirit of prayer was upon us in the evening. It was nearly seven o'clock on this first of January that it came into my heart to ask Brother Parham to lay his hands upon me that I might receive the gift of the Holy Spirit. It was as his hands were laid upon my head that the Holy Spirit fell upon me and I began to speak in tongues, glorifying God. I talked several languages, and it was clearly manifest when a new dialect was spoken.[12]

Charles Parham later recounted: "I laid my hands upon her and prayed. I had scarcely completed three dozen sentences when a glory fell upon her, a halo seemed to surround her head and face, and she began speaking the Chinese language and was unable to speak English for three days.[13] When she tried to write in English to tell us of her experience, she wrote the Chinese, copies of which we still have in newspapers printed at that time."[14] Ozman herself relates the following:

> On January 2, some of us went down to Topeka to a mission. As we worshiped the Lord, I offered prayer in English and then prayed in another language in tongues. A Bohemian who was present said that he understood what I said. Some months later at a schoolhouse with others, in a meeting, I spoke in tongues in the power of the spirit and another Bohemian understood me. Since then, others have understood other languages I have spoken.[15]

In chapter 8 of Sarah Parham's biography, Thistlethwaite gives abundant evidence that everyone present at the Topeka revival meetings believed that "speaking in tongues" was a miraculous gift of previously unlearned foreign languages. She writes, for example:

> On one occasion a Hebrew Rabbi was present as one of the students, a young married man, read the lesson from the Bible. After services, he asked for the Bible from which the lesson was read. The Bible was handed to him, and he said, "No not that

---

12. Parham, *Life of Charles F. Parham*, 66.

13. This is contradicted by Ozman, "Personal Testimony," para. 8, where she says she prayed in English the next day (January 2).

14. Charles Parham, as quoted in Parham, *Life of Charles F. Parham*, 42–53. Images of Ozman's writing in tongues may be found in "Agnes Ozman's Writing," 32, col. 2; Sullivan, *GOTP*, s.v. "Solutions," s.v. "Writing and Singing in Tongues."

15. Ozman, "Personal Testimony"; cf. Frodsham, *With Signs Following*, 20.

one, I want to see the Hebrew Bible. That man read in the Hebrew tongue."[16]

In chapter 13 of her biography, Sarah Parham herself relates how a
professor who spoke five languages came to one of their meetings where
he witnessed the miracle of "tongues" and shared his impressions with her
husband:

> He said to him the most marvelous thing about the use of these
> languages was the original accent they (the workers) gave. They
> demonstrated that under instruction [that] it was impossible for
> an American to learn. They gave the *real foreign accent so per-*
> *fectly*, that when he closed his eyes, it seemed to him as though
> he were listening to utterances from his native masters in the
> Old World.
>
> To me this was very convincing, coming from those unbi-
> ased and competent judges. They ofttimes interpreted for me
> when languages they knew were spoken. Many foreigners came
> to the meetings and were frequently spoken to in their native
> tongue, with the original accent that could not be perfectly
> acquired. This, more than anything else, convinced them that
> it was wrought by some power above the human. Their hearts
> were always touched and they frequently went to the altar for
> prayer, convinced that it was the real power of God.[17]

When Parham and his group of students visited Galena, Kansas, in
late January, the wire services picked up the story, which now included the
following extraordinary assertions:

> A remarkable claim made during these meetings was that the
> students, Americans all, spoke in twenty-one known languages,
> including French, German, Swedish, Bohemian, Chinese,
> Japanese, Hungarian, Bulgarian, Russian, Italian, Spanish, and
> Norwegian. In a conversation with a *Kansas City Times* corre-
> spondent, Parham claimed that his students had never studied
> these languages and that natives of the countries involved had
> heard them spoken and had verified their authenticity. Taking
> these events at face value, Parham immediately began to teach
> that missionaries would no longer be compelled to study foreign
> languages to preach in the mission fields. From Henceforth, he
> taught, one need only receive the baptism with the Holy Ghost

16. Parham, *Life of Charles F. Parham*, 62; cf. Frodsham, *With Signs Following*, 22.

17. Parham, *Life of Charles F. Parham*, 116–17.

and he could go to the farthest corners of the world and preach to the natives in languages unknown to the speaker.[18]

William Seymour and the Azusa Street Revival

William Seymour (1870–1922) was an African-American from Louisiana who moved to Texas early in his life. Raised a Baptist, he was exposed to holiness views at a Black Methodist Episcopal Church in Indianapolis in 1895 and classes at Martin Wells Knapp's Bible school in Cincinnati from 1900 to 1902. In 1903 he returned to Houston, a short, stocky, poverty-stricken southern black man with one eye damaged by smallpox and a hunger to learn more about the Bible and theology. Several years later, he learned about "The Bible Training School" that Parham had established in Houston after closing his Bible college in Topeka and taking a four-year whirlwind revival tour across Kansas and Missouri. In 1906, Lucy F. Farrow, who had taken a position with Parham's evangelistic team as his children's nanny and was the first African-American recorded as having "spoken in tongues," encouraged Seymour to attend Parham's school. Southern racial mores prevented Seymour, a black, from attending Parham's school, but Parham allowed him to sit in the hallway just outside of the classroom and hear his lectures through the open door. Seymour adopted Parham's teaching that speaking in "tongues" was a sign of "Spirit baptism." He broke with Parham, however, over theological differences, such as Parham's unorthodox belief in the annihilation of the wicked, and Parham's disapproval of interracial revival meetings. The same year, Seymour moved to Los Angeles, where he began preaching his own Pentecostal message, drawing large crowds that sparked the Azusa Street Revival. His leadership—his establishment of *The Apostolic Faith* newspaper in 1906, which at its height had a circulation of fifty thousand (not to be confused with Parham's newspaper by the same title), and his organization of the *Apostolic Faith Movement* independent of Parham's—launched him into national prominence.[19]

The first issue of *The Apostolic Faith* newspaper sported the headline: "Pentecost Has Come," and opened with a paragraph describing how "Pentecost as recorded in the Book of Acts" had "surely come" to Los Angeles, with "many being converted and sanctified and filled with the Holy Ghost,

18. Synan, *Holiness-Pentecostal Tradition*, 92.

19. Synan, *Holiness-Pentecostal Tradition*, 92–93; Robeck, *Azusa Street*, 22–24, 32–33, 46–49; Robbins, *Pentecostalism in America*, 26, 46–49.

speaking in tongues as they did on the day of Pentecost."[20] The paper included accounts of the origins of the Pentecostal revival in Parham's Topeka Revival and even carried an amicable message from Parham stating: "I rejoice in God over you all, my children, though I have never seen you; but since you know the Holy Spirit's power, we are baptized by the one Spirit into one body."[21] Five years after the beginning of Parham's revival, this gospel is described as "spreading everywhere," with "something like 13,000 people" now involved. It is also clear that the gift of "tongues" was clearly understood to be a miraculous *xenolalic* gift of speaking in actual foreign languages:

> Many are speaking in new tongues, and some are on their way to the foreign fields, with the gift of language. . . .
>
> The Lord has given the gift of writing in unknown languages. . . .
>
> A Mohammedan, a Soudanese by birth, a man who is an interpreter and speaks six languages, came into the meetings at Azusa Street and the Lord gave him messages which none but himself could understand. He identified, and wrote [a] number of the languages. . . .
>
> In about an hour and a half, a young man was converted, sanctified and baptized with the Holy Ghost, and spoke with tongues. . . . He has received many tongues, also the gift of prophecy, and writing in a number of foreign languages, and has a call to a foreign field. . . .
>
> The gift of languages is given with the commission, "Go ye into all the world and preach the Gospel to every creature." The Lord has given languages to the unlearned. Greek, Latin, Hebrew, French, German, Italian, Chinese, Japanese, Zulu and languages of Africa, Hindu and Bengali and dialects of India, Chippewa and other languages of the Indians, Esquimaux [Eskimo], and the deaf-mute language.[22]

This *xenolalic* interpretation of the gift of tongues as the miraculous speaking of actual human languages continued beyond the original revivals of Topeka (1901) and Los Angeles (1906), which gave birth to Pentecostalism. V. P. Simmons, although a relatively unknown name in Pentecostal history, wrote an early Church history of tongues, which was serialized in the Pentecostal newspaper called the *Bridegroom's Messenger* in 1907. He linked the gift of tongues in the recent Pentecostal revivals with the discussions of

20. "Pentecost Has Come," 1.
21. "Pentecost Has Come," 1.
22. "Pentecost Has Come," 1.

tongues found in early Church Fathers like Irenaeus, whose understanding of tongues was clearly *xenolalic*.[23] When the editors of the Azusa Street Revival newspaper (*The Apostolic Faith*), Clara Lum and Florence Crawford, moved their publishing house to Portland, Oregon, shortly after it was founded by Seymour, they continued to adhere to the view that "tongues" were actual languages, even though they had already begun allowing a distinction between the "gift of tongues," on the one hand, as a voluntary exercise under the speaker's control, and "utterances" in the Spirit, on the other hand, as an involuntary phenomenon.[24] In fact, as we shall see below, after the Pentecostal crisis of Missionary Tongues between 1906–8, references to "utterances" became increasingly frequent among Pentecostals and nearly came to replace "tongues" when indicating their own practice.[25] Nevertheless, the traditional *xenolalic* view continued to prevail for some time. The September 1906 issue states: "Different nationalities are now hearing the Gospel in their own 'tongue wherein they were born.'"[26] The July-August, 1908, issue references "preaching in tongues" that was "understood by those present" in their own languages of Russian, Spanish, African, and Indian dialects.[27]

The September 1911 issue reports that "hundreds of people all over the world have received the gift of . . . speaking in new tongues, the languages of the nations."[28] Seven years later, the September 1918 issue reports people "getting saved, sanctified and baptized with the Holy Ghost" at various meetings, and "speaking in the Chinese languages," which were understood by missionaries from China.[29] A British Pentecostal periodical edited by A. A. Boddy, called *Confidence*, reports in its January 1913 issue that a Chinese girl who did not know English "spoke in purest English."[30] In Frank Bartleman's *How Pentecost came to Los Angeles* (1925), we read:

> A. B. Simpson [founder of the Christian and Missionary Alliance] said: "We are to witness before the Lord's return real missionary 'tongues' like those of Pentecost, through which the heathen world shall hear in their own language 'the wonderful works of God' and this perhaps on a scale of whose vastness we

23. Sullivan, *GOTP*, s.v. "V. P. Simmons," para. 10.

24. Sullivan, *GOTP*, s.v. "Early Pentecostal Tongues," s.v. "Apostolic Faith (Portland)."

25. Sullivan, *GOTP*, s.v. "Utterance Versus Tongues," para. 1–5.

26. "Russians Hear in Their Own Tongue," 4.

27. "The Promised Latter Rain," 1, s.v. "Preaching in Tongues."

28. "Power of the Blood," 8, s.v. "Shanghai, China."

29. "Power of God," 4, para. 3.

30. "Utterance in Tongues," 4.

have scarcely dreamed, thousands of missionaries going forth in one last mighty crusade from a united body of believers at home to bear swift witness of the crucified and coming Lord to all nations."[31]

Again, the first seventeen chapters of Stanley H. Frodsham's classic, *With Signs Following: The Story of the Pentecostal Revival in the Twentieth Century* (1926), documents people miraculously speaking in foreign languages.[32] Examples could be multiplied.

Immediate Historical Antecedents

Parham's Topeka Revival, and even more so Seymour's Azusa-Street Revival, gave national attention to an underground movement spreading across the United States and to other countries. They gave a much wider platform for speaking in tongues, which went viral throughout a diverse range of religious communities, bringing the phenomenon into the court of public opinion. This outbreak initially perpetuated the traditional view of tongues that dominated Christian history for over two thousand years. The Pentecostal understanding was that certain individuals were inspired by the Holy Spirit to miraculously speak in foreign languages. This understanding was accompanied by attendant convictions about tongues serving as "initial evidence" for "Spirit baptism," and debates about whether such baptism was a second or third "work of grace," and about how it related to sanctification. The revivals were also accompanied by a sense that everyone was now living in the "end times," that the prophecy of Joel 2:28 meant that God was pouring out his Spirit on all people and that the reference to a "latter rain" in Joel 2:13 meant that this latter-days outpouring would be greater than the first outpouring at Pentecost, as described by David Wesley Myland's *The Latter Rain Covenant and Pentecostal Power* (1910).[33] Recipients of the gift of tongues also understood it as implying a divine missionary commission, often related to the language they were told they were speaking, exciting a sense of urgency about foreign mission work and sharing the Gospel of Christ.

31. Bartleman, *How Pentecost Came*, 65.

32. Frodsham, *With Signs Following*, chs. 1–17.

33. Early Pentecostal references to the "latter rain," despite their common reference, should not be confused with the "Latter Rain Revival" of 1948–52, which began in Saskatchewan, Canada, or the "Latter Rain Movement," which continued from 1952 into the 1960s.

Seymour was confirmed in the substance of his Pentecostal theology largely by Parham's instruction. Parham himself was heavily influenced by A. B. Simpson, the Canadian founder of the Christian and Missionary Alliance, who promoted kindred views, and by two other controversial notables during this period: Alexander Dowie and Frank Sandford. What they all had in common was the aim of restoring the faith and practice of the primitive Church, and a sense that the end of the world was imminent. Dowie's influence effectively provoked Parham's interest in the world of supernatural phenomena, empowering and authorizing him to inquire directly into its mysteries. Sandford was a passionate speaker, revivalist, and mystic with apocalyptic ideas who mixed British Israelitism with an urgent sense of mission and an immediate sense of divine interventions in daily life. Most importantly, he exposed Parham to his first experience of witnessing people speaking in tongues during a visit to one of his revivals at his Shiloh community in Durham, Maine, which filled Parham with a firsthand feeling of the immediacy of the supernatural. Parham also read Sanford's tract, *The Everlasting Gospel*, in which he learned about a woman named Jennie Glassey who was endowed with the miraculous ability to speak and draw and sing in foreign languages, which further confirmed his conviction that the miraculous manifestation of foreign languages was a precursor to the imminent end of the world.[34] These were all deeply formative experiences for Parham.

These ideas did not emerge in a cultural vacuum, however. They emerged from the larger context of the Second Great Awakening and the Holiness movements rooted in the post-Civil War Wesleyan realignment, defined by its emphasis on the doctrine of a second work of grace leading to Christian perfection, its conviction of an end-times renewal of miraculous spiritual gifts and missionary fervor. Links between a *xenolalic* view of tongues and a missionary mandate can be found also in earlier Holiness evangelists. Two examples are A. B. Simpson and W. B. Godbey. In 1882, A. B. Simpson launched the *Christian Missionary Alliance Weekly*, the official magazine of the denomination he founded. While not generally considered a pioneer of the Pentecostal movement, his contributions to the Holiness movement and his desire for the renewal of the spiritual gifts were immensely important in the development of early Pentecostalism. The February 12, 1892 issue of his *Weekly* (8/7) carries an article entitled "The Gift of Tongues," which argues for a cautious openness to *xenolalia*: "But does the Bible really warrant the expectation of the gift of tongues for the

---

34. For the relationship between Parham, Sandford, and Glassey, see Lie, "Origin"; Hunter, "Beniah."

purpose of preaching the Gospel to the heathen? We must frankly say that we are not quite clear that it does, and yet we would not dare to discourage any of God's children from claiming and expecting it if they have faith to do so and can see the warrant in His word. . . . We should not be surprised in any case to hear of the direct bestowal of the power to speak an unknown language."[35] William B. Godbey, one of the most influential evangelists of the Wesleyan-Holiness movement in its formative years preceding the Pentecostal movement, wrote, in his book, *Spiritual Gifts and Graces* (1895): "Bishop Taylor . . . says this power to speak unknown languages is enjoyed at the present day by some of his missionaries in Africa. . . . The Gift is destined to play a conspicuous part in the evangelization of the heathen world, amid the glorious prophetical fulfillment of the latter days. All missionaries in heathen lands should seek and expect this Gift to enable them to preach fluently in the vernacular tongue."[36] William Arthur, a leader in the great Ulster revival of 1859, wrote:

> "THEY began to speak with other tongues, as the Spirit gave them utterance." It is not said, "with unknown tongues." In fact, the expression, "unknown tongues," was never used by an inspired writer. In the Epistle to the Corinthians, it is found in the English version but the word "unknown" is in italics, showing that it is not taken from the original. Speaking unknown tongues was never heard of in the apostolic days. That *miracle* first occurred in London some years ago. On the day of Pentecost, no man pretended to speak unknown tongues; but just as if we in London suddenly began to speak German, French, Spanish, Russian, Turkish, and other foreign languages, so it was with them.[37]

Where did the idea of tongues as "initial evidence" come from? Parham has been called "father of the doctrine of tongues as the initial physical evidence of the baptism of the Holy Spirit."[38] This is a generally accepted view, and he indeed stressed this relationship. A hint of a significant earlier precedent for his views, however, is found in a comment Parham makes in his work, *A Voice Crying in the Wilderness* (1902). He writes: "We have found . . . that the Irvingites, a sect that arose under the teaching of Irving . . . during the last century, received not only the eight recorded gifts of 1

35. "Gift of Tongues," 98–99.
36. Godbey, *Spiritual Gifts*, 42–43.
37. Arthur, *Tongue of Fire*, 68.
38. Jones, "Holiness Movement," 727.

Cor 12, but also the speaking in other tongues, which the Holy Ghost reserved as the evidence of His coming."[39]

The Irvingite Antecedent

Edward Irving (1792–1834) was a Scottish-Presbyterian pastor, theologian, and revivalist in London during a time of prophetic expectation some seventy years before the birth of Pentecostalism. There were pockets of excitement in both Scotland and England about the imminent return of Christ and restoration of the supernatural gifts found among the original Apostles. David Bundy writes: "Influenced by the ideas of Samuel Taylor Coleridge and Thomas Carlyle, Irving became convinced that he was to function as a prophet and priest. His study of the biblical accounts of the early church persuaded him that since the fivefold offices of apostles, prophets, evangelists, pastors, and teachers had been abandoned, the Holy Spirit had, as a result, left the church to its own devices."[40] With the support of a wealthy patron, Henry Drummond, who had his own apocalyptic views, Irving began preaching sermons on the end of the world, later published under the title of *Babylon and Infidelity Foredoomed by God* (1826). The comparatively recent French Revolution likely fed some of this apocalypticism. Margaret Oliphant, one of Irving's foremost biographers, offers one of the most comprehensive and detailed accounts of his life, which incorporates a firm understanding of the Irvingite mindset. Describing the end-times anticipation among her generation that inflamed Irving's popularity, she describes the popular conviction that the "unclaimed and unexercised supernatural endowments, which had died out of use so long, would be restored only at the time of the Second Advent, in the miraculous reign, of which they form a fitting adjunct," embodying the belief that "the Holy Ghost ought to be manifested among us all, the same as ever He was in any one of the primitive Churches."[41]

At this time, according to Bundy, "prayer groups were established to seek a new outpouring of the Holy Spirit, and many were led, by Irving's assistant, Alexander Scott, to seek the charismata ['gifts'] described in the [New Testament] as part of early Christian spirituality."[42] Anticipation increased during Irving's preaching tours of Scotland in 1828 and 1829. From 1830–33, a revival broke out in the west of Scotland, which was largely

---

39. Parham, *Voice*, 29; cf. McGee, "Initial Evidence," 785.
40. Bundy, "Edward Irving," 803.
41. Oliphant, *Life of Edward Irving*, 2:104–5.
42. Oliphant, *Life of Edward Irving*, 2:104–5.

lay-led despite initial inspiration by clergymen such as Irving, John McLeod Campbell, and A. J. Scott. On April 14, 1830, as David Dorries relates, a woman named Margaret McDonald, while suffering from a terminal illness, prophesied to her brothers: "There will be a mighty baptism of the Spirit this day."[43] She reportedly was healed almost immediately, as well as a family friend named Mary Campbell, who had herself been dying of a lung disease. "Mary Campbell burned with a passion to see the church ministering supernaturally as Jesus had in his earthly ministry," says Dorries, adding that she "sought to set an example for others," on one occasion even announcing publicly that she would pray for the miraculous healing of a lame boy and then commanding him to walk, although the boy never overcame a limp.[44]

Irving believed that in the final outpouring of the Holy Spirit at the end of the world, one of the significant signs would be the occurrence of supernatural tongues identical to those described in the Book of Acts. According to Oliphant, Irving and his movement held that the initial sign of the Spirit's outpouring was fulfilled in the person of Mary Campbell when she spoke in "tongues":

> When in the midst of their devotion, the Holy Ghost came with mighty power upon the sick woman as she lay in her weakness, and constrained her to speak at great length, and with superhuman strength, in an unknown tongue, to the astonishment of all who heard, and to her own great edification and enjoyment in God—"for he that speaketh in a tongue edifieth himself." She has told me that this first seizure of the Spirit was the strongest she ever had.[45]

Another biographer, Washington Wilks, refers to other women who also spoke in tongues:

> When, therefore, in the spring of 1830, [Irving] heard of Scottish women speaking as did the Twelve on the day of Pentecost, he suspected no travestie of that wondrous story, but felt only hope and thankfulness. He dispatched an elder to inquire into the thing, who brought back a good report, and found the tongues of flame sitting on his own wife and daughters.[46]

Oliphant nevertheless claims that the modern "tongues" movement began with Mary Campbell's experience of this gift: "It was thus that agitating and

---

43. Dorries, "West of Scotland Revival," 1189.
44. Dorries, "West of Scotland Revival," 1191; cf. 1190.
45. Oliphant, *Life of Edward Irving*, 2:129.
46. Wilks, *Edward Irving*, 204.

extraordinary chapter in the history of the modern Church, which we have hereafter to deal with, began."[47]

When Irving realized in early 1830 that parishioners in Scotland were beginning to experience charismata, especially the gift of "tongues," and that they understood these charismata in light of his own interpretation, this had a profound effect on him, leading him to shift his ministry in the direction of preparing his own church in London for similar manifestations of the Spirit. In 1831 charismata first broke out in his early morning prayer services, then spread to regular Sunday services in his two-thousand-member church, and his ministry in London quickly became the focus of a major revival. Oliphant describes how the movement soon became a national phenomenon: "There is not a corner of this part of the island where the subject of Prophecy and the Second Advent have not in the Church firm and able supporters."[48] Their gatherings became spectacles, attended by thousands— one time by upwards of thirteen thousand people.[49] Church seating became such a problem that they took to selling tickets![50] The concept of a "tongues revival" became a top story in "every periodical work of the day," even in the then-popular *Fraser's Magazine*, where Irving wrote three articles on the topic.[51] Wilks remarks on the wide range of Irving's influence:

> The Duke of York repeated his visit, and carried with him other members of the royal family. . . . The parliamentary leaders of both sides, and even the Tory premier, Lord Liverpool (much to the lord Eldon's horror)—the judges, and barristers of every degree—fashionable physicians and medical students—duchesses, noted beauties, city madams—clerics and dissenters—with men and women who rather followed the fashion than made particular to either intellect or religion.[52]

Acquaintances of Irving came to include members of the royal family, parliamentary leaders, and notables such as Charles Dickens, Ralph Waldo Emerson, Alfred Tennyson, John Stuart Mill, and Thomas Carlyle.

Over the years, Irving's emphasis on tongues became so central to his ministry that it became a serious point of disagreement with Carlyle, as the

---

47. Oliphant, *Life of Edward Irving*, 2:130.

48. Oliphant, *Life of Edward Irving*, 2:118.

49. Oliphant, *Life of Edward Irving*, 2:85.

50. Wilks, *Edward Irving*, 32.

51. Wilks, *Edward Irving*, 170; cf. Sullivan, *GOTP*, s.v. "Irvingites and the Gift of Tongues," s.v. "Tongues according to Irving," para. 2–3.

52. Wilks, *Edward Irving*, 31.

latter noted in some of his letters, calling him *"gift-of-tongues Irving."*[53] Carlyle actually had a deep respect for Irving as an intellectual, but Irving's fixation on tongues eventually led Carlyle to regard him as mentally unstable. Irving and his followers initially believed that their tongues were identical to the supernatural tongues of Pentecost described in Acts 2 and that they were actually speaking foreign languages. On one occasion, however, Carlyle and some friends had the gift of tongues demonstrated for them at Irving's home by a woman (possibly Irving's wife) in an adjoining room with some other devotees, who *"burst forth* [with] *a shrieky hysterical, 'Lah lall lall!' (little or nothing else but l's and a's continued for several minutes),"* to which Irving, with singular calmness, said only, "There, hear you, there are the Tongues!"[54] Carlyle noted that they "answered him nothing, but soon came away full of distress, provocation, and a kind of shame."[55] In October of 1831, Carlyle wrote to his brother expressing his distress about Irving:

> Of poor Edward Irving I have seen little and wish I had heard nothing since you went away. Alas! the "gift of tongues" has now broken loud out (last Sunday) in his Church, the creature Campbell (or Caird or whatever she is) having started up in the forenoon; and (as the matter was encouraged by Irving) four others in the evening, when there ensued as I learn something like a perfect Bedlam scene, some groaning, some laughing, hooting, hooing, and several fainting. The Newspapers have got it, and call upon his people for the honour of Scotland to leave him, or muzzle him. The most general hypothesis is that he is a quack; the milder that he is getting cracked. Poor George is the man I pity most: he spoke to us of it almost with tears in his eyes and earnestly entreated me to deal with his Brother; which, when he comes hither (by appointment on Tuesday) I partly mean to attempt, tho' now I fear it will be useless. It seems likely that all the Loselism [lazy rascality] of London will be about the church next Sunday; that his people will quarrel with him; in any case, that troublous times are appointed him. My poor friend! And yet the punishment was not unjust; that he who believed without inquiry, should now believe against all light, and portentously call upon the world to admire as inspiration what is but a dancing on the verge of bottomless abysses of Madness! I see not the end of it; who does?[56]

53. Carlyle, *Carlyle Letters*, "Letter of TC to John A. Carlyle (August 15, 1834)."
54. Carlyle, *Reminiscences*, 252.
55. Carlyle, *Reminiscences*, 252–53.
56. Carlyle, *Carlyle Letters*, "Letter of TC to John A. Carlyle (October 21, 1831)."

Meanwhile, as A. Drummond noted in his book, *Edward Irving and His Circle* (1937), Irving had allegedly changed his definition of "tongues" to a dual one: (1) the original *intelligible* "tongues" of Pentecost used for evangelizing but no longer in general use for that purpose, and (2) the modern *unintelligible* variety, which resembled those of Corinth and were rationally indefinable. Referring to Irving's final contribution to *Fraser's Magazine* where he made the distinction, Drummond writes:

> The final article in *Fraser's Magazine* appeared in April 1832. He opens by claiming that tongue-speech was the *same* form of utterance given at Pentecost; whereas in his March article he distinctly denied that glossolalia in his time was designed as a miraculous way of evangelizing by languages unlearnt—Pentecost being unique and modern manifestations resembling rather those at Corinth.[57]

In fact, in his first article, Irving did not explicitly indicate that the gift of tongues was *xenolalic* and involved the speaking of actual foreign languages. Others who followed the initial outbreak of tongues understood it to be so; but when they began tracking the phenomenon, they eventually sensed a change in definition. By the time of his March 1832 article, Irving was revisioning his interpretation of "tongues" in light of what was happening in his congregation and in light of 1 Corinthians 14, where tongues are described as a language "which no man understandeth," and in which one speaks "not unto men, but unto God," proceeding, as Irving wrote, from a "hidden and invisible power which uttered the words unknown."[58] It is in light of this revised interpretation, as well as his later elaboration upon the gifts of "interpretation of tongues" and "prophecy," that we must seek clarity concerning what he says about tongues:

> So far from being unmeaning gibberish, as the thoughtless and heedless sons of Belial have said, ['tongues' constitute a well-pronounced discourse] which evidently wanteth only the ear of him whose native tongue it is to make it a very masterpiece of powerful speech. But as the apostle declareth that it is not spoken to the ear of man, but to the ear of God . . . we ought to stand in awe, and endeavour to enter into spiritual communion with that member of Christ, who is the mouth of the whole Church unto God. . . . Ah me! it is the standing symbol of the "communion of the saints, and their fellowship with the Father

---

57. Drummond, *Edward Irving*, 164; cf. Irving, "Recent Manifestations," parts 2 and 3.
58. Irving, "Recent Manifestations," 2:198.

and the Son," not by means of intelligence, but by means of the Holy Ghost.[59]

Given his revised understanding of "tongues," Irving would seem to have accepted the view that if the tongues of Pentecost in Acts were *xenolalia*, that species of tongues would not occur again. The question naturally arises then, what did Irving think about the "tongues" of Corinth? Drummond supplies the answer: when asked this question, "Irving replied that he had not the least idea of the meaning of Tongues," and "aspired to be no more than the humble pastor of the flock."[60] While Irving's reply may suggest that he was simply avoiding a definition, his studied agnosticism about the identity of "tongues" was an essential part of his doctrine. When George Pilkington, who aspired to be a "tongues interpreter" in Irving's assembly, reported his doubts about their intelligibility as actual languages and their supernatural origin, he was told by Irving: "You cannot interpret by human understanding; interpretation must be given by the Spirit."[61] Irving's transformation was now complete: he now believed that the "tongues" of his day were an entirely other-worldly and divinely-inspired phenomenon with no admixture of ordinary human intelligibility.

Irving's followers believed the gift of tongues was *xenolalic*. Mary Campbell initially believed herself to have miraculously spoken the language of the Pelew Islands (now Palau), a group of distant islands between the Philippines and Indonesia where less than twenty thousand people spoke the language.[62] With limited travel conditions, the difficulty of confirming the claim renders it a trifle suspect. On at least one occasion, her language was believed to be Turkish or Chinese.[63] The definition immediately became a source of discussion. One member of Irving's original Regent Square Church argued, for example, that the gift of tongues was not a shortcut to missionary success, from which we may infer that most Irvingites continued to believe that the gift of "tongues" was *xenolalic*.[64] Wilks gives a commonsense observation about the entire matter:

> The mental condition out of which it arose was just then a very common one in the religious world and is not without parallel in ecclesiastical history—namely, despair of the world's conversion

59. Irving, "Recent Manifestations," 2:199.

60. Drummond, *Edward Irving*, 172.

61. Pilkington, *Unknown Tongues*, 19–22, 27–30; cf. "Revelation: The 'Tongue,'" an anonymous review of Pilkington's book.

62. Drummond, *Edward Irving*, 160; cf. Oliphant, *Life*, 2:206.

63. Drummond, *Edward Irving*, 160; Oliphant, *Life*, 2:206.

64. Pilkington, *Unknown Tongues*, 19–22, 27–30; "Revelation: The 'Tongue,'" 21–40.

by the ordinary methods of evangelization; and the desire of supernatural manifestations as a prelude to the Lord's second advent.[65]

An unavoidable problem, however, was the emerging discrepancy between the definition of tongues at the beginning of the movement and the understanding that emerged later. Oliphant notes this when she says that "the hypothesis of actual languages conferred seems to have given way to that of a supernatural sign attestation of the intelligible prophecy."[66] Writing about William Harding, a member of Irving's Regent Square Church in London, Drummond states: "Harding protests against the popular misconception of the Tongues as a shortcut to missionary success, and quotes Conyers Middleton, the liberal eighteenth-century divine."[67] This begs the question: what led to the shift away from the traditional view of tongues as the spontaneous utterance of a foreign language unknown to the speaker beforehand—to a heavenly language unknown on earth? It had become sadly apparent that the traditional understanding of the gift of tongues based on the Book of Acts fell somewhat short of defining what was happening in the Irvingite community in London.

Irving's refusal to censure the expression of spiritual gifts in his Regent Square Church led to his expulsion by the London Presbytery in 1832, which considered the practice disruptive when allowed in regular Sunday worship services. The London decision barred him from his church but did not affect his ordination. Shortly after this, however, he was required to appear before the Presbytery of Annan, in his Scottish hometown. At his trial, he wanted the discussion to revolve around the question of supernatural gifts; but the Presbytery instead decided to charge him with heresy because his Christology maintained "the sinfulness of the Savior in His human nature," and he was defrocked.[68]

Irving led about eight hundred members from his church to form the first congregation of what would become the Catholic Apostolic Church.[69] He was increasingly marginalized by the emerging leadership in the new church and died two years later in 1834 of tuberculosis. Irving's movement, because of its claim to have revived the New Testament gift of "tongues," awakened widespread popular interest and provoked intense scrutiny and

65. Wilks, *Edward Irving*, 203.

66. Oliphant, *Life of Edward Irving*, 206.

67. Drummond, *Edward Irving*, 183.

68. *The Trial of the Rev. Edward Irving*, 4, 8, 23–24, 26, 31–34, 92; cf. Martindale, "Irving's Incarnational Christology"; Oliphant, *Life of Edward Irving*, 2:261.

69. Bundy, "Edward Irving," 803.

critical analysis among religious scholars throughout Europe, particularly in connection with the emerging new theory of *glossolalia*. The broad evangelical movement in that century, however, did not accept the theology of the Irvingites or the Catholic Apostolic Church as a new standard. Instead, many, if not most, regarded Irvingites as frauds and charlatans, dismissing them as victims of "supernatural delusion."[70] The Irvingite tongues controversy must be understood from one of two perspectives: either the tongues phenomenon in London was a novelty not previously recognized by the Church, or it was a fraud with people pretending to speak in tongues, as popular opinion held. Some seventy years later, the same confusions and controversies appeared in an even more embarrassing crisis that occurred across the Atlantic in the American Pentecostal revival of the early 1900s.

The Pentecostal Crisis of Missionary Tongues

The problems posed by the definition of "tongues," not to mention questions about how they may be related to "end times," "Spirit baptism," "water baptism," sanctification, and evangelism, were not resolved by Irving and his followers, but were transmitted *en bloc*, unresolved, to the Methodist-Holiness and Pentecostal movements and revivals that followed. Vinson Synan, one of the pillars of Pentecostal historiography and theology, explains: "The Pentecostal movement arose as a split in the holiness movement and can be viewed as the logical outcome of the holiness crusade that had vexed American Protestantism, and the Methodist Church in particular, for more than forty years. The repeated calls of the holiness leadership after 1894 for a 'new Pentecost' inevitably produced the frame of mind and the intellectual foundations for just such a 'Pentecost' to occur."[71] The doctrine of sanctification as a subsequent or second work of grace following water baptism was already present in Methodist-Holiness circles before Parham. Parham's defining contribution was to link "Spirit baptism" as a second work of grace with "tongues" as the "initial evidence" of this work of grace, and this contribution became a defining feature of Pentecostalism. Thus, Parham's act of laying his hands on Agnes Ozman's head, and Ozman's reception of "Spirit baptism" and subsequent manifestation of "tongues," set an enduring pattern for others. Synan explains, "Ozman's experience thus became the prototype experience for all the millions of Pentecostals who were to follow."[72] Despite the much larger impact of the later Azusa Street Revival,

70. R. Y., "New Gift of Tongues," 419.

71. Synan, *Holiness-Pentecostal Tradition*, 105–6.

72. Synan, "Touch," 84, quoted in MacArthur, *Strange Fire*, 20n4; cf. 271n4.

it was Parham's earlier ministry that was, in many ways, pivotal. As Pentecostal historian James R. Goff observes, "Parham, then, is the key to any interpretation of Pentecostal origins. He formulated the connection between Holy Spirit baptism and tongues, oversaw the growth and organization, and initiated the idyllic vision of xenoglossic missions. The story of his life and ministry reveals the sociological and ideological roots of Pentecostalism."[73]

Speaking-in-tongues as "ecstasy," "prayer," a "language of praise," or a "heavenly language" were not part of Parham's religious vocabulary. He remained certain that the gift of tongues was the miraculous, spontaneous utterance of a language unknown beforehand by the speaker for evangelistic or missionary purposes. He was convinced that these were the kinds of tongues he heard Ozman and others speaking during his Topeka Revival, and he never departed from this conviction. Within weeks of the revival sparked by Ozman's initial tongues event, newspapers across the country were echoing Paham's aforementioned boast to the *Kansas City Times*, that "missionaries would no longer be compelled to study foreign languages to preach in the mission field." Half-way across the Pacific, the *Hawaiian Gazette* of Friday, May 31, 1901, carried an article entitled "New Kind of Missionaries: Envoys to the Heathen Should Have Gift of Tongues," featuring Parham's Topeka school:

> His plan is to send among the heathen, persons who have been blessed with the "gift of tongues"—a gift which, he says, no others have ever had conferred upon them since apostolic times. His missionaries, as he points out, will have the great advantage of having the languages of the various peoples among whom they work miraculously conferred upon them and will not be put to the trouble of learning them in the laborious way by which they are acquired by other prospective missionaries.
>
> "Our summer Bible school will begin in Topeka June 10," said Rev. Mr. Parham last night. "It will be held on the campus of the college. We are expecting thousands of ministers, evangelists, and other people from all parts of the United States who desire to become missionaries to attend."[74]

Not all of Parham's students at his school, however, were convinced. In an interview with *The Topeka Daily Capital*, S. J. Riggins said of Parham and his fellow students, "I believe the whole of them are crazy."[75] Holiness leaders like William B. Godbey also grew skeptical of the tongues at Azusa

---

73. Goff, *Fields White unto Harvest*, 16.

74. "New Kind of Missionaries," 10, col. 5; cf. Lie, "Origin."

75. Newman, *Race*, 50.

Street.[76] National newspapers were not long in turning the corner from credulity to skepticism. In its April 18, 1906 issue, the *Los Angeles Times* published a piece entitled, "Weird Babel of Tongues," describing the tongues of Azusa Street in condescending and outright mocking tones:

> "You-oo-oo gou-loo-loo come under the bloo-oo-oo boo-loo;" shouts an old colored "mammy" in a frenzy of religious zeal. Swinging her arms wildly about her, she continues with the strangest harangue ever uttered. Few of her words are intelligible, and for the most part, her testimony contains the most outrageous jumble of syllables, which are listened to with awe by the company. . . .
>
> Undismayed by the fearful attitude of the colored worshipper, another black woman jumped to the floor and began a wild gesticulation, which ended in a gurgle of wordless prayers which were nothing less than shocking.
>
> "She's speaking in unknown tongues," announced the leader, in an awed whisper, "Keep on sister." The sister continued until it was necessary to assist her to a seat because of her bodily fatigue.[77]

The following April, the *New Zealand Herald* reprinted an article from the *London Express*, with some added commentary in a mocking tone about similar happenings in London:

> The newest sect of rabid revivalists had a fit of temporary insanity last night (says the London Express of April 3) at a small hall in Upper-street, Islington. . . . The "gift of tongues" was loudly invoked, and the gift arrived a little more quickly than anyone anticipated. An anemic-looking girl in the middle of the hall rose to her feet, and let out a yell like a steam siren:—"Ouchicka—ouchicka—ouchicka, Hoo—hoo—hoo. Havaa—howaa."[78]

Even Parham seems to have believed that "tongues" were sometimes faked, and a persistent theme in his wife's biography is that speaking in tongues was definitely not gibberish; but it was nothing less than such fraudulence that Charles Parham believed he witnessed at Seymour's Azusa Street Revival when he was invited to preach there in October of 1906:

> I hurried to Los Angeles, and to my utter surprise and astonishment I found conditions even worse than I had anticipated.

76. Synan, *Pentecostal Tradition*, 127.

77. "Weird Babel of Tongues," 1.

78. "Weird Travesty of Religion," 2, col. 4.

Brother Seymour had come to me helpless, he said he could not stem the tide that had arisen. I sat on the platform in Azusa Street Mission, and saw the manifestations of the flesh, spiritualistic controls, saw people practicing hypnotism at the altar over candidates seeking [Spirit] baptism; though many were receiving the real baptism of the Holy Ghost.

After preaching two or three times, I was informed by two of the elders, one who was a hypnotist (I had seen him lay his hands on many who came through chattering, jabbering and sputtering, speaking in no language at all) that I was not wanted in that place.[79]

Undaunted, the Topeka and Los Angeles revivals nevertheless managed to inspire a group of missionaries to take the Gospel of Christ overseas to Asia, trusting their ability to communicate using their supposedly-miraculous gift of tongues. Unfortunately, however, this strategy backfired rather embarrassingly. As charismatic authors, Jack Hayford and David Moore, admit in *The Charismatic Century* (1977), "Sadly, the idea of xenoglossalalic tongues [i.e., foreign languages] would later prove an embarrassing failure as Pentecostal workers went off to mission fields with their gift of tongues and found their hearers did not understand them."[80] Robert M. Anderson elaborates:

S. C. Todd of the Bible Missionary Society investigated eighteen Pentecostals who went to Japan, China, and India "expecting to preach to the natives in those countries in their own language," and found that by their own admission "in no single instance [were they] able to do so." As these and other missionaries returned in disappointment and failure, Pentecostals were compelled to rethink their original view of speaking in tongues.[81]

The tension between the sincere, trusting, confident expectation of being able to communicate the Gospel in foreign lands using a gift of *xenolalic* tongues, and the bitter disappointment of discovering upon arrival that they did not work, is poignantly noted in the communications of a well-known missionary couple, Alfred and Lillian Garr. They were high-profile personalities in the Holiness movement who were among the first of those to receive Spirit baptism along with speaking in tongues at Azusa Street in Los Angeles. Their names appear frequently in early Pentecostal literature. They came from a Methodist background and were educated at

79. Parham, *Life of Charles F. Parahm*, 163.

80. Hayford and Moore, *Charismatic Century*, 42.

81. Anderson, *Vision of the Disinherited*, 90–91.

the well-known Asbury Theological Seminary in Kentucky. They eventually felt drawn to join a Holiness movement called "Burning Bush," which commissioned them to lead a church in Los Angeles. Not long after their move to Los Angeles, Alfred visited the Azusa Street revival meetings where he received Spirit baptism and began speaking in tongues. His wife soon joined him in this experience. While speaking in tongues in church on one occasion, Alfred believed that a man from India understood him to be speaking Bengali, as well as some other languages of India. This inspired Alfred and Lillian with a desire to go to India with the first wave of Pentecostal missionaries to carry their Gospel abroad. Their story is quite representative of what happened to such missionaries and is chronicled in fascinating detail in the pages of *The Apostolic Faith* newspaper.[82]

The September 1906 issue reports how Alfred and Lillian were both "powerfully baptized with the Holy Ghost and received the gift of tongues" at the Azusa Street Mission, and how Alfred Garr was able to speak Bengali to "a native of India," and Lillian Garr spoke Chinese; and how, when they spoke in tongues, the sick were "immediately healed."[83] The October 1906 issue relates their preparation for departure to the mission field in India; and, in the context of discussing how a girl miraculously spoke in German so that a native speaker could understand her perfectly, reports that "Sister Garr improves every day in her Thibetan [*sic*] and Chinese."[84] In the February-March issue of 1907, a missionary in India named Mary Johnson reports that the Garrs had arrived in India. She does not mention any language problems, but it soon becomes apparent that something is afoot because the focus of the Garrs decidedly shifts in their subsequent communiqués.[85] In the April 1907 issue, Lillian Garr reports: "God is spreading Pentecost here in Calcutta, and thirteen or fourteen missionaries and other workers have received it"; but she omits any reference to speaking in tongues. Rather, she shifts the emphasis: "The Spirit is giving the interpretation, song and writing in tongues, and other wonderful manifestations of His presence among us."[86] The June-September, 1907 issue features a letter from the Garrs about the work in India, announcing that they are no longer involved directly in evangelistic efforts because of the linguistic barrier, but shifting their focus from evangelizing native Indians to equipping long-term missionaries who

82. For subsequently archived issues of the *Apostolic Faith* newspaper, see https://pentecostalarchives.org/.

83. "Good News from Danville, VA," 4.

84. "Pentecost in Danville, VA," 2.

85. "In Calcutta, India," 1.

86. "In Calcutta, India," 1.

already have the needed language skills: "The only way the nations can be reached is by getting the missionaries baptized in the Holy Ghost," writes Garr.[87] The October-January, 1908 issue reports: "Brother and Sister Garr are in Hong Kong, China, last report. God is using them blessedly. A glorious revival is breaking out. Several souls in Hong Kong have received their Pentecost."[88]

What happened? Upon their arrival in India, the Garrs discovered that their gift of tongues did not work. Sometime after their arrival, A. A. Boddy, a Pentecostal leader in England, directly asked Alfred about his gift of tongues. Did this supernatural endowment help Garr when he arrived in India? Could he actually communicate in Bengali? Did other, similarly empowered missionaries also demonstrate this phenomenon? The May 1908 issue of Boddy's Pentecostal periodical, *Confidence*, carries an article entitled "Tongues in the Foreign Field: Interesting Letters," which features (on p. 1) a reply by Alfred Garr: "As to whether I know of any who have received a language, I know of no one having received a language so as to be able to converse intelligently, or to preach in the same with the understanding, in the Pentecostal movement. . . . I supposed [God] would let us talk to the natives of India in their own tongue, but He did not, and as far as I can see, will not use that means by which to convert the heathen."[89] Garr wrote that the supernatural "language" he was given in Los Angeles and believed was Bengali had changed many times before he arrived in India and was no longer of use in his present circumstances. His faith that he had been endowed with the gift of *xenolalic* tongues remained unshaken, however; and he believed it was from God, even if it was of no use in his mission work.

It was not as if this sort of thing had not happened before, however, even since the Irvingite controversy. A decade before the Pentecostal revival of the early 1900s, a young missionary with the China Inland Mission named C. T. Studd wrote about departing for the mission field while claiming, in faith, the promise of Mark 16:17 that believers would be empowered to "speak in new tongues." When he and several others arrived in China in 1889, they expected to be able to speak Chinese supernaturally, but discovered that "they did not understand us at all" and that the Chinese "thought us idle fanatics." Following this embarrassment, they quickly discerned that God required the hard work of language study.[90] In the fevered excitement

87. "The Work in India," 1.

88. "Good Tidings of Great Joy," 1, s.v. "China."

89. For Garr's complete letter, see Garr, "A Letter from Bro. Garr," 2; cf. Sullivan, *GOTP*, s.v. "Garr's Missionary Crisis," para. 7–12.

90. Broomhall, *Evangelisation*, 53.

of the Pentecostal revivals a decade later, however, it was easy to discount such disappointing reports.

Allan Anderson, one of the foremost authorities on Pentecostal history, states that many supposedly "endowed" missionaries were disillusioned upon arrival but does not elaborate.[91] The experience of disillusionment is rarely documented in Pentecostal works. Why no effort was made to confirm their presumed "languages" by a reputable authority before embarking on foreign missions adds another level of mystery to the whole narrative. A doctoral student named Charles Shumway, after trying in vain to prove that the Pentecostal tongues were authentic *xenolalia*, criticized the *Houston Chronicle* in his 1919 doctoral dissertation for credulously reporting that government interpreters had validated the supposed languages, when, in fact, "letters are on hand from several men who were government interpreters" at the time, which "are unanimous [in] denying all knowledge of the alleged facts."[92] In 1908, George B. Cutten, a Baptist minister who subsequently became a psychologist and then president of Colgate University, considered the question from a psychological perspective and concluded that it was nothing more than an emotionally-charged state of those from the "lower classes" who did not know any better.[93]

Redefining "Tongues"

Despite dauntless faith, irrepressible zeal, and unflagging enthusiasm, the early Pentecostal adventure of "missionary tongues" in foreign nations was a decided failure, leaving the movement with a serious theological and public-relations challenge on the home front. The leaders of the movement had the choice of admitting that they had been wrong but never did so. No publication exists in early Pentecostalism that makes such an admission. Forty years later the Pentecostal leader, Donald Gee, in his book, *The Pentecostal Movement: A Short History and An Interpretation for British Readers* (1941), called the view that the gift of tongues could be used for mission work "mistaken and unscriptural."[94] By that time, however, it no longer mattered and had little if any impact on the movement, since a redefinition of "tongues" had already been tacitly accepted, and there was no longer a "problem." The closest thing to an admission of error is the concession of a serious misunderstanding acknowledged much later by the great Pentecostal professor of

91. Anderson, "Azusa Street," 107–18.

92. Goff, *Fields*, 76.

93. Cutten, *Psychological Phenomena*, 52.

94. Gee, *Pentecostal Movement*, cited in Sullivan, *GOTP*, s.v. "Solutions," para. 6.

Church history, Gary B. McGee, in his well-researched article, "Shortcut to Language Preparation? Radical Evangelicals, Missions, and the Gift of Tongues" (2001), in which he writes:

> Not surprisingly, though claims of bestowed languages had the potential of being empirically verified, such claims severely test-ed the credulity of outside observers. Corroborating testimony that Pentecostals preached at will in their newfound languages and were actually understood by their hearers proved difficult to find. By late 1906 and 1907 radical evangelicals began re-viewing the Scriptures to obtain a better understanding. Most came to recognize that speaking in tongues constituted worship and intercession in the Spirit (Rom 8:26; 1 Cor 14:2), which in turn furnished the believer with spiritual power. Since on either reading . . . the notion of receiving languages reflected zeal and empowerment for evangelism, most Pentecostals seemed to have accepted the transition in meaning.[95]

It is certainly surprising to find an Assemblies of God teacher admitting this flaw in the "missionary tongues" expectation, even though the admis-sion is muted by the presumed discovery of "a better understanding," which he says emerged "by late 1906 and 1907." Unfortunately, however, he does not delve into who was responsible for the reinterpretation of "tongues."

Many Pentecostals have simply ignored that the crisis ever occurred. This can be observed, for example, in the writings of the important early Pentecostal editor, writer, and pioneer, Stanley Frodsham, who first encoun-tered Pentecostalism in A. A. Boddy's church in Sunderland, England, and later moved to the United States where he became editor of the *Pentecostal Evangel* magazine of the Assemblies of God—one of the largest Pentecostal denominations in the United States. His book, *With Signs Following: The Story of the Pentecostal Revival in the Twentieth Century* (1926), which has been long considered definitive, is excellent and well documented, and is very likely the best of any early Pentecostal histories. The first seventeen chapters of his book document people who were miraculously speaking in foreign languages. Then an unexplained shift occurs in the last portion of the work. He concludes at the end of the book that Christian tongues are a secret speech, something between a man and God, without ever delving into what necessitated or caused this shift in definition.[96] The grassroots Pentecostal-Charismatic movement today continues this tradition of ac-cepting a revisionist interpretation of "tongues" and does not generally

95. McGee, "Shortcut to Language Preparation?," 122.
96. Frodsham, *With Signs Following*, 269.

acknowledge the theological crisis created by the "missionary tongues" in the early days of Pentecostalism.

Other early Pentecostals shifted the emphasis to writing or singing in "tongues." Some early leaders also introduced the term "utterance," as we have seen, keeping the definition loosely related to language, yet ambiguous enough to admit various interpretations and make it easier to defend than the traditional *xenolalic* definition suggested by the expression "gift of tongues." For example, the February 1, 1908 issue of *The Bridegroom's Messenger* declared that "speaking in tongues as the Spirit gives utterance is not the gift of tongues"; but it left "utterance" undefined, except to state that, unlike the "gift of tongues," it is involuntary.[97] References to writing and singing in "tongues," and to "tongues" as a language of prayer and praise and adoration further broadened the semantic range of the word. "Writing in tongues" was mentioned quite frequently in early Pentecostal literature by Parham, Lillian Garr, and many others, though it faces challenges common to the "tongues" crisis. When a photograph of Agnes Ozman's "Chinese" writing-in-tongues was published in 1901 in the *Topeka Daily Capital* and taken to a Chinese man for translation, he found it utterly incomprehensible.[98] "Singing in tongues" faces similar challenges; but "tongues" understood as "language of prayer and praise," "heavenly language," or "private prayer language," do not face any such obstacles because there is no way to empirically test their authenticity. "Singing in tongues" was unique to the Pentecostal movement at its beginning. *The Apostolic Faith* newspaper described it as "heavenly singing by a chorus of voices in supernatural sweetness and harmony"; and others described learning to sing "in the Spirit" even when they never knew how to sing before.[99] *The Apostolic Faith* newspaper also expanded upon its "utterance" idea by suggesting that when one "utters" something in the Spirit, the utterance is converted into a prayer of adoration and praise: "The tongues they speak in do not seem to be intended as a means of communication between themselves and others, as on the Day of Pentecost, but corresponds more closely with that described in the 14th [chapter] of 1 Corinthians, 2nd verse, and seems to be a means of communication between the soul and God."[100] By definition, such "tongues" cannot be humanly authenticated.

97. "Questions and Answers," 2, s.v. "Question Two." Sullivan, *GOTP*, s.v. "Utterance," para. 2–4, says that a distinction between "utterance" and the "gift of tongues" developed less than a year after the Azusa Street Revival of 1906.

98. *Topeka Daily Capital*, January 6, 1901, 2; cited in Gelbart, "Pentecostal Movement," 3.

99. "Heavenly Choir," 1; Bartleman, *How Pentecost Came*, 74–75.

100. "The Work in India," 2.

The shift from "missionary tongues" to "utterances" thus allowed the definition of "tongues" to develop in a new direction. An example of this is the idea of tongues as a "heavenly" or "angelic" devotional language.[101] The first occurrence of this was in a 1916 article, published "in the interest of the General Assembly of God" in their denominational periodical, *Weekly Evangel*, which interpreted the "tongues" of 1 Corinthians 14 thus: "This is not a gift of different languages as some have believed, but is an emotional or heavenly language, in which the speaker speaks only to God," citing the *Pulpit Commentary*'s assertion that it was "an unintelligible vocal utterance," that might be either a human language or a heavenly or angelic language.[102] Two months later, an article in the same periodical appeared, crediting the teaching of A. A. Boddy and the influence of W. J. Conybeare and J. S. Howson's *Life and Epistles of St. Paul* (1856) and Philip Schaff's *History of the Apostolic Church* (1853). The article endeavored to integrate the old and new definitions:

> We see that the belief that the gift was for the preaching of the Gospel to foreigners is unfounded. Foreign people did certainly hear their own languages on the day of Pentecost (the disciples were not, however, on that occasion, preaching the Gospel but magnifying God—the common use of the gift) therefore the Spirit must have sometimes given a known language.[103]

One can already detect similarities in these accounts to the contemporary Charismatic views we explored in chapter 2, particularly in connection with the statements of Francis Sullivan and Mary Healy. The reference to Schaff also signals another development that would soon come to play a role in the Pentecostal reinterpretation of "tongues." Schaff was affiliated with the German academic movement of biblical-theological "Higher Criticism," from which the term *glossolalia* would also be imported into Pentecostal circles and eventually be given a Pentecostal meaning. The development of the *glossolalic* interpretation of "tongues" in many ways dovetailed nicely with the Pentecostal experience following the "missionary tongues" crisis, when an opening was made for new understandings of "tongues." The Higher-Critical theory of *glossolalia* was destined to overtake the traditional

101. No credible evidence has been found supporting the idea of "tongues of angels" or a "heavenly language" in the Dead Sea Scrolls, the Testament of Job or the Book of Enoch. See "Testament of Job," lxxii–cii, 103–37; *Book of Enoch*, 58(sec. x):1—61:12; Martínez and Tigchelaar, *Dead Sea Scrolls*, 1:4Q401 8; 4Q400 12 17; 4Q403 27 40; Sullivan, *GOTP*, s.v. "Testament of Job," para. 1–8, and s.v. "Dead Sea Scrolls," para. 106 and "Conclusion."

102. Mercer, "Speaking in an Unknown Tongue," 6.

103. Lawrence, "The Works of God," 4.

definition in scholarly circles in the last two decades of the nineteenth century and eventually dominate the interpretation of "tongues" to such an extent that it would also help shape the framework for Pentecostal "tongues" as well. *Glossolalia*, then, is another major clue in our archeological "dig," and is the subject of our next chapter.

CHAPTER 4

Who Coined the Word *Glossolalia* and Why?

From the twenty-first century back to 1830 (German Higher Critics)

ONE OF THE MOST interesting claims of contemporary Charismatics, one that seems to be regarded as having the most promise of providing biblical validation for the Pentecostal redefinition of "tongues" examined in the last chapter, is the claim that the origins of *glossolalia* can be traced back to what the Apostle Paul describes in 1 Corinthians 12–14. In making this claim, contemporary Charismatics typically equate the meaning of *glossolalia* with the Pentecostal redefinition of "tongues" in one or another of its recent versions. For example, the Catholic Charismatic, Mary Healy, categorically dismisses the idea that *glossolalia*, understood as an unintelligible private "language of prayer and praise," is alien to the traditions of the ancient Church and could have been introduced by a novel theory introduced in the nineteenth century by Protestant biblical scholars.[1] She finds it "difficult to see how anyone who has read 1 Corinthians 12–14 carefully" could fail to note that "St. Paul clearly refers to the gift of 'tongues' as a form of non-conceptual yet vocalized prayer."[2] This assertion is not surprising. The assumptions behind it are now so widespread that they are generally considered standard and unexceptional, if not incontrovertible. Yet these assumptions are problematic and debatable, as we shall see. They fail to note the distinctive features of the concept of *glossolalia* that originated in nineteenth-century Higher

1. Healy, "Answers," sec. on *glossolalia*.
2. Healy, "Answers," sec. on *glossolalia*.

Critical scholarship and how that scholarship influenced the understanding of tongues in the Pentecostal and Neo-Pentecostal traditions that have shaped contemporary Charismatic views, both popular and academic. The burden of this chapter is to excavate this theory of *glossolalia* at its source in nineteenth-century scholarship, and then to examine why the traditional doctrine of tongues as a supernatural endowment of a foreign language all but died out and came to be replaced by a definition adapted from the Higher Critical doctrine of *glossolalia*. The question as to what was going on in the church of Corinth, and whether the tongues of Corinth can be equated with *glossolalia*, will be addressed in volume 3 of this work.

Let us begin with some pertinent facts: the word *glōssolalia* (γλωσσολαλία) appears nowhere in Scripture. It is a hybrid neologism—a made-up word—cobbled together from two Greek words, *glōssa* (γλῶσσα), meaning "tongue" or "language," and *lalein* (λαλεῖν), meaning "to speak" or "to babble." This neologism is now so widely accepted that there is even a prevailing consensus as to its supposed meaning. The following definitions are typical. *The Encyclopedia Britannica* (2019) defines it as "utterances approximating words and speech, usually produced during states of intense religious experience."[3] *The New International Dictionary of the Christian Church* (1978) defines it as "the spontaneous utterance of uncomprehended and seemingly random vocal sounds."[4] There are no definitions of *glossolalia*, however, before the nineteenth century because the word did not yet exist. Why is this?

If the word "*glossolalia*" is nowhere in the Bible, where did it come from? Who coined the word, and why? The word was introduced into English by Frederic W. Farrar, the well-known Dean of Canterbury and friend of Charles Darwin, in his book, *The Life and Work of St. Paul* (1879). The idea behind the word, however, arose about half a century earlier. The concept of "tongues" as a humanly *unintelligible* language first gained traction after it was introduced as an alternative definition in the early 1830s by Edward Irving and his followers during the British revivals when he discovered that the "tongues" he was witnessing were not intelligible languages, as we saw in the last chapter. The key player in formulating the concept of *glossolalia*, however, was not Irving, but members of an early nineteenth-century movement called Higher Criticism in Protestant biblical theology, originally in Germany, whose interest in the long-dormant subject of "speaking in tongues" was awakened by the Irvingite revival of tongues-speaking in Britain.

3. "Glossolalia," in *EB87* 11:842.
4. "Glossolalia," in *NIDCC* 415.

The term "Higher Criticism" was first used in eighteenth-century German biblical scholarship as a contrast to "Lower Criticism," or Textual Criticism, which aimed to sort through textual variants and different versions of ancient biblical manuscripts in order to prepare the best possible version of a text based on available sources. "Higher Criticism," by contrast, aimed at Historical-Critical analysis of the "world behind the text," in an attempt to reconstruct its original meaning in its historical context and its literal sense independently of ecclesial traditions of interpretation, which were judged to be "unscientific" and therefore unacceptable.[5] Protestant Higher Critics in Germany introduced the concept of *glossolalia* under the influence of Enlightenment Rationalism. They rejected the testimony of Patristic and medieval Catholic sources as overly credulous and superstitious, particularly because Catholic medieval writers seemed to find miracles happening everywhere and because Catholic tradition viewed the gift tongues—naively, it was supposed—as a continuing miraculous gift of communication in previously unlearned *intelligible* foreign languages. Non-Catholics often dismissed such beliefs as medieval foolishness. The growing skepticism of the era toward miracles was not only apparent on the Continent. It was also evident among British philosophers, from the early materialists like Thomas Hobbes (1588–1679), up through empiricists like John Locke (1632–1704), and skeptics like the Scotsman, David Hume (1711–76). Miracles were increasingly interpreted as improbable, or as naturally-occurring phenomena with natural explanations, or, in some Protestant "Cessationist" circles, as having ceased altogether. The latter view was enshrined in Conyers Middleton's Cessationist manifesto, which struck a death blow to the continued influence of the Church Fathers in the Protestant world. It sported the ponderous but telling title, *A Free Inquiry into the Miraculous Powers Which Are Supposed to Have Subsisted in the Christian Church from the Earliest Ages through Several Successive Centuries, by Which It Is Shown That We Have No Sufficient Reason to Believe, upon the Authority of the Primitive Fathers, That Any Such Powers Were Continued to the Church after the Days of the Apostles* (1749).[6]

This was the cultural context in which German Protestant theologians formulated the doctrine of *glossolalia*. The doctrine is not an old one in the history of the Church. It is an innovation scarcely two hundred years old. It represents an alternative framework designed by these theologians to explain the "tongues" mentioned in the New Testament, particularly in Acts

5. Soulen and Soulen, *Handbook of Biblical Criticism*, 78; Ebeling, *Word and Faith*, 17–60.

6. Middleton, *Free Inquiry*.

2 and 1 Corinthians 12–14. The doctrine was thus intended to explain both the "tongues" of Pentecost and Corinth, using pre-Christian Greek sources and second-century Montanist sources as its basis. Significantly, these theologians virtually ignored the entire tradition of ecclesiastical writings in arriving at their conclusions. The rise of the *glossolalic* definition of "tongues" was influenced by the growing atmosphere of skepticism toward traditional ecclesiastical writings, which led to such writings being omitted from lists of "credible" historical sources in academic circles and being consigned to the category of "legends" and "myths." This tendency is reflected in the noticeable decline of references to any writings published after the first three centuries of Church history in the primary, secondary, and tertiary sourcebooks from the nineteenth-century onwards. The principal reasons for this decline were twofold: (1) the rise of Enlightenment Rationalism in the "Age of Reason" and (2) the rise of Protestant anti-Catholicism. Both of these promoted skepticism towards medieval supernaturalism, as Protestants vied with Catholics for the higher moral ground in the conflict sparked by the Reformation in the sixteenth century.[7]

The subject of "tongues" first appeared on the horizon for the German theologians as a subject worthy of serious investigation in the early 1800s due to the heightened interest created by the Irvingite movement. The London-based revival had garnered international attention by its claim that, for the first time since Pentecost, it was witnessing the renewal of the gift of miraculous "tongues" as a sign of an end-time outpouring of the Holy Spirit. In their response to the Irvingite phenomenon, these German theologians formulated their own alternative to the traditional tongues-doctrine, which they called *glossolalia*. The new theory was first broached in the early 1830s by Frederick Bleek and F. C. Baur, then reinforced when Augustus Neander published his highly popular 1832 book, *History of the Planting and Training of the Christian Church by the Apostles* (*Geschichte der Pflanzung und Leitung der christlichen Kirche durch die Apostel*). Although Neander does not seem to have introduced the term *glossolalia* in his writings, he established the general idea and gave it what appeared to be a credible framework. The highly esteemed Anglican theologian, Dean of Canterbury Cathedral, F. W. Farrar, made the doctrine an international phenomenon when he published his book, *The Life and work of St. Paul* (1879), which marked the first time the term *glossolalia* entered into the English vocabulary. The concept was further reinforced by the theologian, Philip Schaff, a Swiss-German professor who immigrated to the United States and contributed immeasurably to the English-reading audience in Church history and theology through

---

7. Lecky, *History*, 27–201; Carus, *History*; Trevor-Roper, *Crisis* chs. 1–3.

his work at the German Reformed Theological Seminary in Mercersburg, Pennsylvania, and Union Theological Seminary in New York City.

What these theological Higher Critics discovered was an alternative way of explaining the idea of unintelligible tongues by reference to extra-biblical antecedent sources. They believed they had found these sources in the ancient ecstatic utterances of the Oracles of Delphi (prophetess-priest-esses at the Temple of Apollo in Delphi in ancient Greece) and the bizarre babblings of the Montanists (a heretical Christian sect in the second-century Phrygia, in Asia Minor). They no longer considered the biblical or Patris-tic narratives about Pentecost to be authoritative historical sources on the subject. Therefore, they turned to ancient pre-Christian, pagan narratives about the Delphic Oracles and to the heretical sectarian narratives of the second-century Montanists.

The Greek Oracles at the Temple of Apollo at Delphi in ancient times participated in a rite in which they would sequester themselves in a chamber where volcanic fumes would reportedly induce a state of ecstatic trance in which they were empowered to speak prophetically, essentially "channeling" the words of the Greek god, Apollo. Members of the public, from commoners to kings, would go before the Oracles seeking divine guid-ance for their concerns, just as Chaerephon, in Plato's early fourth-century BC dialogue, the *Apology*, famously visited the Delphic Oracle to inquire whether any man was wiser than Socrates.[8] Whether these Oracles spoke in ecstatic utterances, hexameter verse, or foreign languages is a matter of dispute. The German theologians and their followers maintained that these oracular prophecies were "ecstatic utterances." They later also drew con-nections between their doctrine of *glossolalia* and the bizarre vocalizations of Montanus, and his two prophetesses, Maximilla and Prisca (sometimes called Priscilla), which they also called "ecstatic utterances." Throughout their writings, the Higher Critics steadfastly ignore the writings of Church Fathers such as Augustine, Gregory of Nazianzus, Cyril of Jerusalem, and a host of many other prominent ecclesiastical writers, even though they clearly wrote about the gift of tongues, and even though some of them, such as Eusebius of Caesarea and Epiphanius of Salamis, explicitly and critically addressed the question of Montanist utterances. According to the Higher Critics' interpretation, then, the Greeks and Montanists were the only cred-ible sources on tongues, and the tongues of Pentecost and Corinth were both to be interpreted in light of them, therefore, as "ecstatic utterances."

---

8. Cf. Plato, *Apology*, 20e, where Chaerephon was told by the Pythian prophetess that there was no one wiser than Socrates.

The doctrine of *glossolalia* has expanded widely since the nineteenth century and has become the *de facto* authoritative framework for virtually all primary and secondary source studies on the subject of tongues. This understanding of tongues has now become so popular, even among Pentecostals, that it has almost extinguished any vestige of the traditional ecclesiastical doctrine of tongues that may be traced back over the previous 1800 years. As we saw in the last chapter, the Pentecostal understanding of tongues began changing between 1906 and 1907 when their concept of "missionary tongues" failed. Not long afterward, probably by around 1910, Pentecostals had concluded that *xenolalia*, or the speaking of foreign languages, was no longer viable as a stand-alone definition for "tongues." Their solution came from an amalgamation of two sources. First, it stemmed from the disappointing experience of "missionary tongues" that turned out not to be actual languages but unintelligible utterances, both in the Irvingite and Pentecostal revivals. Second, it involved a convenient adaptation of a respected academic framework for interpreting the gift of tongues as unintelligible vocalizations, a framework provided by the works of Farrar, Schaff, and a few other like-minded individuals, promoting the theory of *glossolalia* as mysterious "ecstatic utterances." This new definition diverges radically from the traditional consensus of ecclesiastical theologians who guarded the old definition of "tongues" as a miracle of a person either spontaneously speaking a foreign language or hearing sounds in his native language. Rarely, however, has the new hybrid definition of *glossolalia* ever been critically examined or traced from its initial beginnings to the present as we shall do here.

The term *glossolalia* and its associated definitions did not enter into the theology of tongues until the mid-nineteenth century. After that, the traditional view was increasingly marginalized and excluded. This shift erroneously leads the unsuspecting Bible student to think that there is no other option. It forces the reader to conclude that the phenomenon must be some form of ecstatic utterance, as in the theory of *glossolalia*, or at least something like it. Modern historians have also reframed the Christian doctrine of tongues to fit into this *glossolalia* paradigm. Instead of tracing the tradition of speaking in tongues back through Church literature, the majority have chosen to follow the Higher Critical trajectory back to classic Hellenistic literature (and sometimes to the Montanists) instead.

Origins of "Glossolalia"

It may be said without exaggeration that it was the Irvingite move-ment's claim in the 1830s to have revived the long-lost gift of tongues that brought the study of tongues out of a long slumber and to the attention of religious scholars throughout Europe. Without Irving's controversial and apocalyptic tongues-speaking revival, international scholarly inquiry into the doctrine of tongues would never have occurred. There would have been no catalyst for developing and propagating a new definition.

Although the German theologians referred to "ecstatic utterances" to express their new definition of "tongues," a word of caution is in order here. The word "ecstasy" has a long and venerable history and was in use long be-fore these Higher Critics took up the term. Medieval Catholic mystics and theologians defined "ecstasy" as a state accompanying a divine encounter—somewhat similar to, yet different from, what Pentecostals and Charismatics today sometimes associate with "baptism in the Spirit."[9] Indeed, the word "ecstasy" was so essential to the late medieval vocabulary that the massive sixteenth-century Greek dictionary by Henri Estienne (Stephanus), the *The-saurus of the Greek Language*, allotted considerable space for the definition of this Greek word, *ekstasis* (ἔκστασις).[10] *Ecstasy* was a well-known concept in Catholic circles at this time, as seen in artistic representations of the spiritual ecstasy of saints such as Teresa of Avila or Catherine of Siena. The German academic community took this familiar religious term to express its definition of "unintelligible tongues." The idea of *ecstasy*, however, was not sufficient for its purposes in the long run. It served as the starting point, however, in the evolution of its doctrine of *glossolalia*.

The rise of the concept of *glossolalia* can be traced to Germany in the early 1800s. This era represents an apex where the influences of the Renais-sance, Reformation, Humanism, and anti-Catholic fervor all converged to produce some of the most significant historical and philosophical works that have been formative in their influence on the modern Christian concept of "tongues." The story of *glossolalia* begins in this period with five German scholars, all of whom were involved in the developing Higher Criticism movement, through which they intended to promote a fresh new approach to biblical interpretation that purposely avoided the trappings of traditional, ecclesiastically-authorized interpretations of biblical texts. These five schol-ars include:

9. The rapture and exaltation associated with the ecstasy of medieval mystics lack the elements of learned behavior, hypnotic suggestibility, frenzy, and bizarre conduct manifested in circles such as the Toronto Blessing revivals.

10. Estienne et al., *Thesaurus* (1865), s.v. "ἔκστασις," 3:570–72.

- *Friedrich Schleiermacher* (1768–1834), often called the "father of modern liberal theology," who was known for his attempt to reconcile the Enlightenment's critical outlook with Protestant Christianity, his influence in the evolution of Higher Criticism and biblical "hermeneutics" (interpretation), his resistance to institutional dogma, and his use of sociological and psychological perspectives in theology.

- *W. M. L. de Wette* (1789–1850), a fellow teacher with Schleiermacher at the University of Berlin, an Old Testament specialist who accepted the prejudices of Enlightenment Rationalism, even reworking the idea of *myth* into a category of biblical interpretation that influenced the controversial David Friedrich Strauss and Old Testament critic, Julius Wellhausen, but, like Schleiermacher, continued to defer to the value of subjective religious feelings.[11]

- *Ferdinand Christian Baur* (1792–1860), the celebrated professor at the Tübingen School of Theology, who was deeply influenced by Schleiermacher and G. W. F. Hegel, and created a radical new framework for biblical interpretation that represented second-century Christianity as a synthesis of Jewish ("Petrine") and Gentile ("Pauline") Christianity, which allowed speculative constructions such as the *glossolalia* theory to germinate, and also wrote an essay "On the True Concept of *Glossolalia*."[12]

- *Friedrich Bleek* (1793–1859), a student of De Wette, highly praised by Schleiermacher, who became one of the foremost German Biblical scholars of all time, first rising to prominence with his publication of two articles, "Origin and Composition of the Sibylline Oracles," and "Authorship and Design of the Book of Daniel."[13]

- *August Neander* (1789–1850), a more conservative and less theologically speculative disciple of Schleiermacher, who taught at the University of Berlin with Schleiermacher and De Wette, and was likely more influential than any of the others in shaping the modern definition of "speaking in tongues."[14]

Of these five, only the names of Baur, Bleek, and Neander appear as key figures in the direct development of the *glossolalia* doctrine; but all of

---

11. Howard, *Protestant Theology*, 195.

12. Baur "Über den wahren Begriff," pt. 2, 78–133.

13. "Friedrich Bleek," in *EB02*, para. 1.

14. "August Neander," in *EB02*, para. 2–3.

them contributed to the culture of Higher Criticism that formed the framework within which the doctrine emerged.

In the late 1800s, the historian, author, and biblical exegete, Heinrich A. W. Meyer, stated that the first known academics to publish a critical work on "tongues" defined as "ecstatic utterances," were Bleek and Baur, immediately preceding the main outbreak of the Irvingite revival around 1830.[15] In his *Critical and Exegetical Handbook to the Epistles to the Corinthians* (1887), he writes:

> Bleek believes that *glōssai* is a poetic, inspired mode of speech, whereas Baur believes it to be "a speaking in strange, unusual phrases which deviate from the prevailing use of language"— partly borrowed from foreign languages.[16]

He adds that before Bleek and Baur came out with their alternative theory, most commentators followed the standard definition, holding that the "gift of tongues" was either the ability to spontaneously speak in a previously-unlearned foreign language or the ability to easily learn a new human language through study.[17]

A German monograph on "tongues" published in 1836, dedicated to Professor Neander (then a professor at Berlin), entitled "The Spiritual Gifts of the First Christians: Especially the so-called Gift of Languages" (*Die Geistesgaben der Ersten Christen: insbesondere die sogenannte Gabe der Sprachen*), by David Schulz, concluded that the most significant thinkers on the subject were Bleek, Baur, and Neander.[18] Chronologically, Neander came a little after the first two, but his contribution had a greater and more universal impact. These three produced the most seminal early works on the subject. Almost all interpretive trends concerning the gift of tongues in modern biblical exegesis and historical scholarship may be traced back to their influence.

Other names occasionally surface as well, though usually as second-tier sources for the *glossolalia* theory. For example, Christopher Wordsworth (1807–85), Bishop of Lincoln and nephew of the poet, William Wordsworth, attributes the *glossolalia* doctrine to the influence of De Wette, Meyer, and Bunsen.[19] Edward Hayes Plumptre (1821–91), also an English divine and Bible scholar, credits the *glossolalia* doctrine to be the "theories of

---

15. Meyer, *CEHEC*, 366.

16. Meyer, *CEHEC*, 371.

17. Meyer, *CEHEC*, 365.

18. Schulz, *Geistesgaben der ersten Christen*, 3.

19. Wordsworth, *New Testament*, 9.

Bleek, Herder, and Bunsen."[20] *Christian C. J. Bunsen* (1791–1860), just mentioned, was a German diplomat and scholar who favorably cites De Witte and Neander, along with their newer, more figurative interpretation "the Pentecost miracle," but denounces "convulsive utterances" and the "ecstatic state" as falling short of a "healthy manifestation of the spirit of Christianity" and "the religion of the Spirit."[21] *Johann Gottfried Herder* (1744–1803), the famous German philosopher, poet, and literary critic, wrote extensively on language and authored a treatise on the gift of tongues at Pentecost, in which he embraced the newer, more mystical, and figurative interpretation of the Pentecost event.[22]

A window is opened onto the world of this emerging new scholarship by John McClintock and James Strong's *Cyclopaedia of Biblical, Theological, and Ecclesiastical Literature* (1891), in which they comment on some of the Higher Critics mentioned above:

> Eichhorn and Bardili (cited in Bleek, *Stud. u. Krit.* 1829, p. 8 sq.), and to some extent Bunsen (*Hippolytus*, i, 9), see in the so-called gift [of "tongues"] an inarticulate utterance, the cry of a brute creature, in which the tongue moves while the lips refuse their office in making the sounds definite and distinct. . . .[23]
>
> Bleek (*ut sup.* p. 33) . . . infers . . . that to speak in tongues was to use unusual, poetic language; that the speakers were in a high-wrought excitement which showed itself in mystic, figurative terms. In this view he has been preceded by Ernesti (*Opus. Thelog.*; see *Morning Watch*, iv, 101); and Herder (*Die Gabe der Sprache*, p. 47, 70) . . . who extends the meaning to special mystical interpretations of the Old Test. . . . The direct statement "They heard them speaking, each man in his own dialect," the long list of nations [in Acts 2:1–13] . . . these can scarcely be reconciled with the theories of Bleek, Herder, and Bunsen without a willful distortion of the evidence.[24]

20. Plumptre, "Tongues," 1556.

21. Bunsen, *Hippolytus* 1:9–14.

22. Herder, *Gabe der Sprachen*, 47–70.

23. "Tongues," in *CBTEL* 10:480. References include the treatment of "tongues" by the Enlightenment theologian, Eichhorn, *Eichhorn's Allgemeine Bibliothek*, 2:854–56; the German philosopher and cousin of Friedrich Schelling, Christoph Gottfried Bardili (1761–1808), who opposed "Kantian idealism" with his own "rational realism"; Bleek, "Über die Gabe," 8–10; Bunsen, *Hippolytus*, 1:9.

24. "Tongues," in *CBTEL* 10:480. References include Bleek, "Über die Gabe," 33; Ernesti, *Opuscula*, and Ernesti, "Ernesti on the Gift of Tongues," translated from his *Opuscula*, 101–16; Herder, *Gabe der Sprachen*, 47–70.

Critics of a negative school have, as might be expected, adopted the easier course of rejecting the narrative either altogether or in part. The statements do not come from an eyewitness and may be an exaggerated report of what actually took place—a legend with or without a historical foundation. Those who recognize such a groundwork see in "the rushing mighty wind," the hurricane of a thunder-storm, the fresh breeze of morning; in the "tongues like as of fire," . . . in the "speaking with tongues," the loud scream of men, not all Galileans, but coming from many lands, overpowered by strong excitement, speaking in mystical, figurative, abrupt exclamations. They see in this "the cry of the new-born Christendom" (Bunsen, *Hippolytus*, ii, 12; Ewald, *Gesch. Isr.* vi, 110; Bleek, loc. cit.; Herder, loc. cit.).[25]

Neander, more than any others, seems to have been the scholar most responsible for establishing the new definition of "tongues" throughout the western academic world. He is referred to by more theologians on the doctrine of tongues than any other. His legacy in religious studies was so prodigious that Philip Schaff, who authored the highly esteemed and respected eight-volume *History of the Christian Church*, modestly conceded that his own work was nothing more than an updated and modernized version of Neander's. Schaff had studied in Berlin with Neander, whom he called the "Father of Church History," before moving to the United States, where he widely disseminated Neander's views.[26] The English theologian and writer, Frederick Farrar, was also influenced by Neander, and compellingly presented his views to the favorable attention of English readers.

Neander mentions many other authors, but two with particular consideration for having significantly reinforced or influenced his views. The first is Herder and his aforementioned treatise on the Pentecostal gift of tongues.[27] The second is Baur, whom he credits, "particularly . . . in his valuable essay on the subject in the *Tübinger Zeitschrift für Theologie*, 1830, part ii., to which I am indebted for some modifications of my own view."[28] Neander also knew, like McClintock and Strong, that the new definition clashed with the traditional one, and he readily admitted the sharp deviation: "If, then, we examine more closely the description of what transpired on the day of Pentecost," he wrote, "we shall find several things which favour

---

25. "Tongues," in *CBTEL* 10:482. References include Bunsen, *Hippolytus*, 1:9–13; Ewald, *Geschichte*, 6:110; Bleek, "Über die Gabe," 3–79.

26. Schaff, *History of the Christian Church*, 1:v.

27. Herder, *Gabe der Sprachen*, 47–70.

28. Neander, *Planting*, 1:15n1. For Herder's treatise on Pentecost, see Herder, *Von Der Gabe*; cf. Baur "Über den wahren Begriff," 78–133.

a different interpretation from the ancient one."[29] Neander seems to have believed that the original Pentecost event was redefined by the Church in the third century and that the Church at this time established three concepts bearing on the gift of tongues: (1) Pentecost was a miraculous outpouring, enabling unlearned men to speak in languages they did not know at the time of the Apostles; (2) this event would not recur after the time of the Apostles; and (3) the universal promulgation of the Gospel was achieved through extensive language study. He therefore surmises:

> Accordingly, since the third century it has been generally admitted, that a supernatural gift of tongues was imparted on this occasion, by which the more rapid promulgation of the Gospel among the heathen was facilitated and promoted. It has been urged that as in the apostolic age, many things were effected immediately by the predominating creative agency of God's Spirit, which, in later times, have been effected through human means appropriated and sanctified by it; so, in this instance, immediate inspiration stood in the place of those natural lingual acquirements, which in later times have served for the propagation of the Gospel.[30]

For those who argued that the miracle of foreign languages was necessary for the early establishment of the faith, he built a refutation: the use of *xenolalia* was unnecessary for the expansion of Christianity, he argued, because Greek and Latin were ubiquitous already, serving as either a first or second language for those nations and peoples connected to the Roman Empire. Thus, Neander writes:

> But, indeed, the utility of such a gift of tongues for the spread of divine truth in the apostolic times, will appear not so great, if we consider that the gospel had its first and chief sphere of action among the nations belonging to the Roman Empire, where the knowledge of the Greek and Latin languages sufficed for this purpose.[31]

He believed that the first-century experience was a mystical one involving a spiritual language unrelated to the gift of foreign human languages.

> Thus the speaking in foreign languages would be only something accidental, and not the essential of the new language of the Spirit. This new language of the Spirit is that which Christ

---

29. Neander, *Planting*, 1:12.

30. Neander, *Planting*, 1:9.

31. Neander, *Planting*, 1:10.

promised to his disciples as one of the essential marks of the operation of the Holy Spirit on their hearts.[32]

Therefore, in keeping with the Higher Critics, Neander concluded that the tongues indicated in 1 Corinthians had to be *ecstatic*. That is, he continues, "something altogether different from such a supernatural gift of tongues is spoken of. Evidently, the apostle is there treating of such discourse as would not be generally intelligible, proceeding from an ecstatic state of mind which rose to an elevation far above the language of ordinary communication."[33]

Neander carefully examined the facts concerning the Irvingite congregation in London while Irving was still in charge, and concluded that although the Irvingites believed they were spontaneously speaking in a foreign language unknown to them, that the reality he observed demonstrated otherwise: "Still less can I admit the comparison with the manifestations among the followers of Mr. Irving in London, since as far as my knowledge extends, I can see nothing in these manifestations but the workings of an enthusiastic spirit, which sought to copy the apostolic gift of tongues according to the common interpretation, and therefore assumed the reality of that gift."[34]

Although Schaff later suggested that Neander had failed in his examination of "tongues" and charged him, in this instance, with being a victim of Rationalism and having "yielded too much . . . to modern criticism," it is hard to find the difference between his position and Neander's.[35] Schaff defined the gift of tongues as "an involuntary, spiritual utterance in an ecstatic state of the most elevated devotion, in which the man is not, indeed, properly transported out of himself, but rather sinks into the inmost depths of his own soul, and thus, into direct contact with the divine essence within him."[36] He simply reinforced Neander's position. In fact, one of the analogies he used for these sorts of "tongues" was none other than those of the Irvingites, which were something between gibberish and human languages: "The speaking with tongues in the Irvingite congregations, as it manifested itself in the earlier years of this sect in England, was at first a speaking in strange sounds resembling Hebrew, after which the speakers continued in their English vernacular."[37] He then related the account of an eyewitness

32. Neander, *Planting*, 1:14.
33. Neander, *Planting*, 1:11.
34. Neander, *Planting*, 1:12.
35. Schaff, *History of the Apostolic Church*, 201.
36. Schaff, *History of the Apostolic Church*, 199.
37. Schaff, *History of the Apostolic Church*, 198.

named Michael Hohl, who described an Irvingite episode: a man went into a trance, violently convulsed; and then there came out of him "an impetuous gush of strange, energetic tones, which sounded to my ears most like those of the Hebrew language, poured from his quivering lips."[38] Schaff then inferred the following hypothesis:

> Could we appeal to the Irvingite glossolaly, as a reasonable analogy, we should here have a similar elevation, in which according to Hohl's account above quoted, the ecstatic discourses were delivered first in strange sounds, like Hebrew, and afterwards, where the excitement had somewhat abated, in the English vernacular. Yet this analogy might be used more naturally to illustrate the relation between speaking with tongues and interpretation of tongues.[39]

He references, with some hesitation and caveats, the Irvingites and Montanists as representing points in the evolving history of tongues:

> The speaking with tongues, however, was not confined to the day of Pentecost. Together with the other extraordinary spiritual gifts which distinguished this age above the succeeding periods of more quiet and natural development, this gift, also, though to be sure in a modified form, perpetuated itself in the apostolic church. We find traces of it still in the second and third centuries, and, (if we credit the legends of the Roman church), even later than this, though very seldom. Analogies to this speaking with tongues may be found also in the ecstatic prayers and prophecies of the Montanists in the second century, and the kindred Irvingites in the nineteenth; yet it is hard to tell, whether these are the work of the Holy Ghost, or Satanic imitations, or what is most probable, the result of an unusual excitement of mere nature, under the influence of religion, a more or less morbid enthusiasm, and ecstasis of feeling.[40]

Schaff was clearly intrigued by the gift of tongues, which was a topic of considerable interest in the theological and religious circles of his time. Records of the Society of Biblical Literature indicate that Schaff spoke on the subject at its inaugural meeting in New York in 1880. The minutes state: "Eighteen persons attended the first meeting of the Society . . . and heard Philip Schaff read a paper, "The Pentecostal and the Corinthian Glossolalia,"

---

38. Schaff, *History of the Apostolic Church*, 198.

39. Schaff, *History of the Apostolic Church*, 202n2.

40. Schaff, *History of the Apostolic Church*, 197–98.

[following which they] engaged in spirited discussion."[41] Schaff's discussions of "tongues," however, were limited to academic audiences, as were the views of the Higher Critics in Germany. It was not until Frederic Farrar's book on St. Paul was published that the new doctrine of *glossolalia* met with a much broader audience in the English-speaking world and took the next step toward becoming a universally-accepted standard.

Frederic William Farrar (1831–1903) and his works are largely forgotten today, but he was well known in his time. Not only did this progressive Englishman tirelessly work his way up through the ranks to become Archdeacon of Westminster and Dean of Canterbury Cathedral, but he was the personal friend of Charles Darwin and was later instrumental in securing Darwin's burial at Westminster Abbey and served as a pallbearer at his funeral.[42]

Farrar promoted the view that the tongues of Pentecost had nothing to do with foreign languages. Against the ancient tradition that the *xenolalic* gift of actual languages in Acts 2 should be the standard by which to interpret the tongues of Corinth and later Church history, he turned this view on its head, arguing that the mystical *glossolalia* of 1 Corinthians should set the standard of interpretation:

> The sole passage by which we can hope to understand it is the section of the First Epistle to the Corinthians. . . . It is impossible for anyone to examine that section carefully without being forced to the conclusion that, at Corinth at any rate, the gift of tongues had not the least connexion with foreign languages. Of such a knowledge, if this single passage of the Acts be not an exception, there is not the shadow of a trace in Scripture. That this passage is *not* an exception seems to be clear from the fact that St. Peter, in rebutting the coarse insinuation that the phenomenon was the result of drunkenness, does not so much as make the most passing allusion to an evidence so unparalleled; and that the passage of Joel of which he sees the fulfillment in the outpouring of Pentecost, does not contain the remotest hint of foreign languages. Hence the fancy that *this* was the immediate result of Pentecost is unknown to the first two centuries, and only sprang up when the true tradition had been obscured.[43]

Once again, Farrar acknowledges the influence of Neander: "I do not see how any thoughtful student who really considered the whole subject can

---

41. Saunders, *Searching the Scriptures*, 4.

42. Banerjee, "Frederic William Farrar," para. 1–4; cf. Pleins, *In Praise*, 83.

43. Farrar, *Life*, 1:96–97.

avoid the conclusion of Neander, that 'any foreign languages which were spoken on this occasion were only something accidental, and not the essential element of the language of the Spirit.'"[44] Farrar also adds that he agrees with the view of Döllinger, who says concerning modern counterparts to these New Testament spiritual manifestations that they occur "in a lower sphere, and without any miraculous endowment . . . an unusual phenomenon, but one completely within the range of natural operations, which the gift of the Apostolic age came into to exalt and ennoble it."[45] No less significantly, Farrar introduces a newly-minted noun, *glossolalia*, into the English language with the statement: "The glossolalia, or 'speaking with a tongue,' is connected with 'prophesying'—that is, exalted preaching—and magnifying God."[46] The 1933 edition of the *Oxford English Dictionary* credits Farrar and William Samuel Lily (1840–1919) with introducing the term, as does the current online edition.[47] The current online *Merriam-Webster Unabridged Dictionary* carries no reference to Farrar, but *Webster's Revised Unabridged Dictionary* (1913) traces the introduction of the word *glossolalia* to Farrar.[48]

Did "Glossolalia" Exist before 1879?

When the new interpretation of the "gift of tongues" as *glossolalia* was first introduced in Germany around 1830, it was far from universally accepted even in academic circles. As we have seen, furthermore, the concept of *glossolalia* did not find its way into English publications until Farrar introduced it in 1879. To substantiate the claim that the doctrine of *glossolalia* (not merely the word) was a nineteenth-century novelty that quickly became so entrenched as to become a virtually unquestionable dogma by our own time, it will prove helpful to examine primary, secondary, and even tertiary sourcebooks from this period to confirm that this transition is reflected in these documents and their definitions.

Dictionaries before 1879—Greek Dictionaries published before 1879 demonstrate through their definitions of the Greek word for "tongue," *glōssa* (γλῶσσα), that neither the term *glossolalia* nor the frequently-associated term *ecstasy* or related synonyms exist in any Greek dictionary published before 1879.

---

44. Farrar, *Life*, 1:98, referencing Neander's views in *Planting*, 9–15.

45. Farrar, *Life*, 1:98n2; cf. Döllinger, *First Age*, 321.

46. Farrar, *Life*, 1:96.

47. "Glossolalia," in *OED* 4:232; cf. Lilly, "Mysticism," 631–40.

48. "Glossolalia," in *Webster's Revised Unabridged Dictionary*, 5791.

- 1572—The first exhibit is the mother of all Greek dictionaries, the "Stephanus Lexicon," or *Thesaurus graecae linguae*, which Henri Estienne (Henricus Stephanus) is credited with compiling, and which continued in popularity for centuries and has abiding value even for contemporary ecclesiastical Greek translators. The first edition (1572) has an exhaustive list of almost every variation of the word *glōssa* (γλῶσσα). The only definition given is "language." There is no reference to the hybrid nineteenth-century neologism, *glossolalia*, or to the word for "ecstasy," *ekstasis* (ἔκστασις), in any of its forms.[49]

- 1825—The Second Edition of *The Tyro's Greek and English Lexicon* (1825), edited by John Jones, simply defines *glōssa* (γλῶσσα) as "speech—the tongue—tongue piece," referring to a mouthpiece in a musical instrument.[50]

- 1825—Cornelis Schrevel [Cornelii Schrevelii], *Lexicon: Græco-Latinum* (1825) also defines γλῶσσα simply as "language," with little else noted.[51]

- 1830—John Grove's *Greek and English Dictionary* (1830), admittedly based on Schrevel, defines γλῶσσα as "the tongue; a tongue, language, speech, [to] converse; the tongue in the mouthpiece of wind instruments."[52]

- 1836—James Donnegan's *A New Greek and English Lexicon: Principally on the Plan of the Greek and German Lexicon of Schneider* (1836), lists the primary definition for γλῶσσα as "language," but allows that it can also refer to an antiquated dialect or foreign expression.[53]

- 1858—This edition of the Greek *Hesychii Alexandrini Lexicon* gives a simple definition with no reference to "ecstasy" or "utterance," though it does relate γλῶσσα to divination and Plato.[54]

Latin Dictionaries typically use the noun *lingua* as the equivalent to the Greek *glōssa* (γλῶσσα). The standard definition for the Latin word *lingua* is "language." *Lingua* does not encompass "ecstatic utterance" or "heavenly language" as part of its natural semantic range, and pre-1879 Latin

---

49. Estienne, *Thesauros* (1572), s.v. "γλῶσσα," 1:852–58; cf. Estienne et al., *Thesaurus* (1865), s.v. "γλῶσσα," 2:659–61.

50. Jones, *Tyro's*, 269.

51. Schrevel et al., *Lexicon*, 110.

52. Groves, *Greek and English Dictionary*, 126.

53. Donnegan, *New Greek*, 329.

54. Albertum, *Hesychii*, 136.

dictionary editors show no references to *glossolalia* in their entries for *lingua* in any reference to the Christian doctrine of tongues.

- 1852—E. A. Andrews, in his dictionary with the lengthy title, *A Copious and Critical Latin-English Lexicon: Founded on the Larger Latin-German Lexicon of William Freund with Additions and Corrections from the Lexicons of Gesner, Facciolati, Scheller, Georges, etc.* (1852), contains a simple, brief definition, indicating that *lingua* was understood to mean, simply, *language*. It does not add a special category for the Christian doctrine of tongues. It does contain an entry for *glōssa*, the Latin transliteration of γλῶσσα, which is defined as "an obsolete or foreign word that requires explanation."[55]

- 1866—Peter Bullion's *Latin-English Dictionary, Abridged and Re-Arranged from Riddle's Latin-English Lexicon, Founded on the German-Latin Dictionaries of Dr. William Freund*, has many descriptors. At the very end, it describes *lingua* as also bearing the meaning, "*an obscure or unintelligible expression*," but makes no association between this and the Christian doctrine of tongues.[56]

This Latin survey is brief and requires further study. The central focus here is on William Freund's significant influence on Latin studies. The available information so far, however, demonstrates no awareness of either the term or concept of *glossolalia* in connection with the Christian doctrine of tongues.

Syriac Dictionaries—The traditional Syriac word used for the New Testament passages containing γλῶσσα is ܠܸܫܵܢ (*leshan*). The *Thesaurus Syriacus*, edited by R. Payne Smith and published in 1879—the same year Farrar introduced the word *glossolalia* into the English language—contains no reference to *glossolalia*, ecstatic utterances, or heavenly languages. There is no attempt to expand this word's semantic range beyond the meaning of regular language, speech, or pronunciation; and this stance is not altered by the later editor of the popular revised version in 1903.[57]

Commentaries before 1879—Biblical commentaries before the 1800s do not make a single correlation between "tongues" and "ecstasy" or the Delphic Oracles of ancient Greece. Not a single such reference is contained, for example, in John Lightfoot's 1660 *Commentary on the New Testament from the Talmud and Hebraica: Matthew—1 Corinthians*; Matthew Henry's

55. Andrews, *Copious*, 888 (1852 ed.), 687 (1857 ed.).

56. Bullion, *Latin-English*, 542.

57. Smith, *Thesaurus Syriacus*, 1:1973; cf. Smith, *Compendius Syriac Dictionary*, 245.

Complete Commentary or *Exposition of the Old and New Testaments* (1708–10); or John Gill's *Exposition of the Old and New Testaments* (1746–63).[58] The British Empiricist, John Locke (1632–1704), relies on Lightfoot's interpretation of the Corinthian tongues as involving a problem posed by the liturgical use of the non-vernacular Hebrew language. He does not refer to any other interpretation.[59] The 1752 edition of the British *Monthly Review* carries a review of a book on Christian tongues and concludes that they had ceased their purpose at Pentecost. There is no reference to any other explanation. Almost thirty years later, the same periodical in 1787 published a book review that defines the gift of tongues as musical tones, concerning which the reviewer concludes: "*We think it unnecessary to lay any of the Author's arguments before our Readers; most of them are hypothetical and none of them satisfactory, while the original word militates too strongly against them.*"[60] The first article assumes the standard interpretation of tongues as *xenolalic*, while the second one suggests that any other view is far too deviant for its readership.

"Glossolalia" after 1879—What happened with the *glossolalia* concept after 1879 is even more interesting. When we examine the most widely used and trusted primary, secondary, and tertiary sourcebooks that most Bible researchers used from the late 1800s into the early 1900s, it would be easy to conclude that the concept of "tongues" refers to "ecstatic utterances" and that this is the *only* historically respectable conclusion one could entertain. Most of these texts, however, fail the test of historical comprehensiveness and do not expose the reader to alternative historical theories, ecclesial traditions, or interpretive approaches required by this complex subject. In what follows, we shall endeavor to answer the question: How was the doctrine of "tongues" treated in popular Bible-research resources after 1879, and how were the concepts of "ecstasy" and "ecstatic utterances" interpolated into popular biblical lexicons and language aids of that period?

Dictionaries Published between 1880 and 1890 begin to reveal some cracks between their definitions and those found in older Greek dictionaries. On the one hand, E. A. Sophocles, in his 1887 *Greek Lexicon of the Roman and Byzantine Periods*, keeps the traditional definition for *glōssa* (γλῶσσα), which he defines as a "language"; or, metonymically, as a "nation" or "people."[61] On the other hand, *A Greek-English Lexicon of the New Testa-*

---

58. Lightfoot, *Commentary*, 28, 256–58; Henry, *Exposition*, 6:15–18, 110, 454, 456; Gill, *Exposition*, s.v. 1 Cor 14:2 mentions Lightfoot's opinion that "tongues" referred to Hebrew.

59. Wainwright, *Paraphrase*, 241.

60. "Art. 57," 510.

61. Sophocles, *Greek Lexicon*, 333.

ment, Being Grimm's Wilke's Clavis Novi Testamenti, better known as *Thayer's Greek Lexicon* in the mid to late 1880s, offers a mixture of traditional and novel definitions. The entry for γλῶσσα begins with the traditional definition—"the tongue," "a tongue, i.e. the language used by a particular people," and "foreign *tongues* . . . which the speaker has not learned previously." The entry then proceeds to cite De Wette (and later, Meyer, Schaff, and Farrar) and offer a new definition based on 1 Cor 14, which it describes as follows:

> This . . . is the gift of men who, rapt in an ecstasy and no longer quite masters of their own reason and consciousness, pour forth their glowing spiritual emotions in strange utterances, rugged, dark, disconnected, quite unfitted to instruct or to influence the minds of others: Acts x. 46; xix. 6; 1 Cor xii. 30; xiii. 1; xiv. 2, 4–6, 13, 18, 23, 27, 39. The origin of the expression is apparently to be found in the fact, that in Hebrew the tongue is spoken of as the leading instrument by which the praises of God are proclaimed . . . and that according to the more rigorous conception of inspiration nothing human in an inspired man as thought to be active except the tongue, put in motion by the Holy Spirit."[62]

This description, taken from the 1889 edition of *Thayer's Greek-English Lexicon*, demonstrates that the noun, *glōssa* (γλῶσσα), was in a transitory stage of re-definition. It may be one of the first major Greek-English dictionaries to introduce this new concept.

Dictionaries and Other Reference Works after 1890—The most popular language aide for Greek Bible students remains to this day, Walter Bauer's *A Greek-English Lexicon of the New Testament and Other Early Christian Literature*. This dictionary, originally based on a German work by Erwin Preuschen in 1910, was extensively revised by Bauer and translated and reworked into its first English edition by William F. Arndt and Wilbur Gingerich in 1957. Throughout its several recensions, it has profoundly influenced scholars, ministers, and Greek translators for over a century now. The fourth edition, published in 1957, reflects the evolution of the new "tongues" doctrine, weighing in heavily on the side of the "ecstasy" concept, with only one very brief reference to traditional ecclesiastical usage:

> There is no doubt about the thing referred to, namely the broken speech of persons in religious ecstasy. The phenomenon, as found in Hellenistic religion, is described esp. by E. Rohde (*Psyche* '03) and Reitzenstein; cf. Celsus 7, 8; 9. The origin of the term is less clear. Two explanations are prominent today. The one (Bleek, Henrici) holds that γλῶσσα here means antiquated,

---

62. Thayer, *Greek-English Lexicon*, 118.

foreign, unintelligible, mysterious utterances. The other (Rtzst., Bousset) sees in glossolalia a speaking in marvelous, heavenly languages.[63]

This lexicon goes into much further detail than the quote above. It tracks almost the entire history of the ecstatic tongues doctrine by listing the important authors' names and titles of their articles with no explanation of their special contribution or viewpoint, almost entirely leaving aside any Patristic or medieval opinions. German works, for the most part, are the only ones referenced. One of the more important of these was Erwin Rohde's *Psyche: The Cult of Souls* (1894).[64] This book is one of the monuments to great German classical scholarship of the nineteenth century, an exceedingly erudite and thorough description of classical Greek religion with a substantial portion focusing on the phenomena of ecstasy and frenzy of the Dionysiac cult. Rohde himself did not draw any correlations to the Christian tongues of Corinth or Pentecost, but the reader could easily be drawn to make such a correlation.[65] Bauer's lexicon does cite J. G. Davies' "Pentecost and Glossolalia" (1952)—a short treatise on why the gift of tongues does not consist of "incoherent ecstatic utterances" but is a miracle of foreign languages.[66] Davies' article, however, is too concise and lacks any real historical contributions. It became increasingly normative for translator guides, such as Max Zerwick's *Grammatical Analysis of the Greek New Testament* (1988), to advise the Greek student to translate the word, *glōssa* (γλῶσσα), in 1 Corinthians as "ecstatic utterance."[67] The competitor volume by Fritz Rienecker, *Linguistic Key to the New Testament*, is not so audacious, merely referring the reader to Kittel's *Theological Dictionary of the New Testament* (1957), which, as we shall see below, promotes the pro-ecstatic Hellenic interpretation of tongues.[68] As early as 1926, at least one Syriac dictionary hesitantly includes the concept of "ecstatic utterance" as a debatable option.[69] Even the recently released *Brill Dictionary of Ancient Greek* (2015), which supposedly provides etymologies back to the sixth century AD, demonstrably fails at this undertaking in its entry for *glossa* (γλῶσσα), which lacks a single

---

63. BAG, 161.

64. Rohde, *Psyche*; cf. the original, *Seelenkult*.

65. A portion of Rohde's masterpiece is excerpted in Sullivan, *GOTP*, s.v. "Rohde's *Psyche*," ch. 9.

66. Davies, "Pentecost," 228–31.

67. Zerwick, *Grammatical Analysis*, 525.

68. Rogers and Rogers, *New Linguistic and Exegetical Key*, 381, a revised edition of Rienecker and Rogers, *Linguistic Key*, 433.

69. Jennings, *Lexicon to the Syriac New Testament*, 113.

Patristic reference, reinforcing the stereotypical assumption that the Church was silent on this issue.[70] The same is true of *The New International Dictionary of New Testament Theology* (1976).[71]

Gerhard Kittel's *Theological Dictionary of the New Testament* (*TDNT*), originally published in German beginning in 1933 and introduced to an English audience in the 1960s, follows the approach established by August Neander in the 1850s, with some additional notes. Johannes Behm, the highly controversial contributor for the entry, "γλῶσσα, ἑτερόγλοσσος" (*glōssa, heteroglossos*), writes in this dictionary: "In Corinth, therefore, glossolalia is an unintelligible ecstatic utterance. One of its forms of expression is a muttering of words or sounds without interconnection or meaning. Parallels may be found for this phenomenon in various forms and at various periods and places in religious history."[72] Behm then proceeded to make a boldly-speculative and unsubstantiated assertion:

> Paul is aware of a similarity between Hellenism and Christianity in respect of these mystical and ecstatic phenomena. . . . If the judgement of Paul on glossolalia raises the question whether this early Christian phenomenon can be understood merely in the light of the ecstatic mysticism of Hellenism, the accounts of the emergence of glossolalia or related utterances of the Spirit in the first Palestinian community (Acts 10:46; 8:15; 2:2ff.) make it plain that we are concerned with an ecstatic phenomenon which is shared by both Jewish and Gentile Christianity and for which there are analogies in the religious history of the OT and Judaism.[73]

Around the same time, E. Andrews expressed a similar perspective in *The Interpreter's Dictionary of the Bible* (1962):

> Such ecstatic speech as described above prevailed among the earliest Hebrew prophets, the professionalized *nebi'im*, who, as Yahweh enthusiasts, wandered about the country in bands, working themselves into a religious frenzy by means of music and dancing. . . . The word *nabi*, by which they were called, was probably suggested by their ecstatic babblings and their *hith-nabbe*, "prophesying," may well have corresponded to glossolalia, though scholars are not unanimous. In Hellenistic

---

70. "γλῶσσα," in Montanari et al., *Brill Dictionary of Ancient Greek*.

71. Haarbeck, "γλῶσσα," in *NIDNTT* 3:1080–81.

72. Behm, "γλῶσσα," 1:722. Both Kittel and Behm were Nazis, and Behm was deposed from his academic position after the Second World War for his Nazi collaboration.

73. Behm, "γλῶσσα," 1:724.

circles also, followers of the Dionysian cult, or of some mystery religion, under powerful emotional pressures of ceremonial rites, often slipped into ecstatic states bordering on frenzy, and expressed themselves in forms intelligible only to the initiated. Through the centuries, glossolalia has frequently reappeared among Christian groups, the Montanists, the Camisards, the Irvingites, and many modern sects given to emotional extremes. The psychological aspects are patent.[74]

The monumental 1993 compendium, *The Exegetical Dictionary of the New Testament* (German edition, 1980–83), asserted that the origin of *glossolalia* in the Corinthian Church is found in the "syncretistic piety of the Hellenistic Mediterranean world."[75]

This new view quickly became entrenched in encyclopedias as well. Even the 1917 edition of *The Catholic Encyclopedia*, carries the term *glossolalia* in its entry for the "Gift of Tongues" (originally published in 1912). It also played down the miraculous interpretation of Pentecostal "tongues," suggesting a naturalistic alternative, concluding: "It was the Holy Ghost who impelled the disciples 'to speak,' without perhaps being obliged to infuse a knowledge of tongues unknown. The physical and psychic condition of the auditors was one of ecstasy and rapture in which 'the wonderful things of God' would naturally find utterance in acclamations, prayers or hymns."[76]

The article concedes that in Corinth the charism had "deteriorated into a mixture of meaningless inarticulate gabble" through abuse, but insists that the tongues of Pentecost were "historic, articulate, and intelligible"; and it then concludes: "Faithful adherence to the text of Sacred Scripture makes it obligatory to reject those opinions which turn the charism of tongues into little more than infantile babbling (Eichhorn, Schmidt, Neander)."[77] While the article eschews the notion that genuine tongues are unintelligible and somewhat resists the new Higher Critical interpretations, it underplays the supernatural dimension in the traditional definition of the tongues of Pentecost in Acts 2, and offers hardly any references to Patristic writings, leaving the reader unable to draw any definitive conclusions.

The 1911 *New Schaff-Herzog Encyclopedia of Religious Knowledge* vacillates in its definition, alluding slightly to the traditional view at the outset, but without any compelling development of it.[78] The author then describes

---

74. Andrews, "Tongues, Gift Of," 672.

75. Balz and Schneider, *Exegetical Dictionary*, 253.

76. Reilly, "Gift of Tongues," para. 3.

77. Reilly, "Gift of Tongues," para. 3.

78. Feine, "Speaking," 11:36–39.

the gift of tongues, both in Acts and 1 Corinthians, as one involving ecstatic experience, which the article correlates with antecedents in ancient Greek religion. The 1987 version of the *Encyclopedia Britannica* describes the gift of tongues as consisting in "utterances approximating words and speech, usually produced during states of intense religious excitement," and adds: "Glossolalia occurred in some of the ancient Greek religions and in various primitive religions."[79] The popular *Zondervan Pictorial Encyclopedia of the Bible in Five Volumes* subtly alludes to a relationship between tongues and ecstasy.[80] *The New International Bible Encyclopedia*, a favorite of evangelical Bible Students, first published in 1915, also gives prominence to the view that tongues are ecstatic, drawing correlations between Corinth and influences of the Greek Oracles, citing Rohde's *Psyche* as a source.[81]

Since the turn of the century (1900), commentaries and books have promoted widely the view that tongues are an "ecstatic utterance." One of the most acclaimed commentators of the 20th century, Hans Conzelmann, paved the way for a broader acceptance of the new definition. In his *Commentary on the First Epistle to the Corinthians* (1975), he contends that the solution to the puzzle of the Corinthian tongues is found in the Oracles at Delphi:

> Speaking with tongues is unintelligible to a normal man, even a Christian. On the other hand, it must be meaningful, must be logical in itself. For it can be translated into normal language, which is again made possible by a special gift. . . . If we could explain it, then we must set out from comparable material in the history of religion, above all from the Greek motif of the inspiring *pneuma*, which is expressed especially in Mantic sources, and is bound up more particularly with Delphi. The deity speaks out of the inspired.[82]

In the case of Pentecost, however, he vacillates between ecstatic and ordinary human languages, mixing the two understandings. He writes: "The Pentecost narrative alternates between an account of an outbreak of glossolalia and miraculous speech in many languages. Luke has fashioned it into its present form as an episode with a burlesque impact, a mixture of themes which lead to reflection. In addition to the meaningful event as such, the episode contains instructive material in the description of the scene itself."[83]

79. "Glossolalia," in *EB87* 11:842.
80. Cole, "Tongues, Gift of," 4:775.
81. Easton, "Tongues, Gift of," 5:2995–97; Robeck, "Tongues, Gift of," 874–74.
82. Conzelmann, *First Epistle to the Corinthians*, 234.
83. Conzelmann, *Acts of the Apostles*, 15.

He denies that Luke's account is based on a "naïve legend," but nevertheless suggests that Luke had lost the "conception of the original glossolalia."[84]

The New International Commentary on the New Testament, edited by the revered evangelical author, F. F. Bruce, does not go so far as to impute Greek syncretism to the Corinthian assembly, but he suggests nevertheless that the tongues of Corinth were not human languages.[85] William Barclay, a popular commentator who has attracted a conservative audience, likewise does not accept the idea of Greek influence, but still states in his commentary on *The Letters to the Corinthians* (1975) that ecstasy was at the heart of the experience and was "very common" in the early Church. He writes: "A man became worked up to an ecstasy and in that state poured out a quite uncontrollable torrent of sounds in no known languages. . . . The very desire to possess it produced, at least in some, a kind of self-hypnotism and deliberately induced hysteria which issued in a completely false and synthetic speaking with tongues."[86] Zondervan's *NIV Application Commentary* significantly adds to the idea that tongues and ecstasy are synonymous in its volume on 1 Corinthians. The author, Craig Blomberg, tersely states that the 1 Corinthians passage does "not imply that Paul recognized glossolalia as actual foreign languages spoken by people somewhere on earth, or even that they have a comparable linguistic structure. . . . Various Greco-Roman religions were well-known for their outbursts of ecstatic speech and unintelligible repetition of 'nonsense' syllables."[87]

Contemporary Theological Discussions: The concept of ecstasy has been used by more conservative Christian leaders as a foil for attacking Pentecostals and Charismatics. For instance, John MacArthur has argued that Pentecostals have gone wrong by following the ecstatic practices of Greco-Roman paganism rather than sticking with biblical truth, and by embracing ecstatic "tongues," which were never more than mere gibberish.[88] This connection to pagan Greek antecedents is echoed by British New Testament scholar, James D. G. Dunn, whose work is extensively referenced by Pentecostal and evangelical readers to affirm their doctrine of speaking in tongues. He writes:

> There are some indications that the Corinthian glossolalia was indeed "ecstatic utterance," measured in value by them precisely by the intensity of the ecstasy which produced it and by the unintelligibility of the utterances. . . . These features of Corinthian

---

84. Conzelmann, *Acts of the Apostles*, 15.

85. Grosheide, *First Epistle to the Corinthians*, 317.

86. Barclay, *Letters*, 127.

87. Blomberg, *1 Corinthians*, 293.

88. MacArthur, *Charismatic Chaos*, 270–79; MacArthur, *Strange Fire*, 133–54.

> glossolalia are too reminiscent of the mantic prophecy of the Pythia at Delphi . . . and the wider manifestation of ecstasy in the worship of Dionysus, so the conclusion becomes almost inescapable: glossolalia, as practiced in the assembly at Corinth was a form of ecstatic utterance—sounds, cries, words uttered in a state of spiritual ecstasy.[89]

Modern English Bibles—Most of the standard English translations of the Bible preserve the traditional reading of the "tongues" passages and do not introduce the new definition of unintelligible tongues. The *King James Version* (1611) remains unchanged, although it retains the Reformation-era interpolations of adjectival constructs such as "unknown tongues" and "other tongues," which can mislead many readers (1 Cor 14:2, 4, 13, 14, 19, 27).[90] The adjective "unknown" was not originally intended to express the concept of "ecstatic utterances," as we shall see in chapter 5, but it coincidentally blends quite well with that view. The ubiquitous *New International Version* (1972) and *New American Standard Bible* (1960), as well as the *New Revised Standard Version* (1989) and *New American Bible* (1970), simply follow the traditional approach, maintaining a neutral posture regarding the question at issue.

Two newer English Bible translations have revised their translations toward a *glossolalic* interpretation. The *New English Bible* (1961) translates the "tongues" passages by reference to the new definition. Thus, Acts 19:6 is rendered, "and when Paul had laid his hands on them, the Holy Spirit came upon them and they spoke in tongues of ecstasy and prophesied"; and 1 Cor 14:2 reads, "When a man is using the language of ecstasy he is talking with God." Again, the popular *Message Bible* (2002) translates 1 Cor 14:4 as, "The one who prays using a private 'prayer language' certainly gets a lot out of it, but proclaiming God's truth to the church in its common language brings the whole church into growth and strength."

The additional study notes in these and other Bibles exceed the scope of the present study, though some appear to perpetuate the new narrative of "ecstatic tongues." For example, the notes to the *Harper Study Bible* (1991) state, on the one hand, that the "tongues" of Acts are simply "languages," but, on the other hand, that the "tongues" of 1 Corinthians 14 "are described as ecstatic utterances not corresponding to any known languages but giving direct expression to ineffable emotions with insights of the souls."[91] Such notes obviously call for further study.

---

89. Dunn, *Jesus and the Spirit*, 242.

90. The ISV, by contrast, demystifies the chapter by using "foreign language."

91. HSB, 1714.

Early Objections to the Glossolalia Doctrine

The new definition of "tongues" as an "ecstatic utterance," however, was not universally accepted and initially ran into strong opposition. *Glossolalia* was widely recognized as a departure from the traditional interpretation. Two examples illustrate this within the German academic world. One is the German lexicographer named Hermann Cremer, who simply ignored the new Higher Critical movement in his *Biblico-Theological Lexicon* (1883) and continued to adhere to the old definition, insisting that *glōssa* (γλῶσσα) should always be understood as *language*.[92] Another is the German historian, Joseph von Görres, who wrote a widely-read multi-volume work on magic and miracles throughout the centuries, entitled *On Christian Mysticism* (*Die christliche Mystik*, 1836–42). Remarkably, although his views already show the influence of the German Higher Critical inroads in his association of the gift of tongues with "ecstasy," he nevertheless insisted on the traditional idea of miraculously-spoken foreign languages. Thus, in describing the tongues of Jeanne Delanoue (Joan of the Cross) in the early 1700s, he said that she "had this gift when she was in ecstasy; and she could communicate in various languages, according to the needs of her listeners. . . . She had an ecstasy, and spoke Arabic with them, so that they ended up asking for baptism."[93]

There were also voices in England protesting that the new definition of "tongues" had deserted the received Church tradition. One of these voices was that of Edward Hayes Plumptre, a highly-esteemed scholar, hymnist, and Professor of Divinity at the King's College in London, whose greatest claim to fame came from his opposition to Charles Darwin and his ordination by Bishop Wilberforce, the son of the revered parliamentarian and abolitionist, William Wilberforce. Plumptre wrote a compelling overview of the "tongues" controversy in the 1863 edition of William Smith's *Dictionary of the Bible*.[94] Compared to the ancient definition of "tongues," he found the contemporary definition wanting. His critical survey may be one of the most comprehensive pieces of historical analysis on the topic up to this point. He concludes that the "theories of Bleek, Herder, and Bunsen," cannot be reconciled, "without a willful distortion of the evidence."[95] In his defense, he documented different views throughout history along with the traditionally accepted one.[96]

---

92. Cremer, *Biblico-Theological Lexicon*, 164.

93. Görres, *La Mystique* (1862 French tran. of *Die christliche Mystik*), 181.

94. Smith, *Dictionary of the Bible*, 3:1555–62.

95. Plumptre, "Tongues," 1556.

96. Plumptre, "Tongues," 1557–59.

Another English scholar who echoed these concerns was Christopher Wordsworth, a leading Anglican scholar in the 1850s and the youngest brother of the poet William Wordsworth. He openly challenged the new thinking and reaffirmed the traditional position—a stance that earned him the backing of the Anglican Church:

> One of the most convincing proofs of the truth of the ancient interpretation of this text, as thus declared by the Church of England, is to be found in the almost countless discrepancies of the expositors who have deserted that interpretation.
>
> There is a large and consistent body of interpreters, dating from the second century, and continued for many hundred years in all parts of Christendom, in favour of the ancient exposition; whereas, on the contrary, the expositions at variance with it, which have been propounded in modern times, have no ancient authority in their favour; and are as inconsistent with one another as they are irreconcilable with the teaching of Christian antiquity.[97]

In their 1871 *Commentary: Critical and Explanatory on the Whole Bible*, Jamieson, Fausset, and Brown rejected the new thesis, stating: "Tongue must therefore mean languages, not ecstatic, unintelligible rhapsodies."[98] In 1878 *Churchman Magazine* reflected similar intensity about the matter. Several letters to the editor argue against a minister of the Irvingite Church, John Davenport, who previously had written that the "tongues" of Pentecost neither involved foreign languages nor were intended for the purpose of propagating the Gospel. The magazine published a reader's response to Davenport, which reads: "There is a large and consistent body of interpreters, dating from the second century, and continued many hundred years in all parts of Christendom, in favor of the ancient exposition; whereas, on the contrary, the expositions at variance with it, which have been propounded in modern times, have no ancient authority in their favor, and are as inconsistent with one another as they are irreconcilable with the teaching of Christian antiquity."[99]

Even this small sample of writers demonstrates that there was a traditional definition of "tongues" that many believed was being threatened with unjustified replacement by a novel interpretation. Their objections nevertheless had only a minor effect in the face of the rapidly-gathering momentum of the new doctrine of *glossolalia*. The winds of change and spirit of the

97. Wordsworth, *New Testament*, 9.

98. Jamieson et al., *Commentary*, s.v. "1 Cor 14:5."

99. M. H. W., "Tongues," 14.

times were decidedly behind the new definition. One of the difficulties that defenders of the traditional view had, and still have, in resisting the novelties of these nineteenth-century Higher Critical revisionists and their later twentieth-century scholarly supporters, is the woeful widespread ignorance concerning the extensive ecclesiastical literature on the subject of tongues through Church history. This extensive literature remains largely unread because it is not available in readily-understood modern languages and remains largely untranslated in Latin, Greek, and Syriac. Another deterrence, for any who have actually ventured into this literature, may be that it clearly offers no support for the new revisionist interpretation of tongues.

A visual survey of half the volumes of Migne's *Patrologia Graeca* conducted between 1993–2003 yielded at least thirty-four Patristic texts that explicitly address "tongues," fifty-one more that were strong indicators, and 109 indirect references or parallels, as well as biblical citations, concerning tongues.[100] In addition, there were 360 occurrences of keywords related to the tongues phenomenon that are available for comparative grammatical and syntactical analysis, and thirty-five references to early Church liturgy that can help us better understand the historical context of tongues. This tally is a conservative one. The numbers would likely be much higher if a search of the entire collection were performed today using the digital features now available. Of the thirty-four or more passages explicitly referencing the gift of tongues by ecclesiastical writers in the period spanning upwards of the first thousand years of Church history, only seven are popularly cited in support of the new definition. These include Irenaeus, *Against Heresies* (1.13.3), Origen, *Against Celsius* (7.8–9), Eusebius, *Ecclesiastical History* (5.16), Tertullian, *Against Marcion* (5.8), Epiphanius, *Against Heresies* (48.4), Chrysostom, *Homily* 29 (on 1 Corinthians); and Clement of Alexandria, *Stromata* (1.431.1).[101] The selection is tendentious, to say the least. A key problem is that *none* of these passages includes a single reference to the term *glōssa* (γλῶσσα), meaning "language," except for a hopelessly-obscure sentence from the Tertullian text. Furthermore, passages from the same writers, and numerous others, which *do* refer to the term *glōssa* and suggest (or explicitly state) that "tongues" are human languages are overlooked or omitted.[102] The attempt to harness these seven Patristic texts in support of the revisionist, Higher Critical, and Pentecostal-Charismatic understanding of "tongues," is

100. Sullivan, *GOTP*, s.v. "History of Glossolalia: Patristic Citation."

101. Note that the citation system used in Balz and Schneider, *Exegetical Dictionary*, 253, to reference the passage from Clement of Alexandria (*Stromata*, 1.431.1) is unconventional and difficult to confirm, though it may correspond to 1:21 in *ANF* 2:332.

102. Sullivan, *GOTP*, s.v. "History of *Glossolalia*: Patristic Citation," para. 1–7.

steadfastly contradicted by the vast majority of other Patristic and later texts, concerning which the silence of contemporary scholarship is deafening.

The Delphic Oracles and Christian Tongues

Did the ancient Greek prophetesses—the Pythian priestesses, known as the Oracles of Delphi—speak in the kind of "tongues" found today among Pentecostal and Charismatic Christians? The short answer is no, the Oracle's language was not the same thing as what is now called *glossolalia*. This answer, however, must be demonstrated for skeptics who have assimilated the nineteenth-century doctrine of the Higher Critics. To substantiate our answer, we must identify the primary Hellenistic texts that provide the presumed basis for this connection and evaluate them.

Over the past two millennia, the Christian doctrine of the gift of tongues has been interpreted variously by three major movements; (1) the traditional one that dominated Church history for 1800 years and held that "tongues" referred to a gift of speaking or hearing natural human languages; (2) the movement of *Cessationism* (to be examined in chapter 5) that began shortly after the Protestant Reformation and continues today (especially in Calvinist circles), which holds that all miracles ceased in the early Church and that any subsequent claims of "speaking in tongues" are most likely false; and (3) the nineteenth-century Higher Critical theory of *glossolalia*, which, instead of tracing the history of Christian "tongues" back through Church-approved sources to Pentecost (which they rejected as myth), traced it back through heretical Montanist ecstatics and ancient pagan sources such as Plutarch, Strabo, and others, to the caves of Delphi and Dodona where, well before the advent of Christianity, ancient Greek prophetesses would utter their prophecies. *Glossolalia* has become the dominant interpretive scheme today in academe and has all but erased the memory of the traditional definition. Today reference to *glossolalia* is found ubiquitously throughout all the primary, secondary, and tertiary literature on "tongues." The Hellenistic sources used by Higher Critics to suggest the pre-Christian origins of Christian "tongues" have not been critically examined and properly evaluated. What follows is a brief analysis of these major sources, which include Herodotus, Aristophanes, Plato, Virgil, Lucan, Plutarch, Strabo, Michael Psellos, and Erwin Rohde:

Herodotus (c. 484–425 BC) is remembered for his *Histories* (440 BC), written in the Ionic dialect of classical Greek and now widely considered to be the founding work of history in Western literature. They record the ancient traditions, politics, geography, and conflicts of various cultures from the fifth century BC in Western Asia, North Africa, and Greece. Herodotus also refers to the ancient Delphic Oracles and indicates that they spoke clearly in classic hexameter verse.[103] The actual citations indicate nothing remotely like *glossolalic* "tongues"-speech. In fact, in one passage, we read:

> There (by the providence of heaven) Pisistratus met Amphilytus the Acarnanian, a diviner, who came to him and prophesied as follows in hexameter verses:
> "Now hath the cast been thrown and the net of the fisher is outspread:
> All in the moonlight clear shall the tunny-fish come for the taking."[104]

Plato (c. 428–348 BC) is reputed to have been one of the greatest Greek philosophers of all time, a reputation underscored by Alfred North Whitehead's dictum: "The safest general characterization of the European philosophical tradition is that it consists of a series of footnotes to Plato."[105] In all of Plato's works, there are only two references to a Greek priestess speaking in a way that even comes close to being interpretable as ecstatic. But neither is compelling or substantial. The first is from his dialogue, the *Phaedrus* (c. 370 BC):

> And the priestesses at Dodona when they have been mad have conferred many splendid benefits upon Greece both in private and in public affairs, but few or none when they have been in their right minds; and if we should speak of the Sibyl and all the others who by prophetic inspiration have foretold many things to many persons and thereby made them fortunate afterwards, anyone can see that we should speak a long time. And it is worthwhile to adduce also the fact that those men of old who invented names thought that madness was neither shameful nor disgraceful.[106]

The second is from Plato's *Timaeus* (c. 360 BC), where he describes how the human mind can touch the divine only in an altered state and insists that whatever vision, apparition, or speech that occurs in such an altered state must be interpreted by a person of a stable, rational mind.

> No man achieves true and inspired divination when in his rational mind, but only when the power of his intelligence is fettered

---

103. Herodotus, *Histories*, bk. 1, §47, 53; §62, 73.
104. Herodotus, *Histories*, bk. 1, §62, 73 (cf. Greek original on opposing page).
105. Whitehead, *Process and Reality*, 39.
106. Plato, *Complete*, 1:244b; cf. Plato, *Platonis Opera*, 244b.

in sleep or when it is distraught by disease or by reason of some divine inspiration. But it belongs to a man when in his right mind to recollect and ponder both the things spoken in dream or waking vision by the divining and inspired nature, and all the visionary forms that were seen, and by means of reasoning to discern about them all wherein they are significant and for whom they portend evil or good in the future, the past, or the present.[107]

The speech to which Plato refers cannot be the same thing as *glossolalia*, because it consists of utterances whose intelligible meaning must be rationally discerned behind difficult imagery and words, so that what was uttered in an altered state of mind may be interpreted in an understandable way—something that cannot be said of today's "private language of prayer and praise."

Virgil (70 BC–19 BC) is the celebrated first-century Roman author of the well-known epic poem entitled the *Aeneid*. His alleged contribution to the "tongues" debate is small. He wrote:

> "Then to Phoebus and Trivia will I set up a temple of solid marble, and festal days in Phoebus' name. You also a stately shrine awaits in our realm; for here I will place your oracles and mystic utterances, told to my people, and ordain chosen men, O gracious one. Only trust not your verses to leaves, lest they fly in disorder, the sport of rushing winds; chant them yourself, I pray." His lips ceased speaking.[108]

The question that surrounds this excerpt from Virgil is his reference to "mystic utterances." What does he mean? The clause "here I will place your oracles and mystic utterances" in the second sentence of the English translation of the Latin is misleading and would be better translated, "here I shall place your lots and secret fates."[109] It would be a significant stretch to read *glossolalia* into this sequence.

Lucan (AD 39–65), a poet whom the Roman Emperor Nero had executed for treason, wrote a history of the war between Julius Caesar and Pompey, *De Bello Civili* (*On the Civil War*), which contains a narrative about a Delphic priestess. A man named Appius Claudius Pulcher, wanting to know his future, consulted the priestess, Phemenoe, who faked a prophecy. Discovering this, Pulcher forced her back into the ancient cave in Delphi where Oracles received their prophetic inspiration in the past. Although

---

107. Plato, *Complete*, 9:71e–72a; cf. Plato, *Platonis Opera*, 71e–72a.

108. Virgil, *Aeneid*, 6:69–70 (LCL 63:536–37).

109. The Latin is "*hic ego namque tuas sortes arcanaque fata.*"

prophecies had ceased for some time, Apollo returned and Phemenoe, after being violently possessed by Apollo, temporarily went raving mad and uttered a prophecy, foretelling Pulcher's death, saying he would repose in a "broad hollow of the Euboean coast" as his grave. There is no reference, however, to her being in a trance or uttering strange or foreign words. When she is possessed by Apollo, what comes from her mouth is "the sound of articulate speech." For the sake of substantiation, here is an English translation from the Loeb Classical Library, which has the Latin original on the facing page:

> At last Apollo mastered the breast of the Delphian priestess; as fully as ever in the past, he forced his way into her body, driving out her former thoughts, and bidding her human nature to come forth and leave her heart at his disposal. Frantic, she careers about the cave . . . she whirls with tossing head through the void spaces of the temple; she scatters the tripods that impede her random course . . . first the wild frenzy overflowed through her foaming lips; she groaned and uttered loud inarticulate cries with panting breath; next, a dismal wailing filled the vast cave; and at last, when she was mastered, came the sound of articulate speech: "Roman, thou shalt have no part in the mighty ordeal and shalt escape the awful threats of war; and thou alone shalt stay at peace in a broad hollow of the Euboean coast." Then Apollo closed up her throat and cut short her tale.[110]

Plutarch (AD 46–120) was a biographer and essayist who spent the last thirty years of his life serving as a priest at the Temple of Apollo in Delphi. Of all the literature referring to the rites of the Delphic priestesses, Plutarch provides the most information. His essays in his *Moralia* demonstrate that the role of the Delphic priestess was an important one in Greek society and required the prophetess to speak in direct terms. All the prophecies given were coherent and readily understood. There is no hint of strange or incoherent language being spoken. This is apparent in volume 4 of *Moralia*, but even more profoundly in volume 5, where he writes in a letter entitled, *The Oracles at Delphi*, that the prophecies of the priestesses were given in prose and meter, in a formal, eloquent manner:

> Now we cherish the belief that the god, in giving indications to us, makes use of the calls of herons, wrens, and ravens; but we do not insist that these, inasmuch as they are messengers and heralds of the gods, shall express everything rationally and clearly, and yet we insist that the voice and language of the prophetic

110. Lucan, *Civil War*, 251–53; cf. 249.

> priestess, like a choral song in the theatre, shall be presented, not without sweetness and embellishment, but also in verse of a grandiloquent and formal style with verbal metaphors and with a flute to accompany its delivery![111]
>
> ... And as for the language of the prophetic priestess, just as the mathematicians call the shortest of lines between two points a straight line, so her language makes no bend nor curve nor doubling nor equivocation, but is straight in relation to the truth.[112]

Strabo (c. 64 BC–AD 24) was a Greek geographer, philosopher, and historian from Asia Minor who related an account of the Delphic prophetesses very similar to Plutarch's. He said they would go into a trance and prophesy in verse, which was then recorded by priests:

> They say that the seat of the oracle is a cave that is hollowed out deep down in the earth, with a rather narrow mouth, from which arises breath that inspires a divine frenzy; and that over the mouth is placed a high tripod, mounting which the Pythian priestess receives the breath and then utters oracles in both verse and prose, though the latter too are put into verse by poets who are in the service of the temple. They say that the first to become Pythian priestess was Phemonoe; and that both the prophetess and the city were so called from the word *pythésthai*, though the first syllable was lengthened, as in *athanatos, akamatos,* and *diakonos* [italics added].[113]

Michael Psellos (c. 1017–78) was a medieval Christian monk, savant, writer, and public figure from Constantinople, reputed to be one of the most learned men of his time. According to his interpretation, the priestess of Apollo was overcome by Apollo and speaking in turn to Persians, Assyrians, and Phoenicians "all according to metre and also rhythm which she had not known, with beautiful language which she had not learned."[114] In other words, Psellos held that the Pythian prophetess was miraculously speaking in foreign languages. This interpretation is not consistent with any other interpretation. Psellos loved to play with ancient classical literature and parade his literary genius, but this does not explain why he offered this interpretation. He nevertheless believed that the Delphic practice involved

111. Plutarch, *Moralia*, 5:321.

112. Plutarch, *Moralia*, 5:341; cf. 301, 311.

113. Strabo, *Geography*, 4:352–54 (IX.3.5); Strabo, *Strabonis Geographica*, 2:591 (critical edition pagination, 419).

114. Psellos, *Michaelis Pselli Theologica*, 1:293–95; note the context.

a phenomenon similar to the traditional Christian gift of tongues. He believed that the Apostles controlled what they spoke at Pentecost and were personally engaged. By contrast, the Pythian priestess was out of her senses when she spoke. This is an odd addition that needs more scrutiny, but it does not point in the direction of *glossolalia*.

Erwin Rohde (1845–98) was one of the great German classical scholars of the nineteenth century. His *Psyche: The Cult of Souls and the Belief in Immortality among the Greeks* (1890–94) covers ancient Greek religious belief and practice in exceptionally vivid detail and clarity and stands above any other work in its genre. Though over one hundred years old and not widely known outside academic circles, his work has stood the test of time. Yet Rohde's work has been misleadingly cited to promote a view of contemporary "tongues" it does not support. The fourth edition of Bauer's *Greek-English Lexicon of the New Testament and other early Christian literature* (1957) suggests that Rohde's scholarship supports the *glossolalia* doctrine: "There is no doubt about the thing referred to, namely the broken speech of persons in religious ecstasy. The phenomenon, as found in Hellenistic religion, is described esp. by E. Rohde."[115] A closer examination of the pages (289–93) cited by Bauer from Rohde's work, however, belies this assertion. No such connection or evidence resembling anything remotely like *glossolalia* is to be found. The closest reference is this: "In hoarse tones and wild words, the Sibyl gave utterance to what the divine impelling power within her and not her own arbitrary fancy suggested; possessed by the god, she spoke in a divine distraction."[116] One has to be cautious with Rohde because his colorful narrative style may lend itself to reading into the text ideas that are unsupported by it. Nowhere does Rohde offer any substantiation from authorities such as Herodotus, Plutarch, or anyone else, for the idea that the Sibyl's utterances were anything like *glossolalia*.

Aristophanes (c. 446–386 BC) is cited in an obscure reference in support of a syncretistic Hellenic interpretation for the Christian doctrine of tongues by Johannes Behm in his aforementioned entry for "γλῶσσα, ἑτερόγλοσσος" (*glōssa, heteroglossos*) in Kittel's *Theological Dictionary of the New Testament*.[117] Behm writes: "In Corinth . . . glossolalia is an unintelligible ecstatic utterance. . . . In Greek religion there is a series of comparable phenomena from the enthusiastic cult of the Thracian Dionysus with its γλώττης βακχει (Aristoph. Ra., 357) to the divinatory romanticism of the

---

115. BAG, 161.

116. Rohde, *Seelenkult*, 1:68–69; Rohde, *Psyche*, 293.

117. Behm, "γλῶσσα," in *TDNT* 722.

Delphic Phrygi."[118] He cites only the words "γλώττης βακχει" from Aristophanes, making it difficult to locate, and requiring some guesswork. The only reason for including Behm's reference here is that it has been cited by modern scholars in support of the *glossolalia* doctrine. The closest representation to be found in Aristophanes' comedy, *Frogs*, the reference cited by Behm, where the construction "γλώττης βακχει" appears on p. 360 of the critical edition.[119] The Greek word γλώττης is the genitive form of γλῶττα (the first declension Attic form of γλῶσσα), which may suggest something like "bacchic tongues," though the construct remains obscure in popular English translations.[120] A recent translation by Ian Johnson refers to "the ones who've never seen or danced the noble Muses' ritual songs, or played their part in Bacchic rites of bull-devouring Cratinus."[121] The reference *to* Cratinus, a master of Athenian comedy, as a "bull-devourer" (ταυροφάγου γλώττης) is a hyperbolic nod to Cratinus' comedic talent. How this applies to Delphic tongues or anything remotely connected to ecstasy is hard to grasp. The only relationship between the two is that Aristophanes died in Delphi. The closest connection to anything remotely like ecstatic utterances is the word *adontes* (ᾄδοντες), whose primary meaning is to sing or chant; but this still does not correlate to Delphic or Christian tongues.

The works of Herodotus, Aristophanes, Plato, Virgil, Lucan, Plutarch, Strabo, Michael Psellos, and Erwin Rohde demonstrate no viable connection between the ancient Greek prophetesses of Delphi and the modern revisionist Christian doctrine of "tongues." These accounts lack any of the defining characteristics of *glossolalia* that could be used to sustain a connection with the theories of the nineteenth-century Higher Critics. Christopher Forbes, Senior Lecturer in Ancient History and Deputy Chair of the Society for the Study of Early Christianity at Macquarie University in Australia, wrote a dissertation on this subject, later published as a book, entitled *Prophecy and Inspired Speech: In Early Christianity and Its Hellenistic Environment* (1997), in which he writes: "The obscurity of Delphic utterances is not a matter of linguistic unintelligibility at all. It is simply that some such oracles [oracular messages] were formulated at the level of literary allusion and metaphor, in obscure, cryptic, and enigmatic terms. They were, in a word, oracular."[122] A closer parallel might be found between the ancient Greek prophetesses and the Old Testament seers, at least in terms of their role and function in

118. Behm, "γλῶσσα," in *TDNT* 722.
119. Aristophanes, *Aristophanis Ranae*, 37 (critical pagination, 360).
120. Sullivan, *GOTP*, s.v. "Delphi Prophetesses," s.v. "Aristophanes."
121. Johnston, *Aristophanes*, 390.
122. Forbes, *Prophecy*, 109.

their societies. Comparing the prophetic office as found in ancient Israel and Greece may serve as a worthy topic of inquiry in its own right. Yet the parallel still does not fit into the traditional Christian "tongues" paradigm.

Montanism and Christian Tongues

The association between Montanism and the Christian practice of speaking in tongues is a matter of debate. The argument depends on which way one traces the lineage of speaking in tongues. The first way is by using ecclesiastical literature to chronicle the Christian doctrine and practice of the gift of tongues through the centuries. Its trajectory follows tongues as the perceived miracle of speaking or hearing and understanding a foreign language. Montanism does not play a role in this ancient ecclesiastical definition. The second and currently more prevalent way is to trace the lineage of tongues back to pagan Greek antecedents. This path leads to presumed evidence for speaking in tongues as *glossolalia*. Montanism represents one of the critical stops along this second path. Pentecostals and Charismatics push this Montanist association even farther and claim that it represents a historical parallel to their own experience of speaking in tongues. Our goal here is to offer a critical examination of this claim by investigating Montanist source documents.

Originally known by its adherents as the "New Prophecy," Montanism was an early Christian sectarian movement of the late second century founded (c. AD 162) by Montanus and supported by two prophetesses, Maximilla and Prisca (or Priscilla), in Phrygia, a province of Asia Minor. Montanus, a former priest of the pagan Phrygian cult of Cybele (Kybele), was converted to Christianity around AD 155 and continued his prophecies after his conversion.[123] His movement, which called for reliance on the spontaneity of the Holy Spirit's guidance and was condemned as heretical for its belief in new prophetic revelations, lasted up to the sixth century.[124] What we know of the movement is from three primary sources: Eusebius of Caesarea, Epiphanius of Salamis, and Tertullian. The first two, both bishops of the Church, present the Montanists in a negative light, while Tertullian, who was himself a Montanist, defends them. Several modern works allude to Epiphanius correlating Montanism with ecstatic utterances, but no substantiation for such claims has been found in any source texts. Other

123. Burgess, "Montanism," in *DPCM* 339; revised in *NIDPCM* 903–4; cf. Hurst, *History*, 1:235.

124. A good source for a deeper historical overview of the Montanist movement is the time-tested article, "Montanists," in McClintock and Strong, *Cyclopedia*, 6:526–30.

references to Montanists can be found in the writings of Jerome and Didymus of Alexandria, but these have no relevance to the debate over Monanism and its purported relation to *glossolalia*.

The most crucial of these sources for this debate is the account by Eusebius (c. AD 260–339), Bishop of Caesarea and Church historian. One must bear in mind that his account is a critical report on the Montanist movement, with rhetoric that sometimes borders on vitriol. Judging from the severity of Eusebius' attack, one may infer that the Montanists by this time had grown into a populist movement that posed a threat to the institutional Church. Nevertheless, Eusebius himself expressed some doubts about the account provided to him concerning the Montanists by an unknown author, stating: "They say that these things happened in this manner. But as we did not see them, O friend, we do not pretend to know."[125] For this reason, Eusebius' account must be taken under advisement with a degree of circumspection and skepticism.

The key text is found in the *Church History* of Eusebius, which presents a narrative about two Montanist followers who went into a state of ecstasy and uttered strange sounds. What exactly were these sounds? Were they foreign languages, ecstatic speech, or something else? Is this, as some allege, one of the earliest Christian expressions of "tongues" since Pentecost? These questions lie at the heart of the discussion, and our answers must necessarily depend on what we find in the actual text that is used to link Montanist with modern Pentecostal or Charismatic tongues. Here is the text (with key phrases italicized):

> There is said to be a certain village called Ardabau in that part of Mysia, which borders upon Phrygia. There first, they say, when Gratus was proconsul of Asia, a recent convert, Montanus by name, through his unquenchable desire for leadership, gave the adversary opportunity against him. And he became beside himself, and *being suddenly in a sort of frenzy and ecstasy, he raved, and began to babble and utter strange things*, prophesying in a manner contrary to the constant custom of the Church handed down by tradition from the beginning.
>
> Some of those who heard his *spurious utterances* at that time were indignant, and they rebuked him as one that was possessed, and that was under the control of a demon, and was led by a deceitful spirit, and was distracting the multitude; and they forbade him to talk, remembering the distinction drawn by the Lord and his warning to guard watchfully against the coming

125. Eusebius, *Church History*, NPNF 2/1:231–32; cf. Eusebius, *Church History: A New Translation*, book 5.

of false prophets. But others imagining themselves possessed of the Holy Spirit and of a prophetic gift, were elated and not a little puffed up; and forgetting the distinction of the Lord, they challenged the mad and insidious and seducing spirit, and were cheated and deceived by him. In consequence of this, he could no longer be held in check, so as to keep silence.

Thus, by artifice, or rather by such a system of wicked craft, the devil, devising destruction for the disobedient, and being unworthily honored by them, secretly excited and inflamed their understandings which had already become estranged from the true faith. And he stirred up besides two women, and filled them with the false spirit, so that they *talked wildly and unreasonably and strangely*, like the person already mentioned. And the spirit pronounced them blessed as they rejoiced and gloried in him, and puffed them up by the magnitude of his promises. But sometimes he rebuked them openly in a wise and faithful manner, that he might seem to be a reprover. But those of the Phrygians that were deceived were few in number.[126]

The interpretation of this text centers on the meaning of the word *glossolalia*. If *glossolalia* means humanly unintelligible utterances, and if this were what we found in both the ancient Christian gift of tongues and in the Montanists, then a connection between them would be potentially possible. If the phenomena exhibited by either community, however, failed to conform to this definition, then no connection between them is possible, and further discussion is irrelevant. Those who try to make this connection usually assume that *glossolalia* was practiced by the ancient Church. This assumption, however, ignores the fact that *glossolalia* is a modern theory that scholars began using as a framework for interpreting the Christian doctrine of tongues in the early nineteenth century. Technically the term *glossolalia* should not be used to describe antecedents to the Christian doctrine of tongues any earlier than the nineteenth century, because it then becomes an anachronism. Since the term has become so entrenched in the popular mind of contemporary scholars and readers alike, however, the anachronism will be indulged temporarily so as to permit this investigation to run its course.

Pentecostal and Charismatic scholars often take a positive view of Montanism, finding some parallels to their own experience. Some find antecedents to their own tongues-speaking experience in the strange vocalizations of the Montanists. Heidi Baker, for example, ties in this conviction with widely-held Pentecostal assumptions about Church history in her dissertation "Pentecostal Experience: Towards a Reconstructive Theology of

126. Eusebius, *Church History*, NPNF 2/1:231, §§7–9.

Glossolalia" (1995), claiming that the original gift of tongues found in the primitive Church, along with other gifts of the Holy Spirit, were lost when the Church became institutionalized—until Montanus rediscovered them; then they were forgotten again until the Pentecostal movement revived them 1800 years later.[127] In the entry on "Montanism" in the acclaimed *Dictionary of Pentecostal and Charismatic Movements*, Stanley Burgess, the distinguished professor of Christian history at Regent University and Professor Emeritus of Missouri State University, claims that the gift of speaking in tongues flourished with the Montanists and later influenced the *glossolalic speaking* of the eighteenth-century Camisards in south-central France, who then left a legacy for modern Pentecostals to follow.[128] Another theologian who has closely studied the Pentecostal movement, Frederick Dale Bruner, also suggests a connection: "Montanism interests us as the prototype of almost everything Pentecostalism seeks to represent," he writes.[129] Indeed, examining the Montanist movement, especially in light of the kind of thorough coverage offered by the renowned nineteenth-century scholar, August Neander's *History of the Christian Religion and Church during the First Three Centuries* (German original, 1825), suggests many parallels between the two parties.[130]

Such parallels, however, do not of themselves entail an actual Montanist connection with the traditional Christian gift of tongues, as some suggest. A close examination of the details reveals that the actual historical evidence for any such connection is extremely thin. The critical Greek word used throughout the New Testament for "tongues," *glōssa* (γλῶσσα), does not even appear in the text. The presence of this word is indispensable for making a credible connection between the presumed *glossolalia* of Montanism and the Christian gift of speaking in tongues. The absence of this word is a critical point that can be confirmed easily by comparing the Greek, Latin, and English translations of the text.[131]

It is instructive to consider the very different answers to the question about the Montanists and *glossolalia* that two scholars arrived at after researching the question. On the one hand, the aforementioned Christopher Forbes, a specialist in ancient history and early Christianity at Macquarie University, argues that no conclusive evidence exists that the Montanists practiced *glossolalia*. He writes:

127. Baker, "Pentecostal Experience," 79–80.
128. Burgess, "Montanism," in *DPCM* 339; revised in *NIDPCM* 903–4.
129. Bruner, *Theology*, 37.
130. Neander, *History*, 327.
131. See Sullivan, *GOTP*, s.v. "Eusebius on Montanism," para. 4.

If Montanist prophecy was in any sense analogous to glossolalia it is quite remarkable that no ancient writer ever noticed or commented on this fact. Though it is certainly true that Montanist prophecy was characterized by ecstasy (in the modern sense), and occasionally by oracular obscurity, there is no unambiguous evidence whatsoever that it took glossolalic form.[132]

On the other hand, Rex D. Butler, Associate Professor of Church History and Patristics at Baptist Theological Seminary in New Orleans, argues that elements of the Montanist text correlate with *glossolalia*. He directly counters Forbes' claims, first, by focusing on the role of the interpreter. If the prophecy were given in intelligible speech, he asks, then why would the service of the prophetess Maximillia, an interpreter (ἑρμηνεύτην), be required? Second, he suggests that Forbes overlooks the fact that the prophets utilized both intelligible and unintelligible speech. Third, he argues against Forbes' definition of the Greek word, *xenophonein* (ξενοφωνεῖν), in the source text, which Forbes takes to mean "to speak as a foreigner," whereas Butler takes it to mean "to speak strangely." Butler adds that if the term is combined with *lalein* (λαλεῖν), which is found in Eusebius' text in the construction, *lalein kai xenophōnein* (λαλεῖν καὶ ξενοφωνεῖν), then the phrase could be translated as "chatter" or "babble." Finally, Butler concludes: "Forbes' arguments are not sufficient to overturn the historical understanding that Montanists engaged in glossolalia."[133]

Since the arguments on both sides rest on ancient sources and linguistics, the issue requires a closer look. Butler fails to address Forbes' argument fully. He omits mentioning Forbes' observation that if Montanist prophecy was in any sense analogous to *glossolalia*, it is quite remarkable that no ancient writer ever noticed or commented on this fact. Forbes is right here. No ancient writer, Christian or otherwise, made any connection between Montanist and Christian "tongues," a fact amply confirmed by the subsequent chapters of the present work. The *only* historical reference that could connect Montanism remotely with *glossolalia* is an obscure note by Tertullian, a Montanist, who included in a list of the offices in the Church the office of prophecy, healing, and *diverse kinds of tongues*.[134] This confirms the continued existence of "tongues" but fails to go any further. It does not describe what "tongues" were or what role they had within the Church. The text is therefore of little use in resolving this question.

132. Forbes, *Prophecy*, 160.
133. Butler, *New Prophecy*, 32–33.
134. Tertullian, *Against Marcion*, 410.

Butler's strongest argument, at least on first appearance, rests on his question of why an interpreter, Maximillia, would be required if the prophecy were given in intelligible speech.[135] This argument appears to be a strong one, however, only as long as one focuses on classical Greek works without referring to ecclesiastical writings. These Greek sources show that the function of interpretation was most useful in dreams, visions, or prophecy. Plato, for instance, wrote that interpreters were needed for understanding dreams and prophecies since those engaged in prophesying had temporarily lost their wits and could not be expected to explain their thoughts correctly.[136] Aristotle describes how the art of interpreting is a special gift that is especially required when meanings are more difficult to discern.[137] Butler, however, stops here and makes no effort to consider the institutional Church's historical perspective on the subject. Historically, the use of *interpreters* within the Church did not mean the assistance of someone to translate heavenly or divine words or experiences. It had a much more mundane, practical function. For example, in the fourth-century church in Egypt, the role of an *interpreter* was something akin to an ecclesiastical minor order ranking just below that of a *lector*. G. W. H. Lampe attests to this in his *Patristic Greek Lexicon*, citing as his source the *Euchologium* (sacramentary) of Serapion of Thmuis, Egypt (fl. c. AD 330–360), a supporter of Athanasius in the struggle against Arianism.[138] As we will see in volume 3 of the present work, this practice of using *interpreters* is well attested by other sources, such as fifth-century Alexandrian texts and, much later, even in the writings of the great thirteenth-century scholar, St. Thomas Aquinas. These sources did not define the task of the interpreter as having any divine or mystical significance, but simply as serving the duty of translating from one language to another.

When one examines the issue in light of both classical Greek and ecclesiastical literature, it is hard to sustain the view that the Montanists spoke in *glossolalic* tongues. The possibility is too remote from the context and anachronistic. The fact that the speech in question was "wild" and "strange" does not offer strong support for the view that the speech was *glossolalic* or that the interpreter was translating a heavenly language. It could more plausibly have involved a complex form of human speech requiring someone to explain it—speech involving metaphors, symbols, or hexameter poetry, as Herodotus described the language of the Delphic Oracle.

---

135. Epiphanius, *Adversus Hæreses*, 876.
136. Plato, *Complete*, 9:71e–72a.
137. Aristotle, *On the Soul*, 8:348–73 ("On Prophecy in Sleep").
138. Lampe, *Patristic Greek Lexicon*, 459.

Butler also argues that the prophets understood *both* intelligible and unintelligible words so that the interpreter's role cannot be restricted, as he accuses Forbes of supposing, to only intelligible language. Theoretically, Butler could be right about this; but his argument is once again significantly weakened by his omission of any reference to almost eighteen hundred years of ecclesiastical writing on the subject. Ecclesiastical literature overwhelmingly supports the miracle of tongues as involving actual human languages. How this miracle worked was a matter of dispute through Church history right up until the nineteenth century, but it was *never* understood as involving a heavenly or non-human language. Butler fails to address this tension, let alone resolve it.

A critical question in the debate concerning the relation between Montanism and Christian tongues hinges on the meaning of the phrase *lalein kai xenophōnein* (λαλεῖν καὶ ξενοφωνεῖν) in the text of Eusebius above. The first word, *lalein*, simply means "to speak." There is little debate about this verb, just as with the word *kai*, which is simply a conjunction meaning "and," connecting the other two words. The second verb, *xenophōnein*, is where some room for differences of interpretation occurs. The first and most direct translation would be "speaking and saying foreign things"— where the prefix *xeno*, as in the word "xenophobic," means "foreign." This is the translation that Forbes is inclined to accept. Butler, however, takes *xenophōnein* to mean to "chatter" or "babble," and hence, *glossolalia*.

The oldest Greek dictionary, the massive *Thesaurus Graecae Linguae* first published by Henri Estienne (Henricus Stephanus) in 1572 and slightly revised in the 1800s, remains the definitive dictionary for ancient Greek from which subsequent dictionaries generally cull their definitions. This dictionary defines *xenophōnein* (ξενοφωνεῖν) and its cognates in terms of speaking "unwanted" or "unfamiliar" things, or speaking in the "sound of a foreign language."[139] Donnegan's *New Greek and English Lexicon* (1836) defines it as meaning "to speak in a foreign tongue, or in a foreign, or unusual manner."[140] Sophocles' *Greek Lexicon of the Roman and Byzantine Periods* (1900) has "to speak or talk strangely."[141] Lampe's *Patristic Lexicon* (1978) has "to speak strange things," referencing Montanus, then adding as a second definition, "startle, perturb, astonish by strange words or teaching."[142]

These dictionaries fail to offer a definitive resolution to the Butler-Forbes debate. Estienne's dictionary, despite its antiquity, does not give an

---

139. Estienne et al., *Thesaurus* (1865), 5:1657.

140. Donnegan, *New Greek and English Lexicon*, 883.

141. Sophocles, *Greek Lexicon*, 790.

142. Lampe, *Patristic Greek Lexicon*, 932.

adequate background for the word, and the resulting ambiguity is transmitted to the later dictionaries, whether or not they emphasized the theme of foreign languages or strange and exotic utterances. Lampe's 1978 definition strengthens the aspect of strange or exotic utterances by adding the Montanists as a source definition.

The axis of both arguments turns on the understanding of the Eusebian text concerning Montanism. The text itself has received little critical evaluation. Bearing in mind that the English translation quoted above is from the antiquated translation found in *Select Library of the Nicene and Post-Nicene Fathers* (1886–90), a closer examination of this actual text may provide more clues concerning whether Forbes or Butler has the more accurate interpretation

Eusebius' description of Montanist practices points to some form of Montanist synthesis that integrates ancient Greek rites into their sectarian Christian practice, which the Church rejected as alien to its traditions. This position is strengthened when we trace the usage of the word *ecstasy* in the text. Estienne's *Lexicon* refers to "religious frenzy," *enthousian* (ἐνθουσιᾶν), as a divinely inspired frenzy connected with the pagan Greek world of prophecy and the gods.[143] The dictionary offers several definitions, of which the closest relevant application, roughly translated from the Latin, is: "A kind of madness one distinguishes in . . . one who is out of his senses, insane, or inspired. Inspiration by the gods. Having been inspired by the gods, having been transformed, speaking foolishly."[144] Though ecstasy is often a favorable term depending on its usage, it has negative connotations here. The surrounding Eusebian text suggests an egregious syncretism of pagan Greek rites with the Christian practice that the bishop frowns upon as shockingly unacceptable.

No less problematic for the attempt to link Montanism to the Christian gift of tongues is the approach taken by the 1911 entry on "Montanism" in *The Catholic Encyclopedia*. There we read:

> The anonymous opponent of the sect [cited by Eusebius as his source] describes the method of prophecy (Eusebius, V, xvii, 2–3): first the prophet appears distraught with terror (*en parekstasei*), then follows quiet (*adeia kai aphobia*, fearlessness); beginning by studied vacancy of thought or passivity of intellect

---

143. Estienne et al., *Thesaurus* (1865), 3:1088.

144. The full original Latin text, referencing the Greek terms, reads: "*genus μανιας distinguens itidem inter παρακινῶν, Insanus, et ἐνθουσιων. Numine afflatus. Divino numine afflatus et in vatem mutatus ista hariolatur.*"

(*ekousios amathia*), he is seized by an uncontrollable madness (a*kousios mania psyches*).[145]

The article reflects the difficulties of translating Alexandrian Greek, and the author does not declare the source of his information. The question of divine inspiration, however, appears to be an underlying question throughout the Eusebian text. The ecclesial tradition, represented here by Eusebius, does not fault the notion of supernatural illumination. It was a question, rather, of its source: was it truly from God or from some other source? This was the dilemma confronting the Church. Eventually, it was determined that the Montanist practice lay outside the customary practice and doctrine of the Church. Thus, Eusebius condemned Montanus, as we saw, for "prophesying in a manner contrary to the constant custom of the Church handed down by tradition from the beginning." This view is reinforced by a play on words occurring in the Greek: Montanus "grants the *grand entrance* (*parodon*, πάροδον) for himself as one who opposes things," particularly "with respect to the *tradition handed down* (*paradosin*, παράδοσιν)" (emphasis added). In the larger context of the passage, the Greek play on words suggests that Montanus was trying to make out his version of frenzied utterances to be the new prophetic standard for the Church, but that it fell short and was dismissed as mere showmanship.[146]

The most plausible conclusion, in light of available Patristic writings, is that whatever the Montanists uttered in a state of frenzy has no relationship with the Christian doctrine of tongues. The late Notre Dame professor, Josephine Massyngbaerde Ford, refers in her *New Catholic Encyclopedia* article to the Montanist phenomenon as "hypnotically-induced" *xenophoneo* ("strange speech").[147] Even allowing for the loosest possible interpretation of Eusebius, a single passage from his writings is not enough to overturn multiple chapters on the subject produced by Augustine, Gregory Nazianzus, Cyril of Jerusalem, John of Damascus, Cyril of Alexandria, Epiphanius, Michael Psellos, Thomas Aquinas, Francisco Suárez, Pope Benedict XIV, and many others. Furthermore, the absence of the critical Greek word for tongues, *glōssa* (γλῶσσα), in the Eusebian text severely weakens any supposition of a Montanist connection to Christian tongues. Without this, the reference cannot be claimed as direct, substantive evidence, and must be rejected as the contrivance of a doubtful hypothesis. The Montanists were not exercising the Christian gift of tongues, but an entirely different spiritualistic rite peculiar to their sect. Butler is right in noting some correlation

---

145. Chapman, "Montanists," in *CE* 521–24.

146. Eusebius, *Historiæ Ecclesiasticæ*, 20:465–66.

147. Ford, "Glossolalia," 249–50; Ford, "Charismatic Gifts," 115.

between Montanism and ancient Greek prophecy, but any correlation to Christian tongues is tenuous at best. The modern Pentecostal-Charismatic attempt to connect Christian tongues-speaking with Montanism, in light of these facts, is a non-starter.

Near the beginning of this chapter, we noted the growing skepticism toward miracles that was a by-product of the ascendant Rationalism of the Age of Reason. This skepticism dovetailed with the anti-Catholicism of the Reformation era to yield a skeptical view of Patristic and medieval writings concerning miracles found in Catholic ecclesiastical writings. Together, these threads of anti-Catholic skepticism led to the Higher Critical approach to biblical interpretation that yielded the theory of *glossolalia*. Two additional pieces of the puzzle related to the development of contemporary views of "speaking in tongues," both from early Protestant anti-Catholicism, are the Cessationist movement and the interpolation of the "unknown tongues" construct in early Protestant translations of the Bible. These will be examined in chapter 5.

CHAPTER 5

Cessationism and the "Unknown Tongues" Construct

From the twenty-first century (John F. MacArthur Jr.)
back to the 1500s (Protestant Reformation)

IN THIS CHAPTER, WE shall delve back into two developments in the history of the Christian doctrine of tongues that have shaped the modern view of the practice and stem from the widespread anti-Catholicism that followed the Protestant Reformation. These are (1) the movement of Cessationism that developed especially in Calvinist circles following the Reformation, and (2) the Protestant convention of interpolating the adjective "unknown"—in the form of the construct, "unknown tongues"—into their English translations of the Bible. On the one hand, Cessationism, the belief that miraculous gifts ceased in apostolic times, did nothing to change the traditional definition of "tongues" as actual human languages, but it did reinforce a persistent Calvinist prejudice that what passes for "speaking in tongues" today in Pentecostal and Charismatic circles has no relation whatsoever to what went by that name in apostolic times. On the other hand, the "unknown tongues" construct did eventually provide direct reinforcement for the Pentecostal-Charismatic redefinition of "tongues" as a "private language of prayer and praise," although this was not at all its original intent, as we shall see. We shall begin with the Cessationist movement first, and then proceed to the "unknown tongues" construct in English Protestant translations of the Bible.

Cessationism

"Cessationism" (often contrasted with "Continuationism") is a theological term that developed in certain branches of Protestantism in which the belief prevailed, as it still does in some circles, that miracles have died out long ago in Church history.[1] It refers to the belief that the gift of miracles granted to the Apostles—the endowment of the ability to perform supernatural miracles—had the purpose in New Testament times of serving as a powerful, authenticating witness to the truth of the Gospel of Christ. Since those early years of the Church, however, that initial need for the Gospel to be authenticated by miraculous gifts has passed from the scene, it is said, along with Jesus and his Apostles, and has been replaced by the requirement of confident faith in the authority of Scripture. This Cessationist view is typically found in Calvinist circles—which include Presbyterians, various Reformed traditions such as the Dutch Reformed denominations, Reformed Baptists, and others—which adhere strictly to doctrines developed during the Protestant Reformation. The doctrine first emerged in England, peaked in the late 1600s, spread to other English-speaking countries and beyond, waned a bit in the 1800s, made a comeback again in the 1900s, and appears to be in general decline today. Nevertheless, it cannot be overlooked and constitutes an important part of Church history in any study of the doctrine of tongues.

Cessationists understand the gift of tongues to have been a miraculous gift in apostolic times involving the ability to speak in previously unlearned foreign languages. Therefore, they interpret the tongues of 1 Corinthians 12–14 in light of the tongues of Pentecost in Acts 2. They believe that this is the authentic interpretation of the gift of tongues and that this gift has ceased today. In their view, any attempt to interpret miraculous gifts—such as the gift of tongues or the gift of healing—as continuing today is based on an anachronistic misconception and theological error. Thus, the assumptions and practices of contemporary Pentecostals and Charismatics are viewed as fundamentally flawed. Such miracles as being able to supernaturally speak previously unlearned foreign languages, they believe, just don't happen anymore. As such, the Cessationist doctrine does not contribute to the contemporary redefinition of "tongues" as a "heavenly language" or "private language of prayer and praise," except insofar as it agrees that the current Charismatic practice of "tongues" is something non-miraculous and altogether different from the Church's traditional understanding of tongues.[2]

1. Wikipedia, s.v. "Cessationism versus Continuationism," https://en.wikipedia.org/wiki/Cessationism_versus_continuationism, para. 1–3.

2. As noted in ch. 2 above, however, some Calvinist today have come to accept the "Third Wave" claim that biblical miracles continue in present times.

The subject of miracles is one of the most complex of the Christian faith. Theologians have tried for centuries to harmonize the mystery of miracles with both common sense and science, but definitive answers still remain as elusive as the quest to find answers itself remains fascinating. The subject of Cessationism therefore deeply touches on some basic assumptions about the supernatural claims at the heart of the Christian faith.

Cessationism takes some surprising twists and turns historically and cannot easily be defined in simple black and white terms. A better term than "cessation" to describe the prevailing belief at the beginning of the movement may be "de-emphasis," since the earliest Protestant leaders still continued to believe in miracles, albeit in a restricted sense. *Cessationism* properly refers to a later development found in a branch of the movement that came to explicitly deny the continued divine bestowal of miraculous spiritual gifts (*charisms*)—extraordinary powers given by the Holy Spirit—in the present age. The movement arose amidst the controversies of the Protestant Reformation for several reasons, which can be understood from a variety of perspectives.

Firstly, it arose as a Protestant response to what was perceived as an excessive and misguided Catholic preoccupation with miracles and the veneration of miracle-working saints. Protestants, therefore, denounced these features of Catholicism outright and formulated an alternative theological framework that focused exclusively on the precepts and truths they found in Scripture without any emphasis on miracles. In their view, nothing superseded, paralleled, or equaled the authority of Scripture. "Scripture alone!" (*Sola Scriptura!*) was their battle cry. Their view of miracles was that they were intended primarily as authentications of the initial ministry and message of Christ and His Apostles, and that such miracles tended to occur less and less as the New Testament period came to a close. Their inference was that miracles had essentially ceased at that time.

The *Sola Scriptura* emphasis, of course, gave rise to a new problem, especially as it tended to diminish, if not completely marginalize, not only the documents of the official magisterium (doctrinal authority) of the Catholic Church, but the importance of any extra-biblical ecclesiastical literature throughout Church history. This problem also led, in some instances, to an extreme form of "Bibliolatry"—the idolatrous veneration of the Bible as an end in itself. In some cases, it could result in the Bible being interpreted so legalistically (without regard for tradition, reason, conscience, or consent) that the resultant tyranny of the Protestant doctrinal authorities and their interpretations became no less oppressive than the tyranny they imputed to the Catholic Church. The often-technical focus of such authorities on biblical words and semantics led to a world of academic elites holding court over abstract and arcane interpretations that only a few could understand or master.

Secondly, Cessationism developed as a counter-argument against Catholics. Where Catholics argued that Protestantism lacked the backing of divine authority because it lacked confirmation through miracles, Protestants volleyed back that Catholic authorities had condoned and promoted unorthodox views and practices through the manipulation of supposed miracles to the point of overriding Scripture and altering basic Christian identity and doctrine. The rejection of Catholic miracles thus became a rallying point in the Protestant endeavor to secure its own identity.

Thirdly, Cessationism developed in England amidst an era of fear and hatred of Catholicism. England in the late 1600s was politically rife with anti-Catholic prejudices. Any person or idea remotely associated with Catholicism was sure to be disparaged and condemned. There were constant fears of "Popish plots" against the English government, like the Gunpowder Plot of 1606. Virtually any public disaster, such as the Great Fire of London in 1666, was immediately blamed on Catholic sedition. Such fears were exploited and incorporated into English Protestant theology and are reflected in the development of the Cessationist doctrine.

In the earliest phases of this doctrine, the Protestant rejection of the miraculous claims of Catholicism had not yet led to a complete rejection of a belief in the continuing occurrence of the gift of miracles. The Reformers continued to hold a limited view of miraculous gifts, particularly those that could not be traced to Catholic sources. Within a century after the Reformation, however, the Protestant *de-emphasis* on miracles began to expand beyond its original anti-Catholic impetus and develop its own distinctive *Cessationist* characteristics. The doctrine developed into an eclectic mixture of ideas cobbled together from the Rationalist movement and from some uniquely English theological sources.

Protestant writers argued that the majority of the countless miracles reported in Catholic literature throughout Church history were merely exaggerated stories arising from overactive imaginations that amounted to little more than myths and legends. On the one hand, Protestant accusations of exaggeration may seem to have some credibility. When contemporary readers study the accounts of miracles in older Catholic literature, the descriptions of what happened sometimes seem to pass beyond the suspension of normal laws of nature and to venture into the world of utterly credulous fantasy. On the other hand, prudence dictates that not every claim of a miracle should be thrown out simply because it comes from a Catholic source. Each claim should be evaluated on its own merits, and we should be willing to let the resulting judgments surprise us in either direction. Even in those cases where miraculous accounts remain doubtful, they attest to perceptions that should be respected at least for their didactic and historical value.

In time it became clear that the Protestant community was divided on the topic of miracles. The doctrine of Cessationism was not promoted within certain Protestant traditions, like the burgeoning Methodist and Holiness movements of the 1800s. Nevertheless, Cessationists seemed to have some good arguments in their favor. They could cite several high-profile Church Fathers in apparent support of their views, and their claims that miracles had diminished and ceased after the death of the Apostles appeared to have some historical credibility. Some Church Fathers had concluded that the visual display of miracles could easily lead to exhibitionism, pride, and even the temptations of consumerism and personal gain. Miracles, as such, were seen by the Church as ultimately having little value in developing virtuous Christian character; and early Church writers like Origen, Chrysostom, and Augustine regarded spiritual growth in virtue and holiness as far more important than having miraculous gifts.

According to early Protestant writers, it was Chrysostom and Augustine who initially promoted the de-emphasis on miracles in Church history by their observation that the occurrences of miracles had declined since apostolic times. What these Protestant writers failed to note, however, is that this belief in a declining number of miracles and concurrent de-emphasis on them was never affirmed universally throughout the Church. It was absorbed into a Cessationist hypothesis that looked like it could find support in certain passages from Chrysostom and Augustine. For nearly 1,100 years, from the time of these Church Fathers to the rise of Protestant Cessationism, however, belief in miracles continued to flourish unabated.

Nevertheless, once word of Chrysostom's and Augustine's "de-emphasis" on miracles spread among Protestant scholars during the Reformation era, it eventually led to the more radical claims of absolute *Cessationism*, the belief that miraculous gifts had ceased altogether. Yet Cessationism was never a grass-roots movement. It never became a central doctrine of the numerous Protestant sects throughout Europe and the British Isles. It certainly was never embraced by the Catholic Church. It was a doctrine promoted by Puritans and other Calvinist thinkers in the 1600s and has surfaced in various forms ever since.

Medieval Background

Cessationism cannot be understood fully apart from the background of the profusion of miraculous claims in the late-medieval environment, which helped elicit the doctrine as a Protestant reaction. From the tenth to the thirteenth century, there was a pronounced uptick in European intellectual inquiry, culminating in the period of "High Scholasticism," which saw the recovery of Greek philosophy and the formulation of a Greco-Roman intellectual synthesis that combined the claims of faith and reason into a compelling and coherent belief system, largely due to the monumental synthesis of Thomas Aquinas. After Aquinas, however, this synthesis was gradually eroded by competing interpretations and the skeptical movements of the late Middle Ages. No less damaging than these intellectual and spiritual challenges at this time were the devastating plagues that ravaged Europe (as well as Asian and African continents), destroying between 30–60 percent of the European population.[3] In the wake of this devastation, many of the erstwhile leaders of the Christian world were dead and gone. Those who had helped build and sustain the traditional institutions of Catholic Europe, those who had been familiar with the Greek language and culture upon which Europe's Greco-Roman civilization had been built, like those who had been guardians of the classical Roman institutions in earlier years, were simply swept away, leaving a huge social, economic, and religious vacuum. The ensuing political and social instability, the outbreak of wars between European foes (motivated by religion, politics, or economics), the Muslim conquest of Constantinople and later threats they posed to Europe, along with famines and shifts in climate, left many Europeans vulnerable to doubts about the adequacy of their social and religious institutions in confronting the immense challenges of the world. In many respects, the breakdown of the medieval synthesis, the plagues, the social turmoil, and the Protestant Reformation all conspired to launch Europe on a path towards redefining itself in a more secular framework. These and other factors propelled Europeans in early-modern times to venture far beyond their shores in search of new lands, peoples and cultures, opening their doors to new commercial opportunities as well as new ideas.

The emotional scars inflicted by the plagues and religious wars left a lingering impression in many minds that the transcendent religious claims of Christendom had lost some of their earlier luminescence. Christians formed by earlier medieval traditions viewed themselves as witnessing a power struggle between the spiritual forces of good and evil unfolding before them. In times past, Christians had believed that the elements of nature, wars, plagues, health, weather, agriculture, prosperity, success, or failure were due in some measure to spiritual conflict between cosmic forces. As Thomas Howard writes, they believed that "God was in heaven, Beelzebub

---

3. Alchon, *Pest*, 21.

in hell, that the Holy Ghost had impregnated the Virgin Mary, and that the earth and sky were full of angelic and demonic conflict."[4] They believed that the terror of war and pestilence and death was "the terror of devils," and that the thing that was making them scream and foam was not their inability to cope, but the unseen world of demons; and that the thing that was clawing out their entrails was not cancer, but "divine wrath."[5]

In this cosmic battle, there were two ways in which it was thought that peace and stability could be secured. The first was through rigorous attempts to spiritually purify communities and individuals of any perceived evil, ridding communities of witches, divination, and other works perceived to be demonic. Since Satan was perceived as capable of employing natural means against humanity, such as plagues, it was thought that social, physical, and ecological harmony could only be secured by directly defeating Satan. Germs, bacteria, hygiene, and pathogens had not yet been discovered. Thus, there was a heightened sensitivity to things like personal holiness and the tacit belief that if a people pursued absolute purity in the form of sincerely upright and pious lives, they could appease divine wrath and secure divine blessing.

The second means of securing peace and stability was through the mediation and intercession of the saints. The doctrine of the intercession of saints was one of long standing in the Church, but it could also be exploited and abused. The veneration of saints was at an all-time high just preceding the Reformation, and in some cases, as pointed out by Catholics such as Erasmus as well as Protestants, it reached extremes that could almost be mistaken for the polytheistic idolatries of ancient paganism.[6] Sainthood was also big business. The canonization of a saint had significant economic and political benefits for the saint's hometown. This incentivized concerted efforts by communities to promote local causes for canonization. Franco Mormando, in a book on St. Francis Xavier (1506–52) published by The Jesuit Institute of Boston College in 2006, relates the intense campaign for his canonization, involving enormous amounts of time and money, and the patronage of "powerful people in high places" to succeed.[7] Xavier was the Jesuit missionary to India and the Far East whose evangelistic exploits opened up the European imagination to new and exotic worlds. He was also an admirable example of Catholic veracity in a time when the Church was losing many followers to Protestantism. His legendary status was

4. Howard, *Chance, or the Dance?*, 11.

5. Howard, *Chance, or the Dance?*, 12.

6. Cunningham, *Brief History*, 25, 51–52.

7. Mormando, "Introduction," 9–22.

challenged after his canonization by evidence that purportedly contradicted the claim that he was able to miraculously speak in foreign languages during his mission work. The canonization process had referenced this claim of miraculous tongue-speaking without what many viewed as adequate attention to scientific criteria for evaluating evidence. The refusal of ecclesiastical officials to retract what many contemporaries regarded as mere "myth" appeared to demonstrate serious flaws in the canonization process, seized upon by Protestant critics, which took well over a century for the Church to adequately address. Pope Benedict XIV (1675–1758) finally wrote a major treatise that was instrumental in correcting these defects concerning evidential criteria, addressing the question of tongues, and tightening up the canonization process.[8]

Accounts of miraculous events, both past and present, may strike readers today as hyperbolic or fanciful, and it is often difficult to sort out fact from fiction due to the lack of adequate evidential criteria by which to evaluate claims. Yet contemporary Christians would do well to remember that such accounts are not the exclusive preserve of the ancient or medieval Church, but are found throughout Scripture as well. Many of the Old and New Testament accounts of miracles may strike secularized contemporary readers as no less fanciful than those of medieval history. For example, sepulchers of saints have served as famous pilgrimage sites throughout history (and even into modern times), because it was believed that the relic bones of saints could bring healing simply by touching them—much as the bones of Elisha were reported to have caused the dead body of an ancient Israelite to be miraculously resurrected when it was dropped into his grave and touched his bones (2 Kgs 13:21); or as even the handkerchiefs or aprons touched by the Apostle Paul, when carried to the sick, were said to have cured them of diseases and evil spirits (Acts 19:12); or as those who first touched the water in the pool of Bethesda after it was stirred by an angel were said to have been healed (John 5:2–9). Princeton Professor Peter Brown, credited with creating the field of study known as Late Antiquity (AD 250–800), offers an illuminating description of the beginning of Christian veneration of the relic remains of early saints and martyrs and the role of tombs, shrines, relics, and pilgrimages connected with their bodily remains in his book, *The Cult of the Saints: Its Rise and Function in Latin Christianity.*[9] Like biblical history, Church history is rife with miraculous occurrences even up to modern times. An Eastern Orthodox Christian reported in 2010 that when the skull of Chrysostom was brought out for a brief public viewing in 2007 at the

8. Benedict XIV, *Lambertinis*, 547–61; cf. Benedict XIV, *De Servorum*, 724–38.
9. Brown, *Cult of the Saints*, chs. 1, 4.

Monastery of Mt. Athos, some people who were present were miraculously healed of illnesses.[10]

While there is no good reason to doubt the historical occurrence of miracles, if one believes in the supernatural at all, it is nevertheless not always easy to know where to draw the line between credible belief and sheer credulity. The most popular book of the Middle Ages, *The Golden Legend* (*Legenda Aurea*), is a compilation of miraculous stories relating to the saints that are easy to dismiss as overblown, especially when not even the original collator reportedly believed them all to be true.[11] Simple child-like faith can sometimes merge toward credulity and even superstition; and compromising mixtures of faith with superstition, myth, and magic, were widespread during the late medieval and Reformation periods. These tendencies were noted by the Anglican historian, William Lecky, in his well-written work, *History of the Rise and Influence of the Spirit of Rationalism in Europe* (1865):

> There was scarcely a village or a church that had not, at some time, been the scene of supernatural interposition. The powers of light and the powers of darkness were regarded as visibly struggling for mastery. Saintly miracles, supernatural cures, startling judgments, visions, prophecies, and prodigies of every order, attested the activity of the one, while witchcraft and magic, with all their attendant horrors, were the visible manifestations of the other.[12]

While one must be mindful of the anti-Catholic Whig proclivities of such a writer, Lecky, to his credit, makes no distinction between Catholic and Protestant communities in his detailed criticism of such tendencies.

Jane Shaw, a historian of religion at the historically Unitarian Harris Manchester College at Oxford, distinguishes between Catholic and Protestant outlooks as follows:

> Holy places and objects, and the rituals associated with those material manifestations of the divine, were vital to late medieval piety. Medieval England was a sacred landscape filled with pilgrimage sites and shrines: the tombs of famous saints such as Thomas Becket at Canterbury; the shrines of local saints such as Frideswide in Oxford; and sites of other relics, such as that of the "true bloo" at the Cistercian Abbey in Hailes, Gloucestershire. The shrines at all these and many other places such as

10. Sanidopoulos, "Contemporary Miracles," para. 1–3.

11. Cunningham, *Brief History*, 32; Voraigne, *Medieval Sourcebook*, 1:1–3.

12. Lecky, *History*, 27–28.

Westminster, Canterbury, and St Albans were places of pilgrimage to which the sick went to be healed, hoping for a miracle.

The belief system that undergirded this set of religious practices was challenged and many of its material manifestations destroyed at the Protestant Reformation. For many of the sixteenth-century reformers and their Protestant heirs, miracles had ceased with biblical times. Miracles were to be viewed with suspicion precisely because they were associated with intermediary figures and objects—saints, relics, and holy places—and all the ritualistic trappings of Roman Catholicism. Most Protestants came to think it wrong to claim that a human institution had the power to work miracles: saints and relics were unnecessary, interrupting the newly privileged relationship between God and the individual, and therefore challenging God's omnipotence. To rely on anything but this relationship with God was, for the strictest of Protestants, blasphemous. Even petitionary prayer was seen as suspicious by some; a person should not tempt providence for the impossible. Only scripture was to be the bedrock of faith. Signs and wonders were to be discarded for the promises made by God in his Word.[13]

Despite the growing influence of the Protestant Reformation and the rising Rationalist and secular influences stemming from the *via moderna* in the late medieval and early modern periods, however, the majority of Europeans and Britons continued to be dominated largely by an otherworldly view of life and history that saw behind mundane events the battle of unseen forces. In this, they displayed their affinity with the outlook of the Apostle Paul who declared, "For we are not contending against flesh and blood, but against the principalities, against the powers, against the world rulers of this present darkness, against the spiritual hosts of wickedness in the heavenly places" (Eph 6:12 RSV). Yet this also showed the degree to which the rational, empirical, and scientific markers that modern historians look for in tracing the development of Western thought were still in their infancy.

Another influence that should be noted at this time is the improvement of literacy and increased availability of literature after the revolution of printing with moveable type launched in 1440 by Johannes Gutenberg of Mainz, Germany, whose first printed book was the Catholic Vulgate, commonly called the *Gutenberg Bible* (1450). Protestants were quick to exploit the invention of the printing press in the propagation of their ecclesiastical revolution in the sixteenth century. Margaret Aston, in her book, *Lollards*

---

13. Shaw, *Miracles*, 21.

and Reformers: Images and Literacy in Late Medieval Religion, described
how the press challenged the traditional role of the Church:

> Ecclesiastical attitudes towards the role of books and the written
> word in the church's main task of making and teaching believ-
> ers, had been fixed long before and were slow to change. They
> were geared to a world in which literacy was a preserve of the
> minority, and the minority were churchmen. The church had
> developed in a society whose culture was predominantly oral,
> and in which it had to be assumed that the mass of believers
> were, and would remain, remote from the world of letters and
> learning.[14]

Aston shows that medieval society was primarily an oral culture and
highly illiterate outside of the clerical ranks. Studies suggest that literacy
was less than 20 percent in the 1400s, with functional literacy being possibly even lower.[15] We must exercise caution, of course, in supposing that
the push for literacy and production of printed literature was exclusively a
Protestant affair. Upwards of twenty Catholic translations of the Bible into
German were in existence before Luther's German New Testament (1522)
saw the light of day, the vast majority of them published in the 1400s.[16] The
best-known Reformation-era English translations of the Bibles were not
published before the seventeenth century—the Protestant King James Version (1603–11), and the Catholic Douay-Rheims Bible (1582–1610), completed one year earlier by exiled English Catholics in France.

Protestant perceptions of this era are indispensable for understanding
the push toward Cessationism among English Protestants; and these perceptions, in whatever degree they were or were not justified, were that the
Catholic Church was rife with abuse, credulity, and a level of superstition
regarding miracles that bordered on a belief in magic. Small wonder that
the Latin words, *Hoc est corpus*—from the priest's consecration of the Body
of Christ in the Catholic Mass, "*Hoc est enim corpus meum*" ("For this is
my body")—quickly became "Hocus-pocus" in the popular imagination. To
justify their de-emphasis on miracles, then, Protestants had to revise their
interpretation of Church history and reframe the history of miracles in the
Church.

---

14. Aston, *Lollards,* 105.

15. Roser and Ortiz-Ospina, "Literacy," para. 7.

16. Wikipedia, s.v. "Bible Translations into German," https://en.wikipedia.org/wiki/
Bible_translations_into_German, s.v. "Overview of German Bibles before Luther";
Maas, "Versions of the Bible," sec. on "German Versions"; Graham, *Where We Got the
Bible,* chs. 5–9.

Patristic Background

From the sixteenth century onward, Protestants began to assert that early Church literature following the apostolic age was silent concerning miracles. Some suggested that miracles declined after the death of the last Apostle around the end of the first century. Others argued that this decline and silence occurred after the canon of Scripture was closed. Still others insisted that the eclipse of miracles occurred after the Edict of Milan in AD 313, in which Constantine gave legal standing to the Church, allowing for the eventual establishment of Christianity as the religion of the Roman Empire.

This Cessationist view, however, has two difficulties.

First, it fails to acknowledge a decisive shift in the Church's focus that accompanied the geographical shift from Jerusalem to Rome as the center of early Christianity. Whereas Christian writers in earlier centuries were members of a minority sect focused primarily on evangelism and missionary activity, those in the fourth century belonged to a respected institution in the Roman Empire and were more interested in seeing how their doctrines stood up against influential Greek philosophical theories. Miracles continued to be reported, but they diminished in apologetic importance as attention shifted towards "faith seeking understanding" (*fides quaerens intellectum*), that is, faith seeking understanding through knowledge that could change one's worldview and offer a framework for applying the life-lessons of the Christian faith in everyday life. The best ready-made analytic tools for building such a framework were those provided by Greek philosophical traditions, and early Christian writers cannot be understood apart from this background of interaction with Greek philosophical traditions. The Apostle Paul attested to this when he stated that the "Jews demand signs while Greeks look for wisdom" (1 Cor 1:22 NIV).

Second, the Cessationist view ignores a wide swath of reported miracles that abound in ecclesiastical literature through Church history. These miracles are all rejected by Cessationists *tout court* because they are Catholic in origin and do not conform to the Cessationist narrative. They are rarely mentioned, even negatively, or even dismissed as myths or legends. This total disregard for the abundant Catholic record of miracles gives the impression that the Church has been silent on miracles during these centuries when it was not. This omission has sadly misled many later students of the Bible on the topic of miracles.

Modern Protestant historians often claim certain Church Fathers as patrons of Cessationism, as we have seen. The first of these is *John Chrysostom* (c. 349–407), the Archbishop of Constantinople and important early leader in the Church. In almost every piece of literature on speaking in tongues that references the Church Fathers, the following quotation from Chrysostom's Homily 29 on 1 Cor 12:1–2 inevitably seems to come up:

> This whole place is very obscure: but the obscurity is produced by our ignorance of the facts referred to and by their cessation, being such as then used to occur but now no longer take place. And why do they not happen now? Why look now, the cause too of the obscurity has produced us again another question: namely, why did they then happen, and now do so no more?[17]

This is a key text for those in the Cessationist movement who believe that the era of supernatural miracles ended with the establishment of the Church. Did Chrysostom really believe, however, that miracles had ceased? A superficial reading may suggest so, but a closer examination yields different results. If one reads deeper into his works, it becomes clear that he demonstrates an openness to the idea of miracles occurring through uniquely anointed individuals, but he never names anyone in his lifetime as having achieved such an "anointed" status. It is possible that he could be following the same line of thinking as Origen, who held that there was a decline of miracles that reflected a decline of virtue and lack of altruistic, pious, holy individuals in his generation.[18] This may be why Chrysostom venerated deceased saints who had achieved great sanctity in their lives. He believed that such individuals had miraculous powers not only during their lives, but that those who visited their graves after their death, venerating their memory and asking for their intercession, could be healed. Chrysostom demonstrates a cautionary approach to miracles. His disposition reflects a man who lived an ascetic life and believed that the goal of every Christian's life does not lie in external displays of dramatic healings or other miracles, but an interior life of humility, purity, and sanctity of one's soul. He also eschewed individualism in favor of the corporate good of the Body of Christ, the Church. In one of his homilies, "On the Holy Pentecost," he bluntly asserts that believers need no outward signs, minimizing the importance of externals. Beyond this, however, he leaves us with many unanswered questions.

Augustine, Bishop of Hippo (354–430) is another key Church Father singled out by Cessationists. Augustine states in *De vera religione* (*On True Religion*) 1:25.47 that miracles had ceased once the Church was established.[19] Thirty-seven years later, he realized his original work was being taken out

17. Chrysostom, *Homilies*, 168.

18. Sullivan, *GOTP*, s.v. "Origen on the Doctrine," sec. (c) *Against Celsus*, 7:8–9, para. 2

19. Augustine, *True Religion*, 248; cf. Augustine, *De vera religione*, 121–72.

of context and revised this comment, stating that when he first wrote *De vera religione* there were incredible miracles of Christian faith still happening within his world. However, he believed the penchant for miracles was a distraction from the building of true Christian character. He felt that if miracles were continually practiced and emphasized as a primary vehicle for propagating the Christian faith, people would become bored with this form of entertainment and disregard the greater message behind it. Jan Den Boeft, former professor of Latin at the Free University of Amsterdam and Utrecht University, states that, based on her research, Augustine maintained that the tongues of Pentecost, along with some other types of miracles (not all) found in the early Church, would no longer be repeated in the future.[20] Thus, Augustine held that the instances of certain kinds of miracles had declined or ceased, but not all miracles. Like Chrysostom, he maintained that individuals obsessed with promoting miracles were vulnerable to pride and inhibiting their spiritual growth. He also held that the gift of tongues in his time was transferred to the whole Church, because the body of Christ was now spread throughout the whole world, speaking all languages, so that the gift was now corporate rather than individual.[21]

Cyril of Alexandria (c. 376–444) is another figure who would seem capable of being enlisted in support of the Cessationist cause, although he is unaccountably overlooked by most parties to that discussion. His *Commentary on Zephaniah* contains the statement that those endowed with the miraculous ability to speak in foreign languages at the first Pentecost retained this miraculous gift for the rest of their lives, but that this gift did not persist after these persons died.[22] The texts of the *Commentary* available today, however, contain passages mixed with added text by the famous theologian and teacher, Didymus of Alexandria (AD 313–398), so that we cannot confidently ascribe proper attribution to Cyril for the original statement. Not all Alexandrians took the view expressed in the *Commentary*. For example, they recognized that the founder of communal monasticism, Pachomius (AD 292–348), was granted the ability to miraculously speak in foreign languages.[23] Why Cyril's text never made it into the Cessationist debate is perplexing. Perhaps it was because of his Alexandrian Greek background, and the fact that his works were marginal to the predominantly Latin scholarship of the Roman Catholic world upon which Protestants

---

20. Boeft, "Miracles," 58.

21. Augustine, *Enarratio*, 147:19 (PL 37:1929); Augustine, *Expositions*, 3:464.

22. Cyril of Alexander, *Commentarius*, PG 71:1005–6.

23. Pachomius, *Chronicles and Rules*, 51–52; cf. the Greek original, Pachomius, *Vitae Graecae*, 154–55.

predominantly relied for their sources; or perhaps because Protestants had exempted Chrysostom and Augustine from their anti-Catholic bias, while Cyril failed to make the cut. In any case, although he held that miraculous tongues had ceased, he did not claim that all miracles had ceased.

Thomas Aquinas (1225–74), the great Dominican friar, Catholic priest, philosopher, theologian, and mystic, is another figure whom Cessationists may think they can enlist in their cause. He is certainly someone no study of the history of miracles in the Church can afford to ignore. Aquinas took up Augustine's idea that the miracle of tongues had shifted from the individual to the corporate Church, arguing, further, that individuals who miraculously spoke in foreign languages were no longer needed because the institutional Church now had available interpreters and native speakers of almost every language in the world.[24] Cessationists are likely to cite his commentary on Matthew in support of the cessation of miracles. Matthew 10:1 says "And [Jesus] called to him his twelve disciples and gave them authority over unclean spirits, to cast them out, and to heal every disease and every infirmity" (RSV). Aquinas comments on this verse:

> But if you ask why that power is not given to preachers now, Augustine answers that already visible is the greatest miracle, namely, that the entire world has been converted. Therefore, either there were miracles performed, and then I have proved my point; or if there were not, that is the greatest, because the entire world has been converted by fishermen, the lowliest of men.[25]

This quote is puzzling since even a cursory reading of his works reveals that Aquinas readily believed in the miraculous and supernatural. In his *Summa contra Gentiles*, his description of miracles demonstrates serious attention to their occurrence in the present and not merely in the past.[26] An in-depth reading of his lectures on 1 Corinthians also reflects his persisting belief in the continued infusion of extraordinary gifts, and his portrayal of the supernatural gift of prophecy as still in use.[27] It is thus difficult to understand Aquinas apart from his sense of divine interaction in both the personal affairs of Christians and in the corporate affairs of the Church.

Jon Ruthven, a professor at Regent University, took a deep look at the question of Aquinas and miracles and concluded:

---

24. Aquinas, *ST*, II–II, q. 176, a. 1, ad. 3.

25. Aquinas, *Super Evangelium S. Matthaei*, 303, §811.

26. Aquinas, *SCG*, bk. 3, pt. 2, chs. 101–2.

27. Aquinas, *Super epistolas s. Pauli lectura*, §758, §§812–18; Aquinas, *Commentary on the Letters of Saint Paul to the Corinthians.*, 285 §758; 308–11, §§812–18.

According to Aquinas, the central function of miracles was to serve as a *signum sensibile*, a *testimonium* to guarantee the divine source and truth of Christian doctrines, particularly the deity of Christ. To explain the lack of visible miracles in his day, Aquinas asserted that Christ and his disciples had worked miracles sufficient to prove the faith once and for all; this having been done, no further miraculous proof of doctrines could be required. In a number of other places, however, he vitiates this position by maintaining that miracles can recur if they aid in confirmation of preaching and bringing mankind to salvation. But even beyond this, Aquinas suggested that believers of great sanctity may exhibit miraculous gifts of the Spirit, a doctrine that strengthened the veneration of shrines and canonization of saints via miracles. A widespread belief in these last two exceptions, which essentially contradicted cessationism, resulted in the excesses surrounding miracles which precipitated the Reformation.[28]

To draw a Cessationist conclusion from the comment by Aquinas on Matt 10:1, therefore, seems precipitous. Such a conclusion is simply too out of step with the rest of his writings. Neither this odd quote from Aquinas, nor the earlier-cited passages from Chrysostom, Augustine, and Cyril of Alexandria considered above ever gained traction among ecclesiastical writers as sufficient ground for promoting a Cessationist interpretation of miracles. The gift of tongues, healing, prophecy, visions, exorcism, and more, thus continued to be subjects of interest throughout the Middle Ages.

Protestant Beginnings

It is not without significance that the doctrine of Cessationism arose within a Protestant theological framework, which defined its understanding of divine revelation by way of contrast to the Catholic doctrine. The Protestant textbook tradition expresses this contrast by insisting that Protestants define divine revelation as "closed" and Catholics as "open." On this view, Protestants hold that nothing can be added to or subtracted from the deposit of divine revelation in Scripture (cf. Deut 4:2; Rev 22:18–19), whereas Catholics hold that the miracle of divine revelation is unfinished and new doctrine may be revealed later and added to what is found in Scripture. The Catholic textbook tradition would agree with Protestants that the canon of Scripture is closed but would insist that Scripture is only one of

28. Ruthven, *Cessation*, 20–21.

three channels by which divine revelation is received by the Church, the other two being "Tradition" (cf. 2 Thess 2:15) and "Magisterium" (cf. 2 Pet 1:20–21; Matt 23:1–3). On this view, John Henry Newman argued in his *Essay on the Development of Christian Doctrine* (1845) that doctrine may "develop" as the Church grows in its understanding of Scripture and offers increasingly refined articulations of its doctrine, though the Church may never create new doctrines or contradict the biblical deposit of faith that has been believed, as Vincent of Lérins declared, "everywhere, always, and by everyone" (*quod ubique, semper, et ab omnibus*). Catholics would also insist that anything divinely disclosed in *private* revelation—whether to Joseph in a dream (Matt 1:20) or to later saints in visions—cannot licitly contradict what has been disclosed in *public* revelation in Scripture; and that although "disciplines" may be revised to meet changing needs, "doctrines" remain unalterable. What is important for understanding Cessationism, however, is the widespread sixteenth-century Protestant perception that Catholics, far from being bound to an unalterable doctrinal tradition, held a fluid, open-ended conception of revelation that allowed for the multiplication of doctrinal novelties, among which they included the veneration of saints, Mariology, purgatory, celibacy, indulgences, and the "addition" of books of the Bible found in the Septuagint but not in the Hebrew Old Testament. On the Protestant view, there was no continuing need for miracles—including miraculous tongues—to confirm the authenticity of the message revealed in Scripture beyond the final close of the canon of Scripture in the early centuries of the Church. Yet not all Protestants explicitly denied the continuation of miracles.

Martin Luther (1483–1546), the well-known Wittenberg monk whose protest against the Dominican, Johann Tetzel's abuse of indulgences launched the Protestant Reformation, vacillated on the subject of miracles. In the final analysis, he sided with those who de-emphasized the role of miracles in the sixteenth century. More specifically, as the father of the *sola scriptura* doctrine—later amalgamated by Philip Melanchthon into a series of slogans along with *sola fide*, *sola gratia*, and *sola Christus*—he argued that miracles have no value in authenticating or validating any new doctrines. Philip M. Soergel, a medieval and early modern European history specialist, observes:

> Luther's statements held out the possibility that the "age of miracles" had ceased; but his praise of faith's potentialities tended to undercut that conclusion all the same. This tendency—insisting on the one hand that the apostles were able to work miracles for a time only to establish the Church and on the other hand

maintaining that faith has its own miracle-working power—continued to interact in Luther's mature evangelical theology. The interplay between these two notions prevented Luther from articulating a firm doctrine of the "cessation of miracles," as it did for his later sixteenth-century followers as well. As in other areas of his thought, the Reformer proved to be cautious about making blanket pronouncements, since such judgements might presume to know the will of God and the workings of the Holy Spirit.[29]

Although Luther seems to have said very little on the subject of miracles, his vacillation on the subject is evident in the little he does have to say. On the one hand, he could sound like an unabashed Cessationist, and declare, in one of his sermons: "Thanks be to God that we have no longer any need of miracles; the Gospel doctrine has been established by signs and wonders sufficient, so that no one has any cause to doubt them."[30] On the other hand, he could sometimes also grant quarter to the idea of continuing miracles, albeit in a qualified way, as in the following excerpt:

A person may be called into the preaching office in one of two ways. The first one is directly from God, the other through His people, which is also simultaneously from God. Those called immediately must not be believed unless they are certified because their preaching is accompanied by miracles. That is what occurred in the case of Christ, and His apostles, whose preaching was attested with accompanying signs. Then, when a preacher called in this way might come and say to you [Matthew 16], "God is speaking to you here. Receive the Holy Ghost," as they must preach, you must then, of course, ask, "What sign do you give so that we can believe you? If it is only your words then we will pay no attention to them since you, from out yourself, could not say anything worth hearing. But if you work a miracle with it, then we will carefully examine what kind of doctrine you have, and whether or not you speak the Word of God." . . . Do not just believe people because of evidence they give when they attest to the spirit in them with signs and wonders. Do not only look at the fact that they are doing miracles, for the devil can also work miracles.[31]

29. Soergel, *Protestant*, 41.

30. Luther, *Luther's House-Postil*, 246.

31. Luther, *Festival Sermons*, 3–4.

John Calvin (1509–64) was the intellectual synthesizer and administrative genius of the early Reformation. What Luther started in Wittenberg, Calvin organized and structured in Geneva. His writings add some depth to the miracles debate but fall short of making him a strict Cessationist. In response to the Catholic criticism that Protestantism lacked miracles as a sign of divine approval, Calvin argued in his *Institutes of the Christian Religion* (1536–60):

> They are unreasonable when they demand miracles of us. For we are not inventing any new gospel, but we maintain as the truth that gospel confirmed by all the miracles which Jesus Christ and His apostles ever did. You could say that in this distinctive way they go beyond us, that they can confirm their teaching by continuous miracles which are being done up until today. But they claim miracles which are so frivolous or lying that they would undermine the spirit and make it doubt when otherwise it would be at peace. Yet, nevertheless, if these miracles were the most amazing and admirable one could imagine, they would have no value at all over against God's truth, since by rights the Name of God should be hallowed always and everywhere, whether by miracles or by the natural order of things. Those who accuse us would have more semblance of cover if scripture had not warned us about the right use of miracles. . . . So we do not lack for miracles, which are most certain and not subject to ridicule. On the contrary, the miracles which our adversaries claim for themselves are pure tricks of Satan when they draw people away from the honor of their God to vanity.[32]

Nowhere does he claim that miracles have ceased. Rather, he condemns the abuse of miracles. Some authors have quoted Calvin's commentary on John 20:30–31 as expressing his support of miracles; however, his comments do not either promote or rule out modern-day miracles. He simply suggests that miracles can excite the mind to contemplate God's power. This could be construed to suggest that he believed in miracles during his time. Let readers examine his words and judge for themselves:

> Although, therefore, strictly speaking, faith rests on the word of God, and looks to the word as its only end, still the addition of miracles is not superfluous, provided that they be also viewed as relating to the word, and direct faith towards it. Why miracles are called *signs* we have already explained. It is because, by

---

32. Calvin, *Institutes* (2009), 11–12.

means of them, the Lord arouses men to contemplate his power, when he exhibits anything strange and unusual.[33]

The statement is not strong enough to reach a definite conclusion. At most, we can infer from Calvin's hesitancy regarding miracles that he would counsel great caution. His disposition also aligns with the Protestant mantra that miracles must not be used to supersede the authority of Scripture.

The early Protestant *de-emphasis* on miracles shifted decisively to overt *Cessationism* in England during the 1600s. The Church of England was born in the 1530s from the refusal of Rome to grant Henry VIII an annulment from his marriage to Catherine of Aragon so he could marry his mistress, Anne Boleyn. The Church of England initially had no stance on miracles and little if any anti-Catholic sentiment at this time. Earlier in his life, Henry had even been awarded the title "Defender of the Faith" by Rome for his treatise defending the Catholic doctrine of the sacraments against Luther. The Thirty-Nine Articles of 1572 represent Queen Elizabeth's attempt to uphold Reformation doctrines without alienating Catholic liturgical practice. Though the Anglican Reform was influenced by many different sources over the next 150 years, several distinct groups seem to have played defining roles, particularly concerning the development of Cessationism: Puritans, Presbyterians, Latitudinarians, Rationalists, and Deists.

Puritans were those primarily responsible for launching the full-blown doctrine of Cessationism. Though they were never a distinct party or independent religious sect with a definitive leader, they had an immense influence. They can most easily be classified as an activist movement *within* the Church of England that was dissatisfied with the limited extent to which the English Reformation sought to zealously rid itself of any residual influences of Catholicism in its worship and doctrine. Puritans later allied with Scottish Presbyterians on various matters of doctrine, including the cessation of miracles. Their influence reached its zenith between the outbreak of the English Civil War in 1642, which led to the execution of Charles I and subsequent Puritan Protectorate under Oliver Cromwell, and ended with the restoration of the monarchy and the succession of Charles II in 1660. During these 18 years, the public had become fatigued from the impression that the Churches of England and Scotland had traded the superstitions of Catholicism for the dry legalism and captious biblical absolutism concerning even the smallest matters of everyday life. The accession of Charles II brought an end to the dominance of Puritan influence in the English church, state, and society. The Puritans were strong proponents of Cessationism, and it is primarily to them that we owe the legacy of this doctrine, as we shall see.

33. Calvin, *Gospel of John*, 2:281.

Presbyterians were a slightly later offshoot of the Scottish Protestant movement. Their theology is defined by strict adherence to the teachings of John Calvin. John Knox, who visited Calvin's Geneva and observed his reform movement there, was a prominent clerical leader of Presbyterianism in Scotland, which had gained momentum when the English Civil War brought the Puritan Cromwell to power in 1651. Scottish Presbyterians took no position on miracles in the first doctrinal statement they formulated, known as The Scots Confession (1650). They did adhere, however, to the Cessationist doctrine found in the Westminster Confession of Faith (1646)—to be discussed below—and Presbyterians later became one of the more vocal proponents of the doctrine in the 1800s and early 1900s. In any case, it was the Puritan position on miracles that the Presbyterians eventually adopted in their churches. In what follows we shall briefly examine some examples of thinkers and writings that shaped the Puritan doctrine of Cessationism.

William Whitaker (1547–95) was a prominent Calvinistic cleric of the Church of England, theologian, and Master of St. John's College, Cambridge. His Latin-English dictionary is still commonly used by Latin students around the world today. More importantly, he contributed to the first chapter of the Westminster Confession of Faith (1646), which contains a key Cessationist clause: ". . . which maketh the holy Scripture to be most necessary; those former ways of God's revealing his will unto his people being now ceased."[34] Whitaker helped firmly establish the authority of Scripture in the Church of England, over against the value placed on miracles and veneration of saints in Catholicism.[35]

William Perkins (1558–1602) was a Cambridge-educated cleric of the Church of England. He was a gifted orator and popular writer. Although he was a follower of Calvin, his own works outsold those of Calvin by a significant margin in England. He was a staunch and dogmatic conservative but did not join the ranks of the Puritans. His legacy was nevertheless greatly esteemed by both Puritans and Presbyterians, though the extent of his influence is a matter of debate.[36] His writings suggest that a practicing Protestant should avoid any outward exhibition of a miraculous nature, for two reasons: First, because such an exhibition would come too close to being Catholic; and he drew a clear line connecting Catholicism, miracles, and the devil. This was Perkins' primary reason for rejecting miracles. Second, he drew a lesson from what he considered to be an excessive Catholic

---

34. *Confession of Faith*, ch. 1.1; cf. Milne, *Westminster Confession*, 52.

35. Whitaker, *Disputation*, 496–704.

36. Milne, *Westminster Confession*, 50.

interest in miracles and made a general application to human nature: people seek to perform signs and wonders, he argued, for personal or occupational gain. Both of these factors are outlined in his book, *Discourse of the Damned Art of Witchcraft* (1608):

> It were easier to show the truth of this, by examples of some persons, who by these means have risen from nothing, to great places and preferments in the world. Instead of all, it appeareth in certain Popes of Rome, as Sylvester the second, Benedict the eighth, Alexander the sixth, John the 20 and the twenties one [*sic*], etc. who for the attaining of the Popedom (as histories record) gave themselves to the devil in the practice of witchcraft, that by the working of wonders, they might rise from one step of honour to another, until they had seated themselves in the chair of the Papacy. So great was their desire of eminence in the Church, that it caused them to dislike meaner conditions of life, and never to cease aspiring, though they incurred thereby the hazard of good conscience, and the loss of their souls.
>
> The second degree of discontentment, is in the mind and inward man; and that is curiosity, when a man resteth not satisfied with the measure of inward gifts received, as of knowledge, wit, understanding, memory, and such like, but aspires to search out such things as God would have kept secret: and hence he is moved to attempt the cursed art of magic and witchcraft, as a way to get further knowledge in matters secret and not revealed, that by working of wonders, he may purchase fame in the world, and consequently reap more benefit by such unlawful courses, than in likelihood he could have done by ordinary and lawful means.[37]

The important thing to note here is not the inveterate malice with which the author presumes to discern interior motives and libelously impute the iniquitous practices of magic and witchcraft to Catholic leaders. Sorcery, occultism, divination, spiritism, magic, and witchcraft are roundly condemned by the Catholic Church.[38] The important thing is the point Perkins is arguing here: his conviction that since the Gospel had been established already, there was no further need for miracles. He declares: "Therefore if Ministers now should lay their hands on the sick, they should not recover them: if they should anoint them with oil, it should do them no good, because they have no promise."[39] Two refrains he continues to repeat

---

37. Perkins, *Discourse*, 10–11.
38. *CCC* ##2116–17.
39. Perkins, *Discourse*, 232.

are the Catholic abuse of miracles and the Cessationist claim that the age of miracles had passed:

> This gift [of miracles] continued not much above the space of 200 years after Christ. From which time many heresies began to spread themselves; and then shortly after Poperie that mystery of iniquity beginning to spring up, and to dilate itself in the Churches of Europe, the true gift of working miracles then ceased, and instead thereof came in delusions, and lying wonders, by the effectual working of Satan, as it was foretold by the Apostles [in] 2 Thess 2:9. Of which sort were and are all those miracles . . . of the Romish Church, whereby simple people have been notoriously deluded. These indeed have there continued from that time to this day. But this gift of the Holy Ghost, whereof the question is made, ceased long before.[40]

Like many of his Protestant contemporaries, Perkins identified Catholic miracles with superstition. He regarded Catholic ceremony, ritual, and the recitation of prescribed prayers, invocations, etc., as pervaded with superstitious credulity.[41] Perkins, like many others, did not realize that these ceremonies and rituals were instituted by the Church to correct abuses of ad hoc improvisations by individuals and groups hiving off to do their own thing—sometimes leading to self-seeking conceits associated with miraculous gifts. In the fourth century, the Church appears to have shifted the focus of such gifts away from individuals, who could abuse them, towards corporate ceremonies, rituals, and the authority of the institutional Church. This shift is apparent in the writings of both Chrysostom and Augustine, and most notably in the latter who transferred the locus of the gift of tongues from the individual to the corporate Church.[42]

Perkins' logic is confusing. He allows that the Devil may produce enchantments and sorceries that seem like miracles, albeit for diabolical purposes, but denies any alternative endowment by which the Church or individual Christian might receive the power to work miracles. He denies any direct human causative potency in the performance of miracles. Even in discussing miracles performed in biblical times, his emphasis is never on a divine *endowment* of a gift of miracle-working bestowed upon any human

40. Perkins, *Discourse*, 238.

41. Eastwood, *Transactions*, 176.

42. Sullivan, GOTP, s.v. "Chrysostom," para. 6; Augustine, *Enarratio*, 147:19 (PL, 37:1929); GOTP, s.v. "Augustine on the Tongues of Pentecost: English Translations," sec. 11.

being, but purely on the *divine agency*.[43] He denies that Jesus could perform miracles by his human nature alone. By being a divine Person with two natures (human and divine), however, Perkins believed Jesus could perform miracles through his divine nature, or, as in the case of raising Lazarus from the dead, by a combination of his human with his divine faculties.[44] Like many other of his Protestant contemporaries, however, he identified any expression of the Catholic faith with that which is evil and satanic.

James Ussher (1581–1656), a student of Perkins, was a theologian and Archbishop of Armagh in the Church of Ireland (in communion with the Anglican Church, not Rome). He is best remembered for his chronology of world history dating back to the year and date of God's creation of the world. His view of miracles was similar to that of Perkins, and he vehemently attacked Catholic claims of miracles:

> That seeing the Popes Kingdom glorieth so much in wonders, it is most like, that he is Antichrist; seeing the false Christs and false Prophets shall do great wonders to deceive (if it were possible) the very Elect, and that some of the false Prophets prophesies shall come to pass, we should not, therefore, believe the doctrine of Popery for their wonders sake, seeing the Lord thereby trieth our faith; who hath given to Satan great knowledge and power to work stranger things, to bring those to damnation who are appointed unto it.[45]

Asking whether miracles are necessary now, as they were in apostolic times, he answered that they are not:

> No verily. For the doctrine of the Gospel being then new unto the world, had need to have been confirmed with miracles from heaven: but being once confirmed there is no more need of miracles; and therefore we keeping the same doctrine of Christ and his Apostles, must content ourselves with the confirmation which hath already been given.[46]

What inference did he then draw from this premise? "That the doctrine of Popery is a new doctrine, which had need to be confirmed with new miracles; and so it is not the doctrine of Christ, neither is established by his miracles."[47]

---

43. Perkins, *Discourse*, 243.

44. Perkins, *Discourse*, 16.

45. Ussher, *Body of Divinity*, 392.

46. Ussher, *Body of Divinity*, 392.

47. Ussher, *Body of Divinity*, 392.

The Westminster Confession of Faith (1646) was produced at the height of Puritan influence in the Church of England. The authors aimed to codify the Protestant faith in such a way that all the Protestant sects in Britain could be drawn together into a united system of faith. The Confession is still adhered to in certain, largely Presbyterian, religious jurisdictions.

It contains two articles that bear on the question of miracles. The first is in the opening section relating to the authority of Scripture, where it states that what God has revealed in his sacred Word is final and adds: "those former ways of God's revealing his will unto his people being now ceased."[48] The word "ceased" here is ambiguous and controversial. Garnet Milne, in his excellent book, *The Westminster Confession of Faith and the Cessation of Special Revelation: The Majority Puritan Viewpoint on Whether Extra-Biblical Prophecy Is Still Possible*, sums up the interpretation of the word "ceased" as follows:

> An analysis of the writings of the Westminster divines reveals their pervasive commitment to a cessationism of a rather comprehensive kind. In their exposition of the key texts of Eph 1:17–18, Heb 1:1–2, and Joel 2:28–32/Acts 2:17, a large proportion of the divines contend that the possibility of further revelation has ceased, both for the purposes of doctrinal insight and for ethical guidance. They repeatedly contrast the role of Scripture with phenomena such as dreams and visions as means of divine communication, and argue that the latter modalities are firmly confined to the past.
>
> From a range of other biblical texts, the divines adduce further reasons as to why the church ought no longer to expect revelation from a source outside of Scripture itself. Extra-biblical revelation is restricted to the eras of the patriarchs, prophets, and apostles. Special revelation for the governance of the church is said to have ceased. Warnings are issued against the inherent dangers of appeals to immediate inspiration, and the cessation of such revelation is linked to the cessation of miracles. Old Testament texts in particular tend to be read analogically. The Scriptures as a whole are presented and appealed to as the final supernatural revelation of God for all purposes.[49]

Although Milne clarifies the Puritan concept behind the word "ceased," the language of the Westminster Confession was purposely ambiguous to accommodate the non-Puritans within the Westminster Assembly. The ambiguous use of the word "ceased" allowed for a degree of flexibility in

48. *Confession of Faith*, ch. 1.1.

49. Milne, *Westminster Confession*, 145.

interpretation among the various Protestant factions that the authors of the Confession hoped to unite.

A second article of the Westminster Confession relevant to the present topic is one in which the Church is said to have no other head but Jesus Christ and that the Pope of Rome "is that Antichrist, that man of sin and son of perdition, that exalteth himself in the Church against Christ, and all that is called God."[50] Though this passage has been revised in the most recent versions to remove the offensive language, the sentiment in question and opposition to the Catholic Church's "false" miracles continued to serve as a rallying point among various branches of Protestantism.

The Westminster Confession of Faith set the standard for later English Protestant confessions, such as the Savoy Declaration, which was modified for Congregationalists in 1658, and the London Baptist Confession of 1689. Both contained a Cessationist clause.

Latitudinarians were a group of theological liberals that exercised considerable influence within the Church of England, despite being rather small in numbers. They emphasized an alliance of science and religion, which often put them at odds with more conservative and dogmatic Puritan thinkers. Their perception of miracles was defined by their more detached, rationalist, and ostensibly "scientific" approach to the subject. They nevertheless can be viewed as united with the rest of the Anglican communion by their common anti-Catholicism and rejection of Catholic miraculous claims.

Richard Hooker (1554–1600), a prominent Anglican priest and theologian with some Calvinist leanings, was the major contributor to the formation of the Latitudinarian movement and one of the most important theologians of the sixteenth century. He did not, however, address the problem of miracles at all. His contribution lies in another direction. Although he had some doctrinal problems with Catholic theology, he did not absolutely reject the claims of Catholicism. He has been considered the originator of the Anglican *via media* between Protestantism and Catholicism. His works primarily targeted the conservative Puritan faction within the Church of England which he regarded as overly extreme and reactionary in its views.

Several other Latitudinarians notable for their contributions include William Chillingworth (1602–64), who converted to Catholicism, then back to Protestantism, and was accused by both sides of being a rationalist; the Archbishop of Canterbury, John Tillotson (1630–94), known for his integration of reason into theology and his toleration; and the writer, philosopher, and cleric, Joseph Glanvill (1636–80), who envisioned a future in which

---

50. *Confession of Faith*, ch. 15.6.

human beings would be able to communicate throughout the world through the medium of ether. No less significant were the later Latitudinarian scientists and free-thinkers who broke ranks with their British compatriots by becoming proponents of miracles, such as the astronomer, mathematician, and physicist, Isaac Newton (1642–c. 1726); and John Wilkins (1614–72), one of the founders of the Royal Society, Britain's national academy of sciences. Curiously, none of these Latitudinarians promoted the cessation of miracles, even though, as a group, most Latitudinarians maintained a disposition of cautious detachment.

Rationalists and Deists came into prominence in the seventeenth century. The movement of Rationalism refers here, not to the Cartesian theory of innate ideas often contrasted with British empiricism, but to the general cultural outlook that increasingly regarded reason, not faith or feeling, as the only reliable source of knowledge. Deism is often assumed to involve a belief in a distant creator who has little involvement with his creatures, but in fact, covers a spectrum of views. In 1624 the father of English Deism, Lord Herbert of Cherbury published his treatise, *De Veritate* (On Truth), whose full title in English is *On Truth, as It Is Distinguished from Revelation, the Probable, the Possible, and the False*. Yet he was later criticized, not for viewing God as distant and uninvolved, but for being a religious enthusiast who believed in an overly-involved deity who answers prayers and enters into personal relationships with people.[51] Hooker had influenced not only Latitudinarians but the wider English society by urging them, through his writings, to use reason, common sense, and intellectual inquiry in their religious pursuits. The novelty here was not the in the use of reason, which flourished abundantly in the High Scholasticism of the Middle Ages, but rather in the use of reason independently of faith as a purportedly autonomous faculty. The following examples of Rationalists, some of them Deists, may all be classified formally as members of the Church of England, whether or not they assented fully to its articles of faith. Conservative Anglicans and sectarian English Christians were often very critical of these Rationalists and would not even consider them properly Christian.

Thomas Hobbes (1588–1679) was a philosopher who agreed with Hooker's call for the use of reason in matters of faith. Hobbes is difficult to decipher at times, especially since he masked his rejection of the supernatural and the existence of the human soul by the use of biblical references and religious language. He reaffirmed the mantra that miracles had ceased, writing: "Seeing therefore miracles now cease, we have no sign left whereby to

---

51. Brown, *General History*, 2:278; Leland, *Principal Deistical Writers*, 1:25.

acknowledge the pretended revelations or inspirations of any private man."[52] He also believed that the laity was ignorant of the science behind natural events and all too easily fell into calling something a miracle. Occurrences in nature that were not understood were often called miracles. Hobbes was also concerned about those who faked miracles for public attention. He held that any notion of a supposed miracle should be rationally scrutinized by individuals and by the Church and that the natural outcome would be that there was a natural explanation that would ultimately exclude the concept of a miracle. He wrote: "For in these times I do not know one man that ever saw any such wondrous work, done by the charm, or at the word, or prayer of a man, that a man endued but with a mediocrity of reason would think supernatural."[53]

John Locke (1632–1704), one of the most influential English thinkers of the Enlightenment, was a philosopher and physician and has been called the father of political liberalism. He drafted the constitution of the Carolina Colony (before it was divided into two states) and was a major influence behind the restricted, minimalist view of government assumed in the wording and structure of the American Constitution. He also believed that the entire content of Scripture was in agreement with human reason, as he argued in *The Reasonableness of Christianity* (1695). Although he was an advocate of tolerance, authoring *An Essay on Toleration* (1689), he urged authorities not to tolerate atheists because it would lead to social chaos, or Catholics because of their "blind obedience to an infallible pope, who has the keys of their consciences tied to his girdle."[54]

His *Discourse on Miracles* (1701) presents a nuanced but somewhat relativist view of miracles. What one person considers miraculous, may not be so to another. The perception depends on how well or how poorly a person grasps the universal laws of science. He seemed to believe that the claims for miracles far outnumbered the number of actual miracles that occurred. In this respect, his views resemble those of Hobbes, though he is far more accepting of the claims of Christianity. In *Discourse of Miracles*, he sets forth some general rules for assessing the authenticity of a divine miracle.[55]

Conyers Middleton (1683–1750) was a controversial English clergyman and theologian who was often mired in controversy, but he was an outstanding stylist, biographer, and controversialist. He argued that miracles and signs were not necessary for defending Christian truth, practice, or

---

52. Hobbes, *Leviathan*, ch. 32, 198.
53. Hobbes, *Leviathan*, ch. 37, 344.
54. Locke, *An Essay on Toleration*, 152.
55. Locke, *Discourse*, 256–65.

polity. His views are set forth compellingly in his work by the long-winded title, *A Free Inquiry into the Miraculous Powers Which Are Supposed to Have Subsisted in the Christian Church from the Earliest Ages through Several Successive Centuries, by Which It Is Shown That We Have No Sufficient Reason to Believe, upon the Authority of the Primitive Fathers, That Any Such Powers Were Continued to the Church after the Days of the Apostles* (1749).[56] By applying common sense to principles of faith, and rejecting irrational or mystical approaches, he sought to distance a rational Protestantism from a mystical Catholicism. His opinions still resonate with many today.

Middleton's work is impressive in many ways. He quotes a considerable number of Church Fathers when addressing the tongues of Pentecost, which he understood as spontaneously speaking in a foreign language that the speaker did not previously know. He shows no awareness of any doctrine of tongues as a private prayer language or heavenly language. As impressive as his work is, it addresses the doctrine of tongues only in a limited way. He conflates the tongues of Pentecost with those of Corinth without adequate explanation. He leans upon Greek and Latin authors and almost entirely excludes Jewish Hebrew sources. He fails to take account of the larger corpus of historical ecclesiastical literature in drawing his conclusions. By limiting himself to a relatively small selection of writings, it was easy for him to argue that the gift of tongues had died within the first century Church without having to wrestle with numerous other Patristic writers like Augustine or Pachomius, or the historical context of the Corinthian tongues problem, which may not have been mysterious at all in the way most modern Christians seem to believe. He briefly enlists Chrysostom's texts in support of the Cessationist argument. He also elaborates further on the subject in his "Essay on the Gift of Tongues," but the work adds little of any significance to the debate.[57]

The more traditional theologians of the time invested considerable effort in attempting to refute Middleton's claims about miracles. For example, William Dodwell, a controversialist, theologian, and minister, took it upon himself to mount a refutation of Middleton with his book, *A Free Answer to Dr. Middleton's Free Inquiry into the Miraculous Powers of the Primitive Church*. The publication quickly won him a Doctorate of Divinity from Oxford.[58] But the attempted refutation failed to produce the desired result and fell into obscurity while Middleton's work continued to be read and

56. Williams and Waldvogel, "History," 78, says Middleton's work was based on Jean Daillé's *Traité de l'employ des saints Pères* (1632), which was written to discourage "undue reverence" for the Church Fathers.

57. Middleton, "Essay," 77–103.

58. Dodwell, *Free Answer*; Overton, "Dodwell," 182–83.

discussed. Middleton's work had such a great impact that the legendary evangelist, John Wesley, saw the need to try his hand at a refutation in his "Letter to Dr. Conyers Middleton."[59] Wesley's response, however, suffered a similar fate to Dodwell's and is also largely forgotten in the annals of history. It, too, has been powerfully overshadowed by the legend of Middleton's *Free Inquiry*, whose primitive arguments still stand, and have been greatly expanded upon by Cessationist scholars today.

David Hume (1711–76) was a Scottish Enlightenment philosopher, historian, and essayist, best remembered for his system of skeptical empiricism. He can be confusing to read since, like Hobbes, he also masked his skepticism about many supernatural claims of religion and seemed open to rational justifications for Christian beliefs. Hume's radical empiricism, however, led him to take a decidedly skeptical view of miracles. In his view, it would be foolish to believe anything incapable of being verified by first-hand empirical experience. He dutifully conceded that miracles were a logical possibility, but insisted that belief in them would be unconscionably credulous without empirical verification, which he insisted was next to impossible. In fact, he held that not a single miracle had been properly substantiated in human history. He completely rejected, in principle, the credibility of any human *testimony* concerning miracles. He demanded factual evidence of first-hand empirical experience. Short of this, miracles lacked a basis for belief. This meant that Christian claims of miracles, biblical or otherwise, lack credible substantiation, and the entire Christian story might well be pure fiction. Thus, he wrote: "Whoever is moved by Faith to assent to it, is conscious of a continued miracle in his own person, which subverts all the principles of his understanding, and gives him a determination to believe what is most contrary to custom and experience."[60]

Baden Powell (1796–1860), a mathematician and Anglican priest, was influenced by Hume in his writings about faith and science. The social atmosphere of his time was more open and liberal than in Hume's day, and he expressed the view that the word "miracle" is no more than a name used to describe a natural event that we do not understand. Every miracle, thus, is either capable of being explained by natural means or will be explainable naturally once the mechanism at work in it is properly understood. Because of this, he believed that people of higher intelligence with insight into the scientific laws of nature would be far less likely to believe in miracles than the uninformed laity.[61]

59. Wesley, "Letter," esp. para. 1–3.
60. Hume, *Enquiry*, sec. 10, pt. 2 (101), 131.
61. Powell, "Evidences of Christianity," 107.

While many other English Rationalists and deists could be called to witness, this sampling is sufficient for the reader to garner a general understanding of how their view of miracles tends to support the Cessationist doctrine. As a result of their influence, the concepts of the miraculous and supernatural have been relegated largely, with few exceptions, to the realm of rationally unsupportable faith, as opposed to historical and empirical reality. Thus, the issue of miraculous tongues has been relegated by many to the category of a "faith event" that may one day be understood as science advances. While Latitudinarians like Hooker were more open to the supernatural and miraculous than Rationalists like Hobbes, Hume, or Powell, their attitude of "scientific" detachment in many cases had the effect of reinforcing the position of Cessationists, such as the Puritans and Presbyterians. Puritans and Presbyterians, of course, had no trouble believing in the reported miracles of the apostolic era reported in Scripture but rejected the idea that such miracles continued beyond that era.

Later Developments in England and the United States

As mentioned earlier, not all Protestants accepted Cessationism. Later evolutions of Protestantism thus involved a mix of Cessationist and Continuationist views. Accordingly, in what follows, we shall begin by examining the Continuationist position as represented by the Methodist movement of the Wesley brothers and the Irvingite movement associated with Edward Irving. Then we shall turn to examples of the Cessationist position represented by Reformed Baptists such as Augustus Strong and Calvinists such as Charles Hodge, B. B. Warfield, and John F. MacArthur and, others.

Methodism was initially a reform movement within the Church of England. Both John Wesley (1703–91) and his brother Charles (1707–88), who launched and led the movement, were Anglican priests. Their reforms and evangelistic efforts are often classified as part of the great evangelical revival in England and the United States called the First Great Awakening. Both brothers spent time in the United States where they were active in evangelism. Methodism became an independent denomination only in 1795, four years after the death of John Wesley; but in organization, doctrine, and liturgy, Methodism initially remained similar to the Church of England.

In a sermon called "The More Excellent Way," John Wesley addressed the question of miracles. He explicitly rejected the doctrine of Cessationism, explaining that the decline in miracles was due to the faithlessness of the Catholic Church:

It does not appear that these extraordinary gifts of the Holy Ghost were common in the church for more than two or three centuries. We seldom hear of them after that fatal period when the Emperor Constantine called himself a Christian, and from a vain imagination of promoting the Christian cause thereby heaped riches and power, and honour, upon the Christians in general; but in particular upon the Christian clergy. From this time they almost totally ceased; very few instances of the kind were found. The cause of this was not (as has been vulgarly supposed) "because there was no more occasion for them," because all the world was become Christian. This is a miserable mistake; not a twentieth part of it was then nominally Christian. The real cause was, "the love of many," almost of all Christians, so-called, was "waxed cold." The Christians had no more of the Spirit of Christ than the other Heathens. The Son of Man, when he came to examine his Church, could hardly "find faith upon earth." This was the real cause why the extraordinary gifts of the Holy Ghost were no longer to be found in the Christian Church—because the Christians were turned Heathens again, and had only a dead form left.[62]

Wesley conceded that miracles were not occurring because of the faithlessness of Christians, particularly those in the Catholic Church, which he regarded as apostate. Nevertheless, he promoted the belief that miracles could be expected in the life of every true believer as the natural result of a vibrant Christian faith.[63] Thus Wesley defended the continuation of miracles against Conyers Middleton, who had argued that miracles ceased with the apostolic age.[64] His defense consisted in piecing together historical references to miracles without, however, appealing to miracles in his own ministry or time. At the same time, although he recognized the role of mystical spiritual immediacy and charismatic manifestations in the Christian life, Wesley added a cautionary note in response to criticisms in his *An Earnest Appeal to Men of Reason and Religion* (1743):

Are you not convinced, Sir, that you have laid to my charge things which I know not? I do not gravely tell you (as much an enthusiast as you over and over affirm me to be) "that I *sensibly feel* (in *your* sense) the motions of the Holy Spirit." Much less do I make this, any more than "convulsions, agonies, howlings, roarings, and violent contortions of the body," either "certain

62. Wesley, "More Excellent Way," para. 2.
63. Wesley, *Explanatory Notes*, 136.
64. Wesley, "Letter," para. 1–3.

signs of men's being in a state of salvation," or "necessary in order thereunto." You might with equal justice and truth inform the world, and the worshipful magistrates of Newcastle, that I make *seeing the wind*, or *feeling the light*, necessary to salvation.

Neither do I confound the *extraordinary* with the *ordinary* operations of the Spirit. And as to your last inquiry, "What is the best proof of our being led by the Spirit?" I have no exception to that just and scriptural answer which you yourself have given, "A thorough change and renovation of mind and heart, and the leading a new and holy life."[65]

Wesley would not necessarily have fully endorsed either Cessationism or Pentecostalism as it later developed since he did not believe that the extraordinary gifts of the Spirit were necessary as evidence of the Holy Spirit.[66]

The Irvingites, as we saw in chapter 3, represent a proto-Pentecostal movement launched by Edward Irving in the early nineteenth century. Like the Wesleyan movement, the Irvingite movement represents an exception to the Cessationist tradition found primarily in the Reformed or Calvinist branches of Protestantism. Although Irving was a clergyman of the Church of Scotland, his main influence was through his congregation in London, which was controversially engaged in what its members regarded as the restoration of miraculous gifts of the Spirit. Prominent among these was the gift of speaking in an "unknown tongue," which was understood at first as a foreign language, then later interpreted by Irving as a divine unknown language that only God understood; but it functioned preeminently as the mark of a true Christian with a divinely-authorized message. Irving was well aware of two skeptical influences facing him: first, the Scottish Church's belief in the cessation of miracles, and second, the rise of Rationalism within the greater English religious community. He countered both with what he believed was the restoration of miracles. He warned:

> This power of miracles must either be speedily revived in the Church, or there will be a universal dominion of the mechanical philosophy; and faith will be fairly expelled, to give place to the law of cause and effect acting and ruling in the world of mind, as it doth in the world of sense. What now is preaching become, but the skill of a man to apply causes which may produce a certain known effect upon the congregation?—so much of argument, so much of morality; and all to bring the audience into a

65. Wesley, *Earnest*, 41.
66. Adams, "John Wesley," para. 8.

certain frame of mind, and so dismiss them well-wrought upon by the preacher and well pleased with themselves.[67]

He then offered the remedy: "I know nothing able to dethrone this monster from the throne of God, which it hath usurped, but the reawakening of the Church to her long-forgotten privilege of working miracles."[68]

The Church of Scotland took exception to Irving's "unorthodox activities" and he was referred to the London Presbytery for review in 1832. He was not charged ultimately with breaking with Scottish Church tradition in his attempt to revive the extraordinary gifts of tongues and healing found in the early Church, since the denomination had no specific policy on tongues. Rather, he was charged with procedural violations such as allowing church services to be disruptive and permitting unlicensed speakers and women to speak. The London decision barred Irving from his church but did not affect his ordination. Shortly afterward, however, he was required to appear before the Presbytery of Annan in his hometown in Scotland, where he was charged with heresy for promoting a view of the sinful nature of Christ in his human nature, found guilty, and defrocked.[69] Irving was convicted on grounds unrelated to the theological issues surrounding Cessationism, not because they were considered irrelevant, but because the theological controversy surrounding Cessationism made the alternative less politically inflammatory.

The Puritan movement had run its course in the British Isles by the late 1600s, but its influence continued across the Atlantic in the United States as Puritan immigrants began settling in the New World. These included those from Puritan backgrounds in the Church of England, as well as Presbyterians from Scotland. The Pilgrims who came to the New World included not only Puritans, however, but Baptists and Congregationalists, some of whom also brought with them seeds of Cessationism that they planted in America.

Baptists were one of the unofficial Christian sects who fled persecution in England, where they were called "dissenters" or "nonconformists" for refusing to go along with the Act of Uniformity (1660), which required English subjects to follow the prescribed rites of worship established by the Church of England following the restoration of the British monarchy. The Baptist immigrants, especially those known as Reformed Baptists or Particular Baptists, were among those who originally held to the doctrine of Cessationism.

---

67. Irving, *Collected Writings*, 5:479.

68. Irving, *Collected Writings*, 5:480.

69. *The Trial of the Rev. Edward Irving*, 4, 8, 23–24, 26, 31–34, 92; cf. Martindale, "Edward," part 1; Oliphant, *Life*, 2:261.

Augustus Strong (1836–1921) was one of the Reformed Baptist proponents of this doctrine in America. He was a first-rate thinker and well-studied student, who worked his way up from Yale over many years to become President of Rochester Theological Seminary. He wrote a compelling argument on miracles, which was one of the better ones from a traditional perspective in his day. He fully understood the Rationalist criticism that miracles involved a suspension of natural scientific laws. He argued that what a person calls a miracle is personal, involving perceptions within the person's mind, rather than external, measurable properties of an event or act. He makes an interesting argument, but he breaks the momentum of his reasoning by reverting to the doctrine of Cessationism. He writes:

> We may not be able to mark the precise time when miracles ceased. There is reason to believe that they ceased with the first century, or at any rate with the passing away of those upon whom the apostles had laid their hands. So long as the Scripture canon was incomplete, there was need of miracles. When documentary evidence was at hand, miracles were seen no longer. The fathers of the second century speak of miracles, but they confess that they are of a class widely different from the wonders wrought in the days of the apostles.[70]

The Baptist old-world tradition was Cessationist, but Baptist beliefs became more difficult to track as they evolved and subdivisions multiplied in the New World. The independence of local Baptist congregations produced considerable doctrinal diversity in some areas. Baptists dropped the Cessationist clause in The New Hampshire Confession of Faith (1844), which was widely accepted by Baptists in the northern and western states. Why they did so is unknown, but Baptist history has shown that they have remained largely immune to the attractions of enthusiasm and mystical experience involved in seeking presumptively miraculous gifts of the Spirit.

Earlier exceptions exist. For example, the noted historian, Jane Shaw, would disagree with the idea that Baptists were definitive Cessationists. She suggests that new divine healings were alleged, with some caution, among certain Particular Baptists.[71] An article in an 1883 edition of the *Presbyterian Review* takes issue with a Baptist minister from Boston named A. J. Gordon, who wrote a book called *The Ministry of Healing, or, Miracles of Cure in All Ages*.[72] Gordon had argued that miracles found among the Moravians,

---

70. Strong, *Philosophy and Religion*, 146.

71. Shaw, *Miracles*, 49.

72. Vincent, "Modern Miracles," 481; Gordon, *Ministry*, 78.

Huguenots, Covenanters, Friends (Quakers), Baptists, and Methodists were still occurring, confirming that non-Cessationist Baptists still existed.

The Southern Baptist Theological Seminary in Louisville, Kentucky, which is currently among the largest Baptist seminaries in the United States, makes no reference to Cessationism in its doctrinal statement. Nevertheless, there is reportedly within the Southern Baptist community a tacit as well as an oral tradition of commitment to the doctrine. On May 13, 2015, however, the Southern Baptist Convention changed its traditional policy and the denomination's International Mission Board now admits missionary applicants who identify as speaking in tongues.[73]

Presbyterians in the late 1800s and early 1900s championed the doctrine of Cessationism, both in Scotland and in the United States. One example is the Edinburgh theologian and minister of the Free Church of Scotland, Marcus Dods (1834–1909), who translated Augustine's *City of God* for the *Nicene and Post-Nicene Fathers*, edited by Philip Schaff and co-published by the Free Church of Scotland-affiliate, T. & T. Clark publishing house in Edinburgh, and the Christian Literature Company in the United States.

In book 22, chapter 8 of the *City of God*, Augustine recounts numerous miracles he witnessed both as Bishop of Hippo Regis in North Africa, and in his earlier career in Milan. In commenting on the miracle of a blind man restored to sight in Milan, Dods shows his Cessationist as well as anti-Catholic colors when he writes:

> A translation of this epistle in full is given in Isaac Taylor's *Ancient Christianity*, ii. 242, where this miracle is taken as a specimen of the so-called miracles of that age, and submitted to a detailed examination. The result arrived at will be gathered from the following sentence: "In the Nicene Church, so lax were the notions of common morality, and in so feeble a manner did the fear of God influence the conduct of leading men, that, on occasions when the Church was to be served, and her assailants to be confounded, they did not scruple to take upon themselves the contrivance and execution of the most degrading impostures."— p. 270. It is to be observed, however, that Augustin was, at least in this instance, one of the deceived.[74]

In the United States, Cessationism was championed particularly by the theologians of Princeton Theological Seminary, a bastion of Presbyterian

---

73. Horton and Shimron, "Southern Baptists," para. 1.

74. Augustine, *City of God*, 485n2 (Dods, the book's translator and author of this note, was a Cessationist).

orthodoxy and the Cessationist doctrine in the nineteenth century. Most notable in their defense of the doctrine are the writings of the men who headed the Seminary during the late nineteenth and early twentieth centuries.

Charles Hodge (1797–1878), who has been called the "Pope of Presbyterianism," was highly influential on the topic of Cessationism, even though he never directly addressed the subject in writing. He was nonetheless a prodigious writer and widely respected as a principal and professor at Princeton Theological Seminary, one of the leading American seminaries of his time. Through his influence, he helped establish and shape conservative American Protestantism for generations. Cessationism by this time was already lodged deeply within the Reformed psyche and needed no explanation. It was never a matter of debate. This allowed Hodge freedom to address other theological areas, especially the encroachment of Rationalism on the traditional Protestant faith. Charles Hodge excelled at this because his large and comprehensive education demonstrated a well-rounded understanding of the Rationalistic spirit of his era. His three-volume *Systematic Theology* (1871–73) is considered a classic and still read in Reformed circles.[75]

Archibald A. Hodge (1823–86) assumed the leadership of Princeton after the death of Charles Hodge, his father, in 1878. Archibald continued his father's attack on the growing Rationalism of his time, which he saw as subverting Christian orthodoxy. A representative work is his *Commentary on The Confession of Faith, with Questions for Theological Students and Bible Classes*, which was published by the Presbyterian Board of Publications for teaching "theologians, Bible-class scholars, ruling elders, and ministers."[76] The semantics and logic of his work involve a high degree of difficulty. He slightly altered the approach he took toward Cessationism, choosing to use the word *revelation* over *miracle* in his discussions. *Revelation* involves God expressing his divine will through miracles, or supernatural acts, in the order of nature. It is a more comprehensive word than *miracle*. In his view, the concept of "miracle" was too ambiguous to use in the Cessationist clause. He conceded that miracles do exist, but his concession is veiled in confusing circumlocution. He understood miracles as part of a comprehensive order of events that have been "fixed in their occurrence by God's eternal plan" and that the "order of nature is only an instrument of the divine will, and an instrument used subserviently to that higher moral government in the interests of which miracles are wrought."[77] At times his deep and complex

---

75. Hodge, *Systematic Theology*; Gutjahr, *Charles Hodge*; and Noll's excellent *Princeton Theology*.

76. Hodge, *Commentary*, "Preface."

77. Hodge, *Commentary*, 140.

thoughts could seem almost cryptic. Hodge was attempting to work around the Cessationist tenet that miracles have not occurred since the canonization of Scripture in apostolic times. He knew that miracles could still occur today, which left him with the delicate if not impossible job of conceding their possibility without altering the fundamental Cessationist framework. His rationalization was that any miracles after New Testament times were preordained at the creation of the world and part of the course of nature established by God.

Benjamin Breckinridge Warfield (1851–1921) is often considered to be the last of the greatest Princeton theologians before the split in 1929 over growing theological liberalism led to the founding of Westminster Theological Seminary and the Orthodox Presbyterian Church. Warfield represents the pinnacle of Cessationist theology when Princeton Theological Seminary was still a bastion of that doctrine. Unlike Charles and Archibald Hodge, whose language was often abstract and challenging, Warfield used accessible, everyday language to express his arguments for why miracles ceased around AD 100 and did not continue indefinitely. After noting that the apostolic Church was "characteristically a miracle-working church," citing numerous New Testament examples in a note, he writes:

> How long did this state of things continue? It was the characterizing peculiarity of specifically the Apostolic Church, and it belonged therefore exclusively to the Apostolic age—although no doubt this designation may be taken with some latitude. These gifts were not the possession of the primitive Christian as such; nor for that matter of the Apostolic Church or the Apostolic age for themselves; they were distinctively the authentication of the Apostles. They were part of the credentials of the Apostles as the authoritative agents of God in founding the church. Their function thus confined them to distinctively the Apostolic Church, and they necessarily passed away with it.[78]

Warfield's work was not unique. In many ways, it may be viewed as an updating of Conyers Middleton's manifesto, *Free Inquiry*. Warfield cites Middleton's name twenty-three times throughout his book. He also recognizes the compelling force of Middleton's argument:

> After a century and a half the book remains unrefuted, and, indeed, despite the faults arising from the writer's spirit and the

---

78. Warfield, *Counterfeit Miracles*, 5–6; see also 234n5 for his list of New Testament miracles.

limitations inseparable from the state of scholarship in his day, its main contention seems to be put beyond dispute.[79]

Those familiar with Middleton's work will acknowledge the force of Warfield's commendation. Neither the Protestant mainstream nor the current Pentecostal-Charismatic movements have really taken on the specific challenges posed by Middleton in his day. Nobody has either refuted them or reconciled their claims with those of Church history preceding the Protestant Reformation. These tensions remain unresolved.

Warfield spent more time outlining "counterfeit miracles" of Church history than explaining the nature and purpose of miracles, as such. He seems to have been content with his argument that actual miracles had ceased before AD 100. He used this theological template as a basis for attacking the Catholic history of miracles and many of the legends and myths surrounding them in a fairly predictable Protestant manner. He did not limit himself, however, to criticizing *Catholic* claims. A notable section of his book also evaluates *Protestant* miraculous claims, especially those of the Irvingites, the Christian Science movement, and Christian faith healers.

Warfield does not name any individual faith healers, but the most prominent one during his day, the Scottish evangelist and discredited faith healer, John Alexander Dowie (1847–1907), went so far as to oppose the use of physicians, medical assistance, and even pharmaceutical intervention. Dowie was so influential and popular that he founded a city outside of Chicago and called it Zion, where six thousand devotees initially settled.[80] The city still stands today, though its historical origins have been long forgotten. Like the followers of Dowie, the Holiness movement (examined in chapter 3) also had its share of faith healers and believers willing to trust God as the Great Physician, over human doctors and medicine.

An interesting question is what motivated Warfield's skeptical polemic in *Counterfeit Miracles*. Jon Ruthven delves deeply into this question in his book, *On the Cessation of the Charismata*. He notes a variety of influences, including forces eroding the traditional base of Protestantism. One factor he notes, however, is a personal one. Warfield's wife was struck by lightning on their honeymoon and was an invalid for the rest of her life. Ruthven concedes that no inference can be more than speculative, but suggests that this event must have had a significant impact on his thinking.[81]

79. Warfield, *Counterfeit Miracles*, 31.

80. Harlan, "John Alexander Dowie," 117; McDermott, "A. J. Christ Dowie," para. 1–2, 4.

81. Ruthven, *Cessation*, 43.

After the death of Warfield in 1921, the traditional message of Princeton lost its momentum and the Presbyterian Church was confronted with more pressing internal matters related to the inroads of theological liberalism. The era of Presbyterian influence on the American religious conscience was in serious decline. Meanwhile, Cessationism found a home in other quarters within American Protestantism.

Lewis Sperry Chafer (1871–1952) was one of those who promoted the doctrine. Originally, he was a minister of the Congregationalist movement—an offshoot of the Church of England that subscribed to the Savoy Declaration of Faith and Order (1658) of the Reformed tradition, which was Cessationist. Chafer is chiefly remembered for two reasons. The first is his association with Cyrus Scofield, whose annotated *Scofield Reference Bible* promoted the distinct interpretive system of "Dispensationalism," the view that biblical history divides into different ages to which God assigns distinct administrative principles. Although Scofield did not emphasize Cessationism, Chafer's mere association with him brought him national prominence and a ready audience. The second reason Chafer is remembered is for his work in helping found the Evangelical Theological College in 1924, which later became known as Dallas Theological Seminary. Chafer served as the institution's president until his death, leaving a legacy of influence on pastors and teachers that, for nearly a century, has extended to Christian communities throughout the world. As he claimed in his Preface to his eight-volume *Systematic Theology* (1947), "These pages represent what has been, and is, taught in the classrooms of the Dallas Theological Seminary."[82]

Chafer himself was a Cessationist, and this translated into Dallas Theological Seminary being Cessationist. Here is the relevant portion of the institution's doctrinal statement:

> We believe that some gifts of the Holy Spirit such as speaking in tongues and miraculous healings were temporary. We believe that speaking in tongues was never the common or necessary sign of the baptism nor of the filling of the Spirit, and that the deliverance of the body from sickness or death awaits the consummation of our salvation in the resurrection.[83]

The Statement's wording is clearly directed as a polemic against the Pentecostal movements. Pentecostals, like their Holiness brethren from which they branched off in the early 1900s, aimed at restoring the features of the early Church, including miraculous gifts of the Spirit. This provoked a revival of the Cessationist doctrine by way of reaction, which is reflected in

---

82. Chafer, *Systematic Theology*, 1:Preface, xxxviii.
83. Dallas Theological Seminary, "Doctrinal Statement," art. 12.

the Dallas Statement above. Jon Ruthven observes as much when he writes that "the advancing front of charismatic growth has precipitated showers of polemical books and tracts, virtually all of these reiterating this cessationist premise."[84]

Dallas Theological Seminary has by no means been the only institution producing traditional Christian leaders espousing the doctrine of Cessationism. There are others, such as Moody Bible Institute.[85] The perceived importance of the doctrine, however, seems to have quietly diminished in recent years. Moreover, concerns over enrollments, along with growing numbers of applicants from Pentecostals, Charismatics and Third Wavers may be contributing to colleges and seminaries adopting more flexible position statements.

John F. MacArthur Jr. (1939–) is a fundamentalist Calvinist pastor, expository preacher, author, and radio host, and someone whose name comes up almost inevitably in any contemporary discussion of Cessationism. Both loved and hated, he may be one of the most controversial theological figures in the world of conservative Christianity in America today. MacArthur reaffirms the traditional Reformed perspective on miracles. The biggest difference between MacArthur and his Puritan predecessors is that he traded in their old virulent attacks on Catholics for his new virulent attacks on Charismatics. This does not mean, however, that he has entirely shed himself of anti-Catholicism. Indeed, he draws parallels between the excesses of credulous mysticism he finds in both Catholicism and the Charismatic movement. In particular, he exploits numerous Charismatic examples to argue that the miracles they purport to perform are a sham and as further evidence that the divine gift of miracles no longer exists.

MacArthur's arguments are based almost exclusively on Scriptural references, and he offers little philosophical depth in terms of his analysis of the historical or cultural frameworks for the Cessationist interpretations that have developed over the centuries. Nevertheless, his message is straightforward, tailored for a popular audience, and packs a rhetorical wallop. His approach and framework for discussing miracles are very similar to that of Warfield. However, he makes the same mistake that Protestants made at the time of the Reformation by completely discarding all Catholic accounts of miracles without even examining the social and historical context that framed them. MacArthur applies the same lack of consideration in applying his Reformed bias when he shifts his attention from Catholics to

---

84. Ruthven, *Cessation*, 3.

85. Moody, "Sign Gifts," para. 1–2.

Charismatics, as reflected in his blanket condemnation of the movement in his book, *Strange Fire*:

> Charismatics now number more than half a billion worldwide. Yet the gospel that is driving those surging numbers is not the true gospel, and the spirit behind them is not the Holy Spirit. What we are seeing is in reality the explosive growth of a false church, as dangerous as any cult or heresy that has ever assaulted Christianity. The Charismatic Movement was a farce and a scam from the outset; it has not changed into something good.[86]

Much like the sixteenth-century Reformers before him, MacArthur points out some very real and tangible abuses relating to miracles, especially in the realm of faith healing. The problem, however, is that he then extends this into a global condemnation of the whole movement, as if there were nothing of God in it, and juxtaposes adherence to Cessationism as a litmus test of true Christian faith. The intransigent refusal of Charismatics to correct genuine abuses, however, is no less excusable than similar vices Protestants have traditionally attributed to medieval Catholics.

In summary, the Cessationist movement carved out a narrow but significant niche in Protestant history. It is a movement of historical and theological interpretation fundamentally colored by its antipathy toward the abundance of Catholic interest in miracles and supernatural gifts in the late-medieval and early-modern eras. It drew support from Patristic writers like Chrysostom and Augustine who suggested that miracles such as the gift of tongues had declined or ceased altogether by their day, but overlooked the vast tradition of ecclesial writings attesting to the continued occurrence of miraculous tongues throughout Church history. Cessationists did not contribute directly to the modern redefinition of "tongues" as a "heavenly language" or "private language of prayer and praise," because they adhered to the traditional understanding of "tongues" as the miraculous ability to speak in previously unlearned human foreign languages. That fact alone, however, reinforced the Pentecostal-Charismatic redefinition of "tongues" as something utterly novel, discontinuous, and different from the traditional Christian doctrine of the gift of tongues throughout Church history. Not all Protestants are Cessationists, as we have seen. Those groups that descended from the Methodist and Holiness traditions, together with Catholics, affirm Continuationism, the view that miraculous gifts have continued in some form throughout Church history. Even some contemporary Calvinists, although descended from Cessationist traditions, have embraced the Continuationist view that the gift of tongues has continued to the present

---

86. MacArthur, *Strange Fire*, xvii.

day. However, their understanding of what has continued—namely the gift of "tongues"—is not the traditional doctrine of Church history but the novelty introduced to them in the "Third Wave" movement of recent times with roots in the Pentecostal-Charismatic redefinition of "tongues" as a "private language of prayer and praise." Hence, Pentecostal-Charismatic Continuationsim is actually "discontinuous" and represents a novel form of Cessationism effectively affirming the cessation of the gift of tongues as understood in Church history.

The Protestant Tradition of "Unknown Tongues"

The second anti-Catholic development in the debate about speaking in tongues that we shall consider in this chapter comes from a development virtually contemporaneous with the emergence of Cessationism. This was the addition of the adjective "unknown" or "other" or "strange" as a modifier of the word "tongues" in Protestant translations of the Bible. Thus, expressions like "unknown tongues" or "other tongues" are frequently used today by Pentecostals and Charismatics. One finds this, for example, in the title of John Sherrill's *They Speak with Other Tongues* (1965, 2004), now advertised as "The book that lit the flame in millions of hearts." Where did this idea of "unknown tongues" or "other tongues" come from? It was not the Apostle Paul in his first-century epistles. It was not even the Apostle Luke, although the expression "unknown tongues" (*heterais glōssais*, ἑτέραις γλώσσαις) appears just once in his Pentecost narrative in Acts 2:4. It was in the sixteenth century Reformation where these adjectives started being interpolated into biblical texts even where the Greek equivalent didn't exist in the New Testament. The question is, why?

The idiom "unknown tongues" and its variants have a rich tradition that dates back to the earliest days of the Reformation. The idiom has powerful political and religious overtones. When it was first created, it was with the Catholic Church in mind. The Catholic Church asserted its authority through the exclusive use of Latin in its liturgy, theology, and canon law, while the Protestants volleyed back that Latin was an "unknown tongue" that no one understood. The word "unknown" was added to the word "tongues" in the Apostle Paul's famous Corinthian texts, not to facilitate the accurate translation of the text (the word does not appear in Paul's Greek text), but to win the Reformation debate against Rome. The intent of the Protestant translators of the New Testament was to wrest the presumption of divine authority away from the Catholic Church. As we shall see, however, the original intent was lost over the centuries and the interpolated adjectives were later reinterpreted to mean that Paul was referring to a mysterious or mystical heavenly language unintelligible to men.

As we have seen, Pentecostals in the early 1900s relied heavily on this convention of "other tongues" to explain and justify their tongues-speaking experience after their crisis of "missionary tongues," when the miraculous gift of foreign languages they thought they had been given failed them on the foreign mission field. The notion of "other tongues" was critical for their reinterpretation of "tongues" once they abandoned the traditional conviction that the gift of tongues always involved actual human languages. We saw in chapter 3 how the followers of Charles Parham and William Seymour in the Pentecostal revivals of the early 1900s, such as Alfred and Lillian Garr, went off to India believing they had the miraculous ability to speak Bengali or Chinese but were rudely awakened by the discovery that they did not. This problem was so universal and devastating throughout the Pentecostal missionary world that they were compelled to either abandon or redefine the "gift of tongues." They chose the latter. The interpolated idioms, "other tongues," "unknown tongues," and "strange tongues," which found their way into English Bible translations, became key aids in facilitating their reappraisal of the gift of tongues. These idioms allowed for the possibility that speaking in tongues was not a matter of supernaturally speaking an actual foreign language, but something altogether different. They allowed for the possibility that "tongues" referred to a heavenly prayer language or a language of divine worship, something immeasurable and spiritual, something entirely beyond the grasp of the human intellect.

Most Charismatic and Pentecostal leaders today are unaware of the history of the "other tongues" interpolation and its roots in the Protestant Reformation. They usually assume that the English idioms reflect Paul's intentions. The late Charismatic leader Kenneth Hagin made this idiomatic link the cornerstone for his argument in his essay, "Seven Reasons Why Every Believer Should Speak in Tongues."[87] He acknowledges no other possible alternative interpretation of the word "tongues" besides that affirmed by contemporary Pentecostals and Charismatics. He does not qualify his assumption that the "other tongues" idioms serve as a legitimate biblical source text for his understanding, and he rests his entire case upon it.

The only place in the Bible where an idiom of this kind is used is in Acts 2:4, where its usage is incapable of supporting this sort of mystical interpretation but naturally lends itself to the straightforward meaning of "foreign languages." The insertion of such adjectives in Reformation-era translations of 1 Corinthians 12–14 to create neologisms such as "other

87. Hagin, "Seven Reasons," para. 3.

tongues," "unknown tongues," or "strange tongues," allowed for this novel interpretation to develop and perpetuate.

The Pentecostal and Charismatic usage of such idioms outside of Acts 2:4, however, disregards the historical background and proper interpretation of these texts. A brief investigation into the origins and development of the *other tongues* doctrine that predated the Pentecostal movement is therefore necessary. The motivations that caused the addition of "other tongues" to the 1 Corinthians 12–14 texts in English Bible translations were motivated by political considerations rather than theological or exegetical concerns. We shall consider six early English Bible translations below.

One of the most crucial discoveries from researching these translations is how the Authorized King James Version of the Bible, by interpolating the adjective "unknown" into its translation of 1 Corinthians, established "unknown tongues" as a universal idiom in English-speaking Christendom. The Wycliffe Bible, translated into Middle English from the Latin Vulgate and published in 1380, contains no reference to this adjective at all. Instead, it predominantly makes use of the word *langagis* (languages) instead of "tongues" in the key texts. The Tyndale Bible, begun by William Tyndale and completed by Miles Coverdale in 1534, was the first Protestant Bible translated directly from the Hebrew and Greek Texts. It was the first translation to begin inserting the additional adjective "unknown" in the English Bible, but not extensively. The Geneva Bible, a 1557 English translation used as the primary Bible of sixteenth-century English Protestants, significantly expands the frequency of these interpolated adjectives before the King James Bible entrenched the pattern in 1611. This idiom—"other tongues" and its variants—did not exist in early Christian literature.

Only three exceptions have been discovered so far. First, in the eighth century the Venerable Bede (c. 672–735), commenting on Acts 2:4, suggested that the Greek should be understood as "other languages" (*aliis linguis*) rather than "various languages" (*variis linguis*). Bede believed that Pentecost was not about people understanding the languages being spoken, but a fulfillment of Isa 28:11 ("with foreign lips and strange tongues God will speak to this people"), where the people heard languages they did not know; hence, "other" (*aliis*) suited this position better.[88] Second, in the twelfth century, Hildegard of Bingen (1098–1179) used the idiom "unknown tongues" (*lingua ignota*) regarding a self-made "secret" language with an alphabet of twenty-three letters denominated "unknown letters" (*litterae ignotae*); but it is an isolated case completely unrelated to ecclesiastical usage.[89] Third,

---

88. Bede, *Retractionis*, 999.

89. A key reference cited in this connection is Hildegard of Bingen's *Riesencodex*,

in the thirteenth century, the idiom "unknown tongues" (*lingua ignota*) was used once by Thomas Aquinas, but only as a reference to unknown foreign languages without any mystical connotation of the sort one would find in current Charismatic usage.[90] The idiom *lingua ignota* is not found in the Latin Bible. The English equivalent began to proliferate during the Protestant Reformation when it was popularized by the Geneva Bible and especially the King James version. Even then, however, the understanding of "other tongues" or "unknown tongues" among the Protestant Reformers and Cessationists conformed to the unanimous understanding of "tongues" in ecclesiastical writings from the early Church up to the nineteenth century: it was understood to mean nothing more than *actual human languages*.

The Preface to the 1611 Authorized (King James) version holds an important key as to why "unknown tongues" was added in the translation (all grammar and spelling, *sic*):

> But how shall men meditate in that, which they cannot understand? How shall they understand that which is kept close in an unknowen tongue? as it is written, Except I know the power of the voyce, I shall be to him that speaketh a Barbarian, and he that speaketh, shalbe a Barbarian to me. The Apostle excepteth no tongue, not Hebrewe the ancientest, not Greeke the most copious, not Latine the finest. Nature taught a naturall man to confesse, that all of us in those tongues which wee doe not understand, are plainely deafe; wee may turne the deafe eare unto them. The Scythian counted the Athenian, whom he did not understand, barbarous: so the Romane did the Syrian, and the Jew, (even S. Jerome himselfe calleth the Hebrew tongue barbarous, belike because it was strange to so many) so the Emperour of Constantinople calleth the Latine tongue barbarous, though Pope Nicolas do storme at it: so the Jewes long before Christ, called all other nations, Lognazim, which is little better than barbarous. Therefore, as one complaineth, that alwayes in the Senate of Rome, there was one or other that called for an interpreter: so lest the Church be driven to the like exigent, it is necessary to have translations in a readinesse. Translation it is that openeth the window, to let in the light; that breaketh the

---

934, 464v, for which see Higley, *Hildegard*, 3–34, 158, which provides an English translation; Wikipedia, s.v. "Hildegard of Bingen," s.v. "Lingua ignota and Litterae ignotae," https://en.wikipedia.org/wiki/Hildegard_of_Bingen#Lingua_ignota_and_Litterae_ignotae; Wikipedia s.v. "Lingua Ignota," https://en.wikipedia.org/wiki/Lingua_Ignota, para. 1–4; Wikipedia, s.v. "Wiesbaden Codex," https://en.wikipedia.org/wiki/Wiesbaden_Codex, para. 1–2.

90. Aquinas, *Reportationes*, 088 R1C cp 14, 387 lc1.

shell, that we may eat the kernel; that putteth aside the curtaine, that we may looke into the most Holy place; that remooveth the cover of the well, that wee may come by the water, even as Jacob rolled away the stone from the mouth of the well, by which meanes the flockes of Laban were watered. Indeede without translation into the vulgar tongue, the unlearned are but like children at Jacobs well (which was deepe) without a bucket or some thing to draw with: or as that person mentioned by Esau, to whom when a sealed booke was delivered, with this motion, Reade this, I pray thee, hee was faine to make this answere, I cannot, for it is sealed.[91]

The Protestant authors of this Preface were addressing two problems they perceived in the Catholic Church of their day. The first was its longstanding tradition of public liturgical reading of Scripture in Latin, which the majority of worshippers the congregation did not understand. The second was its lack of promotion of private Bible reading in vernacular languages that anyone could understand. These positions were embraced as a powerful argument at the time and went viral throughout the Protestant world. Translations in vernacular languages were promoted as a direct challenge to the authority of the Catholic Church, and this was perceived as such by the Catholic Church.

The Latin language had long been considered a universal sacred language in the western Church. It provided a bridge connecting the past to the present. It was considered to be a language superior in grammatical precision and logical clarity to most others. These virtues of Latin call to mind the popular thirteenth-century writer, Dante Alighieri, best known for his *Divine Comedy*, but also important here for two works he wrote on language: a four-part series of books called *On Eloquence in the Vernacular* (*De vulgari eloquentia*), and another called *The Banquet* (*Convivio*). He only completed one-and-a-half volumes of *On Eloquence*, but he offers an important description of the role of Latin and other languages within Europe in his time. In this challenging work, Dante argued that in contrast to other vernacular languages, Latin was better suited for universal communication and technical details because of its unchanging nature, since it had ceased being spoken as a mutable living language and became, as it were, artificially "frozen" in time. Dante's views are described clearly by the *Dictionary of Untranslatables: A Philosophical Lexicon*:

---

91. Wikisource, s.v. "Bible (King James)/Preface," https://en.wikisource.org/wiki/Bible_(King_James)/Preface, §6.

In the *Convivio*, three reasons are adduced in support of Latin's superiority. The first of these is its "nobility": Latin is perpetual and incorruptible, and this is what allows ancient writings still to be read today. Then, its "virtue": anything that achieves what it sets out to do in the highest degree possible is considered virtuous, and Latin is the vehicle that best allows human thought to become manifest, while the vulgar is unable to convey certain things. And finally, its "beauty": Latin is more harmonious than the vulgar, in that it is a product of art, and not of nature. Latin, or the grammatica, is in any case a human creation, thanks to its inventors (*inventores grammatice facultatis*) which is regarded (*regulata*) by a "common consensus" and is therefore impervious to any "individual arbitrary" intervention. . . . We see, then, how ordinary and everyday variations of different individual ways of speaking (*sermo*) are unable to affect Latin, which remains the same through the ages, this being a necessary condition for the transmission of ancient knowledge.[92]

Dante represents the Catholic mindset throughout Europe. This mindset predictably led in the sixteenth century to the Church's resistance against any encroachments on the Latin language brought by Protestants and any others pressing for change. This mindset assumed not only the primacy of the Latin language but also a fear that the rise of common languages would lead to confusion and ignorance. Educated elites viewed vernacular languages as primitive, lacking sustainable linguistic structures, and unable to transmit or advance the Western cultural heritage with any intellectual acuity. In their view, localized vernacular languages represented a detrimental cultural and historical regression.

The Protestant uprising eventually provoked a reaction from Rome— the Council of Trent (1545–63). Pope Paul III, who presided over the Council, was elected Pope in 1534, the same year that the Tyndale Bible introduced the adjective "other" in the phrase "other tongues shall cease" to translate 1 Cor 13:8. This demanded a response. With an eye to the new vernacular translations that Protestants were producing, the Fourth Session of the Council declared that all publications had to be approved by Church authorities before being printed. Particular emphasis was made on the Latin Bible being the only authentic one, all others being declared inferior, confusing, and misleading. It nevertheless failed to answer the widespread charge that the majority of church audiences did not understand Latin:

---

92. Cassin et al., *Dictionary*, 548.

Moreover, the same sacred and holy Synod,—considering that no small utility may accrue to the Church of God, if it be made known which out of all the Latin editions, now in circulation, of the sacred books, is to be held as authentic,—ordains and declares, that the said old and vulgate edition, which, by the lengthened usage of so many years, has been approved of in the Church, be, in public lectures, disputations, sermons and expositions, held as authentic; and that no one is to dare, or presume to reject it under any pretext whatever.

Furthermore, in order to restrain petulant spirits, It decrees, that no one, relying on his own skill, shall,—in matters of faith, and of morals pertaining to the edification of Christian doctrine,—wresting the sacred Scripture to his own senses, presume to interpret the said sacred Scripture contrary to that sense which holy mother Church,—whose it is to judge of the true sense and interpretation of the Holy Scriptures,—hath held and doth hold; [Page 20] or even contrary to the unanimous consent of the Fathers; even though such interpretations were never (intended) to be at any time published. Contraveners shall be made known by their Ordinaries, and be punished with the penalties by law established.

And wishing, as is just, to impose a restraint, in this matter, also on printers, who now without restraint,—thinking, that is, that whatsoever they please is allowed them,—print, without the license of ecclesiastical superiors, the said books of sacred Scripture, and the notes and comments upon them of all persons indifferently, with the press ofttimes unnamed, often even fictitious, and what is more grievous still, without the author's name; and also keep for indiscriminate sale books of this kind printed elsewhere; (this Synod) ordains and decrees, that, henceforth, the sacred Scripture, and especially the said old and vulgate edition, be printed in the most correct manner possible; and that it shall not be lawful for any one to print, or cause to be printed, any books whatever, on sacred matters, without the name of the author; nor to sell them in future, or even to keep them, unless they shall have been first examined, and approved of, by the Ordinary; under pain of the anathema and fine imposed in a canon of the last Council of Lateran."[93]

Martin Luther in his German translations did not interpolate the German equivalent of the adjective "unknown" in reference to "tongues." In fact, in his translation of the Greek word for "tongues" in 1 Corinthians, Luther

---

93. Catholic Church, *Canons and Decrees*, 17–21.

switched from using the work for "tongues" (*Zungen*) in 1528 to "languages" (*Sprachen*) although he still retained "tongues" in his translation of 1 Corinthians 14 as late as 1545.[94] Why Luther changed from "tongues" to "languages" and continued to vacillate between the two is not known. However, the highly-regarded Pentecostal scholar, R. P. Spittler, insists: "For Luther and his foes, "speaking in tongues" had to do with Roman Mass offered in Latin. Luther said the vernacular."[95]

John Calvin, by contrast, was likely one of the originators behind the addition of the idiom in 1 Corinthians in later Protestant translations. He obviously knew that he was purposely adding the adjective to 1 Corinthians since the Latin text he referenced and printed beside his own text has no such parallel.[96] In his *Institutes of the Christian Religion*, he offers a clear rationale for the interpolation, with the use of some colorful language:

> It is also plain that the public prayers are not to be couched in Greek among the Latins, nor in Latin among the French or English (as hitherto has been everywhere practised), but in the vulgar tongue, so that all present may understand them, since they ought to be used for the edification of the whole Church, which cannot be in the least degree benefited by a sound not understood. Those who are not moved by any reason of humanity or charity, ought at least to be somewhat moved by the authority of Paul, whose words are by no means ambiguous: "When thou shalt bless with the spirit, how shall he that occupieth the room of the unlearned say, Amen, at thy giving of thanks, seeing he understandeth not what thou sayest? For thou verily givest thanks, but the other is not edified" (1 Cor 14:16, 17). How then can one sufficiently admire the unbridled license of the Papists, who, while the Apostle publicly protests against it, hesitate not to bawl out the most verbose prayers in a foreign tongue, prayers of which they themselves sometimes do not understand one syllable, and which they have no wish that others should understand?[97]

Calvin's influence among the many Protestant leaders, like John Knox, who came to witness his religious reforms in Geneva, further reinforced this mindset. The production of the Geneva Bible, an English Bible with a Protestant spin, was a further-developed descendant of the earlier Tyndale Bible

---

94. Meyer, *CEHEC*, 368.
95. Spittler, "Glossolalia," 674.
96. Calvin, *Corinthians*, 435–36.
97. Calvin, *Institutes* (1845), 2:401 (ch. 20, sec. 33).

and became a runaway bestseller in England. The Geneva Bible significantly reinforced the interpolation of the "other tongues" idiom in 1 Corinthians. It set a novel precedent that the King James Bible later adopted and proceeded to completely entrench, ensuring its proliferated in later Protestant traditions of Bible translation.

In summary, the idiom "unknown tongues" and its variants acquired quasi-doctrinal status after 1534, when they were introduced in the Tyndale Bible as a powerful partisan "dig" against the Catholic Church, implying that its liturgical use of Latin, instead of the local vernacular, was spiritually "unprofitable." The idiom carried no suggestion of a mysterious supernatural sense in the sixteenth century such as Pentecostals and Charismatics attach to *glossolalia* today; but in the early twentieth century, it conveniently lent itself to the revisionist interpretation of "speaking in tongues" that became entrenched after the Pentecostal reinterpretation of "tongues." As with the doctrine of Cessationism, the "unknown tongues" idiom was not motivated by any purpose of altering the traditional Christian understanding of "tongues." Both Cessationism and the "unknown tongues" idiom left intact the traditional meaning of "tongues" as ordinary human languages. For Tyndale and the subsequent translators of the Geneva Bible and Authorized King James Bible, the idiom "unknown tongues" simply referred to Rome's use of liturgical Latin. In no case was the idiom used to refer to anything mysterious, such as a humanly unintelligible "heavenly" language or "personal language of prayer and praise," which many today would call *glossolalia*. Yet both Cessationism and the "unknown tongues" idiom inadvertently ended up reinforcing the novel reinterpretation of "tongues" introduced by Pentecostals after their crisis of "missionary tongues" in 1906–8, though in very different ways. Cessationism did so by its insistence that the true gift of tongues, the miraculous gift of speaking in previously unlearned foreign languages, had ceased with the passing of the apostolic age, so that anything subsequently called "speaking in tongues" must be regarded necessarily as different from the historical antecedent—either a fraudulent novelty masquerading as the authentic article or something completely unanticipated. This had the unintended consequence of reinforcing the Pentecostal-Charismatic reinterpretation of "tongues" as something mysterious and wholly other than ordinary human languages. The "unknown tongues" idiom did so by lending itself to a purpose utterly unrelated to its originally-intended one; instead of merely referring to Latin, the sacred liturgical language of the Catholic Church under attack by Protestant critics, the idiom was now enlisted in the service of unintelligible *glossolalia* and assimilated into its mysterious contemporary equivocities—now considered a supernatural gift, now treated as a learned skill. Both of these developments, therefore, play a role—if an unintended one—in the background of the historical development of the modern redefinition of "tongues."

Conclusion

THE GIFT OF TONGUES Project, which was begun by Charles Sullivan in 2008 based on research initiated around 1993, is an ongoing endeavor. Even as we conclude this volume, new details are coming to our attention about Ambrosiaster, Edward Irving, and other thinkers whose ideas we have discussed in the foregoing pages. As such, we can expect the details supporting our thesis in this book to undergo further refinement and expansion in various directions as more facts come to light. One thing this means is that some claims made in support of our thesis may be strengthened by new information in the future, while other arguments may be susceptible to modification and reinterpretation. Another is that we hope our book will encourage friendly debate. While we anticipate that some readers will wish to debate our interpretation of the modern redefinition of "tongues," nearly all of the major claims that we have made in this volume are nevertheless based on irrefutable facts.

It is time to take stock of what we have learned in the foregoing pages, what we have succeeded in demonstrating, what still remains in the realm of conjecture or to be demonstrated in our sequel volumes. Let us begin by reviewing some black-and-white historical facts that have come to light and cannot be reasonably denied.

First, as we already have begun to see, the unanimous tradition of the Church and of ecclesiastical writings before the nineteenth century is that the noun "tongues" in the expression "the gift of tongues" always refers to nothing more than ordinary human languages. As we shall see, this is verified in the writings of ecclesiastical writers back to the beginnings of Church history. This will be demonstrated more fully in volume 2: *Tongues through Church History*, from the encyclopedic eighteenth-century writings of Pope Benedict XIV and seventeenth-century scholastic, Francisco Suárez, back to the earliest Church Fathers, such as Irenaeus (c. 130–202). This fact will also be reinforced in volume 3: *The Tongues of Corinth*, in which we examine

Jewish liturgical sources from the time of Ezra the Scribe in the fifth century BC up to the Talmud Megillah, the tenth Tractate of *Mishnah*, completed about the sixth century AD. Yet, as we have seen, the pervasive historical assumption that "tongues" mean nothing more than human languages is already confirmed to some degree by the widespread *resistance* with which the earliest revisionist theories, such as the Higher Critics' theory of *glossolalia*, were met in the nineteenth century.

Second, when the Pentecostal movement came to national attention with the revivals of Charles Parham in Topeka, Kansas, and of William Seymour in the Azusa Street mission in Los Angeles in the early twentieth century, leaders and participants all initially believed that speaking in tongues involved the miraculous gift of being able to communicate in actual human languages previously unknown to the speaker. This was also the initial view of Edward Irving in the Irvingite revival of the 1830s. There is nothing exceptional about this view. After all, the entire antecedent Church tradition is unanimous in affirming that this is what the word "tongues" has always meant, even where there was some debate over whether the gift of tongues involved a miracle of speaking or hearing (as we shall see in volume 2), or whether it was miraculous or merely a natural "gift" or facility in speaking or understanding and interpreting foreign human languages (as we shall see in volume 3).

Third, after the Pentecostal movement's crisis of "missionary tongues" between 1906–8, it quietly accepted a redefinition of "tongues" as a humanly unintelligible language of the spirit, which later come to be described as a "personal language of prayer and praise." Aside from a very few modern references to "gibberish"-like vocalizations among marginal sectarian groups, the only antecedent to this attempted *redefinition* of "tongues" is found in several briefly-entertained conjectures during the revivals of the Irvingite sect in Britain around 1830; but none of these antecedents gained traction, and the Pentecostal redefinition was clearly the first to stick and proliferate. The Pentecostal movement's acceptance of this redefinition paved the way for the later practice and understanding of tongues in "Third Wave" or Neo-Pentecostal movements such as the Catholic Charismatic Renewal, the Toronto Blessing, and the Signs and Wonders movement in the latter twentieth century and early twenty-first century. Yet if Christian leaders had existed within the Protestant and especially the Pentecostal world who were familiar with the vast untranslated library of ancient ecclesiastical writers and could have read them in their original languages, the modern redefinition of tongues, a definition based on largely on ignorance, might have never emerged.

Fourth, the Cessationist movement's insistence that the miraculous gift of tongues, like all miracles, had ceased after the time of the Apostles, was a Protestant reaction against the profusion of late medieval Catholic attestations of continued miraculous activity, including the continued gifts of miraculously speaking in previously unknown foreign languages. Cessationists nevertheless held the traditional view that "tongues" refer to ordinary human languages. Though not embraced by all Protestants, the Cessationist movement has endeavored to support its position by a selective reading of the Church Fathers, overlooking passages that attest to the continuation of miraculous tongues and exploiting passages from writers such as Chrysostom and Augustine that suggest a discontinuation of miraculous tongues and cessation or diminution in the number of other miracles after apostolic times.

Fifth, the interpolation of extra-biblical adjectives in idioms such as "unknown tongues," "other tongues," and "strange tongues" in early Reformation-era English Bible translations was weaponized by Protestants against the Roman Catholic use of Latin as a sacred liturgical language as well as an official administrative language of the Church. The Apostle Paul's insistence in 1 Corinthians 14 that those who speak in "tongues" should remain silent in the absence of an interpreter (v. 28) because no one understands them (v. 2), was leveraged to attack the Church of Rome's use of Latin, a language widely unknown among the laity and therefore judged "unprofitable" for those ignorant of Latin. In the Reformation era, however, idioms such as "unknown tongues" and "other tongues" were never taken to suggest anything mysterious or mystical, such as may be found in the twentieth-century Pentecostal redefinition of "tongues" as a language of the spirit or a "private language of prayer and praise."

Sixth, the theory of *glossolalia* was a product of the German school of Higher Criticism in the 1830s, and the term, *glossolalia*, was itself introduced into English only in 1879 by Frederick Farrar in his book, *The Life and Works of St. Paul*. This theory sought to establish connections between the Christian doctrine of tongues and practices found in the ecstatic unintelligible babblings of the second-century Montanist prophetesses and the cryptic utterances of the pagan priestesses of the Temple of Delphi in ancient Greece. Elements of this highly-controvertible theory were adapted by Pentecostal and Charismatic scholars as supporting their mystical view of tongues as an unintelligible language of the spirit, even though no support for such a view of "tongues" could be found in any traditional ecclesiastical writings.

Seventh, for those involved in the Catholic Charismatic Renewal, it should be noted that the magisterium (the teaching authority of the

Church) has always classified the gift of tongues among the "extraordinary" or "exceptional" (supernatural) gifts, which, according to Catholic theology, cannot be earned or generated by any human effort because they are gratuitously given gifts (*gratia gratis data*). As such, this classification utterly excludes any learned skill, such as the cultivated ability to speak in language-like utterances widely found in contemporary *glossolalia*. Some Catholic Charismatics have suggested that even a learned skill, like *glossolalia*, can be elevated to the level of an "extraordinary" gift by the Holy Spirit. However, such a conceit fails to square the circle inasmuch as unintelligible *glossolalia* sustains no relation to what the Church has always understood by the "speaking of tongues," which is the speaking of intelligible, actual human languages.

Next, let us consider some claims and suggestions that have not yet been demonstrated but are dealt with substantially in our subsequent volumes. Some elements of these claims can be amply demonstrated. Others, however, are not yet based on conclusively demonstrable evidence but conjecture and probable inference.

In the first place, we know that the theory that the gift of tongues was a gift of *hearing* rather than speaking arose from a confusing translation of the Pentecost Oration of Gregory of Nazianzus by Tyrannius Rufinus in the fourth century. We also know that the debate sparked by this confusion lasted over eight centuries. Finally, we also know that the mainstream of ecclesiastical writers (including writers like Aquinas and Suárez) gave compelling arguments for favoring the view that the miracle of tongues was a gift of speaking. Yet we cannot assert with certainty that one or the other view in this debate represents the "correct" interpretation of the historical tongues of Pentecost. Even Aquinas and Suárez admit that Pentecost could have involved a gift of hearing, and Pope Benedict XIV, who was a consummate scholar, seems to have admitted either possibility. The minor tradition of "one sound" that was heard as "many languages," also raises many questions that have not been entirely resolved.

In the second place, key Patristic writers including Chrysostom attest to a time in Church history when a sacred liturgical language was used in Christian worship, a language that differed from the vernacular, common language of the people. Cyril of Alexandria, Epiphanius, and Ambrosiaster not only attest to this practice continuing in their own time in the fourth and fifth centuries but to the convention of churches employing the services of an interpreter to aid the laity in understanding the readings and liturgy. Epiphanius, for example, explicitly declares that the conflict over tongues in 1 Corinthians 12–14 was over which Greek dialect should be used to translate the sacred liturgical language of Hebrew in the Corinthian assembly. The convention of using an interpreter in liturgies is referenced by the seventeenth-century Anglican theologian and rabbinical scholar, John Lightfoot; by the twelfth-century Jewish scholar, Moses Maimonides; by the Babylonian Talmud (c. AD 200–550); and it can be traced back to Ezra the Scribe (fl. c. 490–440 BC), who employed interpreters to explain the meaning of public readings from the Hebrew Torah to Jews repatriated after their former captivity in Babylon, since their common tongue was now Aramaic, not Hebrew (Neh 8:1–8).

In the third place, we know that during his lifetime, the Apostle Paul was working within a new Jewish sect that would soon come to be known as "Christian." Its composition was still Jewish at the time he addressed his epistles to the Corinthians. Before the destruction of the Temple in Jerusalem in AD 70, Jewish followers of Christ still considered themselves Jews and were regarded as such by fellow Jews. Only after that cataclysmic event were Jewish followers of Christ effectively "excommunicated" from Judaism by Rabban Gamaliel II of Yavneh in the decree, *Birkat Ha-Minim* (c. AD 90). The book of 1 Corinthians dates from between c. AD 52–57, well before these events. Paul, who was not executed until AD 65 in Rome, proudly declared himself "a Hebrew of Hebrews" (Phil. 3:5). These are hard facts; and this is important because this means that if certain liturgical practices can be shown to have occurred in Jewish worship before, during, or after this period, these practices were likely found in the congregations established by the Apostle Paul.

In the fourth place, the claim that the Corinthian assembly described by Paul in 1 Corinthians continued to employ a number of features common in Jewish liturgy is a probable claim based on good evidence, but is not yet capable of definitive demonstration. As we will show in volume 3, the Jewish convention of employing interpreters to help laity understand the Hebrew readings from the Torah and other liturgical prayers and hymns (usually in Hebrew or Aramaic) was continued from the time of Ezra nearly a thousand years until it disappeared from synagogue services around the sixth century AD. This much is fact. There are indications in Paul's epistle that the Corinthian assembly used an interpreter (διερμηνευτής, 1 Cor 14:28), someone assigned to the uncatechized laity (ἀναπληρῶν, 1 Cor 14:16) so that they would know when to say "Amen" during the Eucharistic liturgy. But the words used by Paul for an "interpreter" assigned to the laity differ from those used by later Jewish writers—such as *meturgeman* or *meturgem* (מתרגם), *shaliach tzibbur* (שליח צבור), or *chazzan* (חַזָּן)—as well as from those used by later Church Fathers like Cyril of Alexandria—such as *skopos* (σκοπὸς), and *keimenos* (κείμενος). The function of the interpreter seems to have been similar, but the linguistic labels differ. Inferences about the tongues of Corinth and the role of interpreters, therefore, remain in the realm of probable conjecture.

In the fifth place, although Paul makes clear use of a word that means "interpreter," *diermēneutēs* (διερμηνευτής, 1 Cor 14:28), the role of *anaplērōn* (ἀναπληρῶν, 1 Cor 14:16) is less clear. As we shall see in volume 3, there are some indications that the word *anaplērōn* refers to a person who interpreted or explained what was going on liturgically to the laity. But there is also the complicating factor that the biblical text itself seems to suggest that it was the *anaplērōn* himself who did not know when to say "Amen" in the liturgy, which suggests that rather than being the one assigned to help the laity understand what is going on, the word may refer to the person who himself occupies the place of the laity and needs to have the liturgy explained to him. Thus, although it is clear that Paul refers to the role of interpreters in the Corinthian assembly, it is not entirely clear how his use of the terms *anaplērōn* and *diermēneutēs* correspond to later Christian and Jewish terms or the pre-Christian practice found in Judaism following the exile in Babylon.

In the sixth place, as we also demonstrate in volume 3, there is no basis in fact for the conjecture of Catholic Charismatics that the gift of tongues went by another name and was called "jubilation" in Church history. "Tongues" never meant anything other than intelligible, ordinary human languages. "Jubilation" has such a wide semantic range that it can mean any number of different things—cries of exultation, shouts of triumph, exclamations of joy, etc.—but no historical record exists of any connection between "jubilation" and the traditional Christian doctrine of tongues, much less the novel theory of *glossolalia*, in any recognized encyclopedia or dictionary before the twentieth century. In musicology, *jubilus* refers to the long melisma, or melodic fioritura or roulade, placed on the last syllable of the Alleluia, typical in Gregorian chant. The notion that "jubilation" has anything to do with either the traditional Christian doctrine of tongues or the contemporary Pentecostal-Charismatic practice and understanding of *glossolalia* as a personal language of prayer and praise has no basis whatsoever in the ecclesiastical writings of Church history.

Volume 2 will provide ample evidence that the word "tongues" in sacred tradition has always referred since time immemorial to nothing more than ordinary human languages. This will serve to confirm the reasonable inference that the miracle of tongues described in the Pentecost account in Acts 2, whether it was a gift of speaking or hearing or both, involved ordinary languages that were understood by the pilgrims in Jerusalem from many different countries who comprised the audience of the Apostles. Volume 3 will provide evidence for the claim that the tongues of Corinth almost certainly involved no miraculous gifts of tongues whatsoever, but merely a problem of a foreign sacred language that was not understood by many in the assembly and had to be verbally translated and explained to the laity in the common tongue.

Nevertheless, at the conclusion of the present volume, we can say with certainty that the understanding and practice of "speaking in tongues" found in the Pentecostal-Charismatic tradition today is based on a nine-teenth-century theory of *glossolalia* and a twentieth-century redefinition of "tongues" that are complete historical novelties. Neither the Pentecostal-Charismatic idea of a "heavenly language" or "private language of prayer and praise," nor the Higher Critical idea of unintelligible *glossolalia* based on a theory of antecedents in Montanism or Delphic prophetesses can expect to find any credible support in the facts of Church history. The contemporary practice and understanding of "tongues" as a gift of personal prayer and praise, regardless of how spiritually uplifting they may be, are a historical novelty without precedent before the nineteenth century in Church history. In this respect, we may paraphrase John Henry Newman and say, "To go deep into history is to cease to accept the Pentecostal-Charismatic under-standing of *tongues*."

Bibliography

Adam, Karl. "Die Theologie der Krisis." *Hochland: Monatsschrift für alle Gebiete des Wissens der Literatur und Kunst* 23 (1926–27) 271–86.

Adams, Craig L. "John Wesley and Spiritual Gifts." *Commonplace Holiness* (blog), May 14, 2005. https://craigladams.com/blog/john-wesley-and-spiritual-gifts/.

"Agnes Ozman's Writing." *St. Louis Post-Dispatch*, January 27, 1901.

Albertum, Joannem. *Hesychii Alexandrini Lexicon*. Amsterdam: A.M. Harkert, 1965.

Alchon, Suzanne Austin. *A Pest in the Land: New World Epidemics in a Global Perspective*. Albuquerque: University of New Mexico Press, 2003.

Alnor, William M. *Heaven Can't Wait: A Survey of Alleged Trips to the Other Side*. Grand Rapids: Baker, 1996.

Alpha USA. "Catholic Context: National Advisory Board." https://alpha-usa. squarespace.com/catholic-board.

Anderson, Alan. "The Azusa Street Revival and the Emergence of Pentecostal Missions in the Early Twentieth Century." *Transformation* 23 (2006) 107–18.

Anderson, Allan Heaton. *An Introduction to Pentecostalism*. 2nd ed.. Cambridge: Cambridge University Press, 2014.

Anderson, Robert Mapes. *Vision of the Disinherited: The Making of American Pentecostalism*. New York: Oxford University Press, 1979.

Andrews, E. A. *A Copious and Critical Latin-English Lexicon: Founded on the Larger Latin-German Lexicon of William Freund with Additions and Corrections from the Lexicons of Gesner, Facciolati, Scheller, Georges, etc*. Rev. ed. New York: Harper, 1857.

———. "Tongues, Gift Of." In vol. 4 of *The Interpreter's Dictionary of the Bible*, edited by George Arthur Buttrick, 671–72. New York: Abingdon, 1962.

Aquinas, Thomas. *Reportationes, Opuscula dubiae authenticitatis*. In vol. 6 of *Opera Omnia*, edited by Roberto Busa. Stuttgart-Bad Cannstatt: Frommann-Hoolzboog, 1980.

———. *Summa contra Gentiles*. In *Sancti Thomae Aquinatis Opera omnia*, 13–15. Editio Leonina. Rome, 1918–30.

———. *Summa Theologiae*. In *Sancti Thomae Aquinatis Opera omnia*, 4–12. Editio Leonina. Rome, 1888–1906.

———. *Summa Theologica*. Translated by the Fathers of the English Dominican Province. 5 vols. New York: Benziger, 1948.

————. *Super epistolas S. Pauli lectura*. Vol. 1, *Super primam epistolam ad Corinthios lectura*. Edited by Raphael Cai. Turin. Translated by Fabian Larcher and Daniel Keating. https://isidore.co/aquinas/SS1Cor.htm.

————. *Super Evangelium S. Matthaei lectura, Commentary on the Gospel of Matthew, Chapters 1–12*. In vol. 33 of *Latin/English Edition of the Works of St. Thomas Aquinas*, edited and translated by Jeremy Holmes and Beth Mortensen. Lander, WY: Aquinas Institute for the Study of Sacred Doctrine, 2013.

————. *Commentary on the Letters of Saint Paul to the Corinthians*. In vol. 38 of *Latin/English Edition of the Works of St. Thomas Aquinas*, translated and edited by Jeremy Holmes and Beth Mortensen. Lander, WY: Aquinas Institute for the Study of Sacred Doctrine, 2013.

Aristophanes. *Aristophanis Ranae: The "Frogs" of Aristophanes*. Revised with notes and preface by F. A. Paley. London: Bell and Sons, 1877.

Aristotle. *On the Soul, Parva Naturalia, On Breath*. Translated by W. S. Hett. LCL 288. Cambridge, MA: Harvard University Press, 2014.

Arnott, John. "The Toronto Blessing: What Is It?" *Revival Magazine*, December 31, 1999. http://www.johnandcarol.org/updates/the-toronto-blessing-what-is-it.

"Art. 57, An Essay on the Gift of Tongues." *The Monthly Review* 77 (1787) 510. https://www.google.com/books/edition/The_Monthly_Review_Or_Literary_Journal/VBS2KfQFLgIC?hl=en&gbpv=1.

Arthur, William. *The Tongue of Fire*. London: Hamilton, Adams, 1859.

Aston, Margaret. *Lollards and Reformers: Images and Literacy in Late Medieval Religion*. London: Hambledon, 1984.

Augustine. *City of God*. Translated by Marcus Dods. In *NPNF* 1/2:1–511.

————. *Enarratio in Psalmum*. In *PL* 37:1033–1968.

————. *Expositions on the Psalms, 121–50*. Edited by Boniface Ramsey. Translated by Maria Boulding. The Works of Saint Augustine 20. New York: New City, 2004.

————. *On True Religion*. In *Augustine: Earlier Writings*, translated by John H. S. Burleigh. Library of Christian Classics. Philadelphia: Westminster, 1953.

————. *De vera religione*. In *PL* 34:121–72.

Aumann, Jordan. *Spiritual Theology*. London: Sheed & Ward, 1980.

Baer, Richard. "Quaker Silence, Catholic Liturgy, and Pentecostal Glossolalis: Some Functional Similarities." In *Perspectives on the New Pentecostalism*, edited by R. Spittler, 150–64. Grand Rapids: Baker, 1976.

Baker, Heidi. "Pentecostal Experience: Towards a Reconstructive Theology of Glossolalia." PhD diss., Kings College, University of London, 1995.

Balz, Horst, and Gerhard Schneider, eds. *Exegetical Dictionary of the New Testament*. Grand Rapids: Eerdmans, 1990.

Banerjee, Jacqueline. "Frederic William Farrar (1831–1903)." http://www.victorianweb.org/authors/farrar/bio.html.

Barclay, William. *The Letters to the Corinthians*. The Daily Study Bible Series, rev. ed. Toronto: Welch, 1975.

Bartleman, Frank. *How Pentecost Came to Los Angeles as It Was in the Beginning*. Los Angeles, 1925.

Baumann, Max Peter. "Jodeln." In vol. 4 of *Die Musik in Geschichte und Gegenwart*, edited by Ludwig Finscher et al., 1488–1504. Kassel: Bärenreiter, 1996.

Baur, F. C. "Über den wahren Begriff des γλώσσαις λαλεῖν." *Tübinger Zeitschrift für Theologie* 2 (1830) 78–133.

Bede, The Venerable. *Liber Retractationis in Actus Apostolorum*. In *PL* 92:998–1000.

Behm, Johannes. "γλῶσσα, ἑτερόγλοσσος." In *TDNT* 1:719–27.

Benedict XIV. *Doctrina de Servorum Dei Beatificatione et Beatorum Canonizatione*. Edited by Emmanuel de Azevedo. 1734–38. Reprint, Bruxellis: Typis Societas Belgicae de Propagandis Bonis Libris, Administratore C. J. De Mat, 1840.

———. *Heroic Virtue: A Portion of the Treatise of Benedict XIV on the Beatification and Canonization of the Servants of God*. 3 vols. London: Richardson and Son, 1852.

———. *De Lambertinis Opus De Servorum Dei Beatificatione et Beatorum Canonizatione*. New Ed. Vol. 3. Prati: Aldina, 1830.

———. *De Servorum Dei Beatificatione et Beatorum Canonizatione*. Vol. 3. Rome: Nicolaus et Marcus Palearini, Academiae Liturgicae Conimbricensis Typographi, 1748.

Benedict XVI. *Summorum Pontificum*. https://www.vatican.va/content/benedict-xvi/en/motu_proprio/documents/hf_ben-xvi_motu-proprio_20070707_summorum-pontificum.html.

Beverley, James A. *Holy Laughter and the Toronto Blessing: An Investigative Report*. Grand Rapids: Zondervan, 1995.

———. "Vineyard Severs Ties with 'Toronto Blessing' Church." *Christianity Today*, January 8, 1996. https://www.christianitytoday.com/ct/1996/january8/6t1066.html.

Bieringer, Reimund, et al., eds. *The New Testament and Rabbinic Literature*. Leiden: Brill, 2010.

Blai, Adam. "Exorcism in the Modern Church and How to Keep the Doors to the Demonic Closed." *YouTube*, June 8, 2017. https://www.youtube.com/watch?v=JKnGdr9WMqs.

Bleek, Friedrich. "Über die Gabe des *glossais lalein* in der ersten christlichen Kirke." *Studien und Kritiken* 2 (1829) 3–79.

Blomberg, Craig L. *1 Corinthians*. NIV Application Commentary. Grand Rapids: Zondervan, 1994.

Blosser, Philip. "Questions concerning the Charism of Healing: An Amicus Brief." *Homiletic and Pastoral Review*, November 14, 2018. https://www.hprweb.com/2018/11/questions-concerning-the-charism-of-healing/.

Boeft, Jan den. "Miracles Recalling the Apostolic Age." In *The Apostolic Age in Patristic Thought*, edited by A. Hilhorst, 51–62. Vigilae Christianae Supplements 70. Leiden: Brill, 2004.

The Book of Enoch. http://book-ofenoch.com/.

Broomhall, Benjamin, ed. *The Evangelisation of the World: A Missionary Band: A Record of Consecration, and an Appeal*. London: Morgan and Scott. 1889.

Brown, John. *A General History of the Christian Church*. 2 vols. Edinburgh: Gray and Alston, 1771.

Brown, Peter. *The Cult of the Saints: Its Rise and Function in Latin Christianity*. Chicago: University of Chicago Press, 1981.

Bruce, F. F. "Commentaries on Acts." *Epworth Review* 8 (1981) 82–87.

———, ed. *The New International Commentary on the New Testament*. Grand Rapids: Eerdmans, 1953.

Bruner, Frederick Dale. *A Theology of the Holy Spirit*. Grand Rapids: Eerdmans, 1970.

Bullion, Peter. *Latin-English Dictionary, Abridged, and Re-Arranged from Riddle's Latin-English Lexicon, Founded on the German-Latin Dictionaries of Dr. William Freund.* New York: Sheldon, 1866.

Bundy, David D. "Edward Irving." In *NIDPCM* 803–4.

———. "Suenens, Léon Jozef." In *NIDPCM* 1108–9.

Bunsen, Christian Charles Josias. *Hippolytus and His Age: The Beginnings and Prospects of Christianity.* 2nd ed. Vol. 1. London: Longman, Brown, Green, and Longmans, 1854.

Burgess, Ruth Vassar. "Guerra, Elena." In *NIDPCM* 682.

Burgess, Stanley M. "Montanism." In *DPCM* 339.

———. "Montanism." In *NIDPCM* 903–4.

Burgess, Stanley M., and Eduard M. van der Maas, eds. *The New International Dictionary of Pentecostal and Charismatic Movements.* Grand Rapids: Zondervan, 2002.

Butler, Rex D. *The New Prophecy and "New Visions": Evidence of Montanism in the Passion of Perpetua and Felicitas.* Washington, DC: Catholic University of America Press, 2006.

Charismatic Movement and Catholic Tradition. Est. 2017. https://charismatic.home.blog/.

Calvin, John. *Commentaries on the Epistles of Paul the Apostle to the Corinthians.* Vol. 1. https://ccel.org/ccel/calvin/calcom39/calcom39.

———. *Commentary on the Gospel of John.* Translated by William Pringle. Vol. 2. Edinburgh: Calvin Translation Society, 1847.

———. *Institutes of the Christian Religion.* Translated by Henry Beveridge. 2 vols. Edinburgh: Calvin Translation Society, 1845.

———. *Institutes of the Christian Religion.* Translated by Anne McKee. Grand Rapids: Eerdmans, 2009.

Carlyle, Thomas. *The Carlyle Letters Online: A Victorian Cultural Reference.* https://carlyleletters.dukeupress.edu/home.

———. *Reminiscences.* Edited by James A. Froude. New York: Harper, 1881.

Carus, Paul. *The History of the Devil and the Idea of Evil: From the Earliest Times to the Present Day.* Chicago: Open Court, 1900.

Cassin, Barbara, et al., eds. *Dictionary of Untranslatables: A Philosophical Lexicon.* Translated by Steven Rendall et al. Princeton: Princeton University Press, 2004.

Catholic Church. *The Canons and Decrees of the Sacred and Oecumenical Council of Trent.* https://history.hanover.edu/texts/trent/ct04.html.

———. *Catechism of the Catholic Church.* 2nd ed.. Vatican: Libreria Editrice Vaticana, 2012.

Chafer, Lewis Sperry. *Systematic Theology.* 8 vols. Dallas: Dallas Seminary Press, 1976.

Chevreau, Guy. *Catch the Fire.* Glasgow: Marshall Pickering, 1994.

Chrysostom, John. *Homilies on the Epistles of Paul to the Corinthians.* In *NPNF* 2/12:1–420.

Clark, Randy. "How to Move in the Supernatural without Hype: Conversation with Randy Clark." *Spirit Connection Podcast,* January 31, 2018. https://dougaddison.com/wp-content/uploads/2018/01/Podcast-Transcript-Interview-with-Randy-Clark-01-31-18.pdf.

Clark, Randy, and Mary Healy. *The Spiritual Gifts Handbook: Using Your Gifts to Build the Kingdom.* Minneapolis: Chosen, 2018.

Clark, Steve. *Baptized in the Spirit and Spiritual Gifts.* Pecos, NM: Dove, 1976.

Clement of Alexandria. *Stomata, or Miscellanies.* In *ANF* 2:299–68.

Cole, R. A. "Tongues, Gift of." In *ZPEB* 775.

Colman, Andrew M., ed. *A Dictionary of Psychology.* Oxford: Oxford University Press, 2009.

The Confession of Faith of the Assembly of Divines at Westminster. London: Presbyterian Church of England, 1646.

Congregation for the Doctrine of the Faith. *Iuvenescit Ecclesia.* https://www.vatican.va/roman_curia/congregations/cfaith/documents/rc_con_cfaith_doc_20160516_iuvenescit-ecclesia_en.html.

Conybeare, W. J., and J. S. Howson. *Life and Epistles of St. Paul.* London: Longman, Brown, Green, Longmans & Roberts 1856.

Conzelmann, Hans. *Commentary on the Acts of the Apostles.* Edited by Eldon Jay Epp. Philadelphia: Fortress, 1987.

———. *A Commentary on the First Epistle to the Corinthians.* Edited by George W. MacRae. Philadelphia: Fortress, 1975.

———. *Theology of St. Luke.* London: Faber, 1960.

Cremer, Hermann. *Biblico-Theological Lexicon of New Testament Greek.* Translated by William Urwick. Edinburgh: T. & T. Clarke, 1883.

Crumm, David. "The Rise and Fall of the Word of God Covenant Community." *Detroit Free Press,* September 20, 1992. https://www.scribd.com/doc/51960928/The-Rise-Fall-of-the-Word-of-God-Covenant-Community.

Csordas, Thomas J. *Language, Charisma, and Creativity: The Ritual Life of a Religious Movement.* Berkeley: University of California Press, 1997.

———. "A Phenomenology of Charismatic Music: The Radicalization of Worship through Loud Percussive Praise." *Charismatic Movement and Catholic Tradition* (blog), March 30, 2018. https://charismataexamined.wordpress.com/2018/03/30/a-phenomenology-of-charismatic-music-the-radicalization-of-worship-through-loud-percussive-praise/.

Cullman, Oscar. *Salvation in History.* London: SCM, 1967.

Cunningham, Lawrence S. *A Brief History of the Saints.* Oxford: Blackwell, 2005.

Cutten, G. B. *The Psychological Phenomena of Christianity.* New York: Scribner's Sons, 1908.

Cyril of Alexandria. *Commentarius in Sophoniam Prophetam.* In *PG* 71.

Dager, Albert J. *Vengeance Is Ours: The Church in Dominion.* Redmond, WA: Sword, 1993.

Dallas Theological Seminary. "Doctrinal Statement." https://www.dts.edu/about/what-we-believe/doctrinal-statement/.

Davies, J. G. "Pentecost and Glossolalia." *JTS* 2 (1952) 228–31.

Dead Sea Scrolls: Study Edition. Edited by Florentino García Martínez and J. C. Eibert. 2 vols. Leiden: Brill. 1999.

Dockery, David S. "The Theology of Acts." *Criswell Theological Review* 5 (1990) 43–55.

Dodwell, William. *A Free Answer to Dr. Middleton's Free Inquiry into the Miraculous Powers of the Primitive Church.* London: Birt, 1749.

Döllinger, John J. I. *The First Age of Christianity and the Church.* Translated by Henry Nutcombe Oxenham. 4th ed. London: Gibbings, 1906.

Donnegan, James. *A New Greek and English Lexicon: Principally on the Plan of the Greek and German Lexicon of Schneider.* 2nd ed. Boston: Hilliard, Gray, 1836.

Dorries, David W. "West of Scotland Revival." In *NIDPCM* 1189–92.

Doucet, Diana. "Renewal Excites Canadian Churches." *Charisma*, June, 1994.

Douglas, J. D., ed. *The New International Dictionary of the Christian Church*. Grand Rapids: Zondervan, 1978.

Drummond, Andrew L. *Edward Irving and His Circle*. London: Clarke, 1937.

Dueck, Lorna. "The Enduring Revival." *Christianity Today*, March 7, 2014. https://www.christianitytoday.com/ct/2014/march-web-only/enduring-revival.html?start=1.

Dunn, James D. G. *Jesus and the Spirit*. London: SCM, 1975.

Easton, Burton Scott. "Tongues, Gift of." In *ISBE* 5:2995–97.

Eastwood, David, ed. *Transactions of the Royal Historical Society*. Sixth Series 8. Cambridge: Cambridge University Press, 1998.

Ebeling, Gerhard. *Word and Faith*. Translated by James W. Leitch. Philadelphia: Fortress, 1963.

Eichhorn, Johann Gottfried. *Eichhorn's Allgemeine Bibliothek der biblischen Litteratur*. 10 vols. Leipzig: Widmanns Erben, 1789–1801.

Ensley, Eddie. *Sounds of Wonder: 20 Centuries of Praying in Tongues and Lively Worship in the Catholic Tradition*. 2nd ed. Phoenix: Tau, 2013.

Epiphanius. *Adversus Hæreses*. In *PG* 41:173–1199.

Encounter Ministries. https://encounterministries.us/.

Ernesti, Johann August. "Ernesti on the Gift of Tongues." *Morning Watch* 4 (1832) 101–16.

Estienne, Henri. *Thesauros Tes Ellenikes Glosses*. 4 vols. Geneva: Excudebat Henr. Stephanus, 1572. https://catalog.hathitrust.org/Record/009289969.

Estienne, Henri, et al., eds. *Thesaurus Graecae Linguae Ab Henrico Stephano Constructus*. 8 vols. Paris: Excudebat A. Firmin Didot, 1831–65. https://catalog.hathitrust.org/Record/100163782.

———. *Opuscula Thelogica*. Leipzig: Fritsch, 1773.

Eusebius of Caesarea. *The Church History: A New Translation with Commentary*. Translated by Paul L. Maier. Grand Rapids: Kregel, 1999.

———. *Church History*. Translated by Arthur Cushman McGiffert. In *NPNF* 2/1:81–400.

———. *Historiæ Ecclesiasticæ*. In *PG* 20:43–904.

Ewald, Heinrich. *Geschichte der Volkes Israel Bis Christus*. Vol. 6. Gottingen: Dieterich, 1859.

Fahlsbusch, Erwin, et al., eds. *The Encyclopedia of Christianity*. Translated by Geoffrey W. Bromiley. 5 vols. Grand Rapids: Eerdmans, 1998–2008.

Farrar, F. W. *The Life and Work of St. Paul*. 2 vols. New York: Dutton, 1879.

Faupel, D. William. *The Everlasting Gospel: The Significance of Eschatology in the Development of Pentecostal Thought*. Sheffield: Sheffield Academic, 1996.

Feine, Paul Karl Eduard. "Speaking with Tongues." In *NSHERK* 11:36–39.

Flaherty, John. "Index of all Docs RE: The Sword of the Spirit & Related Topics." https://www.scribd.com/doc/118237557/Index-Of-All-Docs-RE-The-Sword-of-the-Spirit-Related-Topics-by-John-Flaherty-Scribd-com.

Forbes, Christopher. *Prophecy and Inspired Speech: In Early Christianity and Its Hellenistic Environment*. Peabody, MA: Hendrickson, 1997.

Ford, Josephine Massyngberde. "The Charismatic Gifts in Worship." In *The Charismatic Movement*, edited by Michael P. Hamilton, 114–23. Grand Rapids: Eerdmans, 1975.

———. "Glossolalia." In *NCE2* 6:249–50.

———. "Toward a Theology of 'Speaking in Tongues.'" *Theological Studies* 32 (1972) 25–29. http://cdn.theologicalstudies.net/32/32.1/32.1.1.pdf.

Frodsham, Stanley Howard. *With Signs Following: The Story of the Pentecostal Revival in the Twentieth Century*. Springfield, MI: Gospel, 1941.

Garr, A. G. A Letter from Bro. Garr." *Confidence*, May, 1908.

Gee, Donald. *The Pentecostal Movement: A Short History and An Interpretation for British Readers*. Redditch: Read, 2010.

Gelbart, Jean. "The Pentecostal Movement—A Kansas Original." https://ksreligion.omeka.net/items/show/1023.

"Gift of Tongues." *Christian Missionary Alliance Weekly*, February 12, 1892.

Gill, John. *Exposition of the Old and New Testaments*. https://www.biblestudytools.com/commentaries/gills-exposition-of-the-bible/.

Godbey, William B. *Spiritual Gifts and Graces*. Cincinnati: Knapp, 1895.

Goff, James R., Jr. "Charles Fox Parham." In *NIDPCM* 955–57.

———. *Fields White unto Harvest: Charles F. Parham and the Missionary Origins of Pentecostalism*. Fayetteville, AR: University of Arkansas Press, 1988.

———. "Topeka Revival." In *NIDPCM* 1147–49.

"Good News from Danville, VA." *AF*, October, 1906.

"Good Tidings of Great Joy." *AF*, October–January, 1908.

Gordon, A. J. *The Ministry of Healing, or, Miracles of Cure in All Ages*. London: Hodder and Stoughton, 1882.

Görres, Joseph von. *Die christliche Mystik*. 2nd ed. 5 vols. Regensburg: Manz, 1879.

———. *La Mystique Divine Naturelle et Diabolique*. Translated by Charles Sainte-Foi. 2nd ed. Paris: Librairie de Mme Ve Poussielgue-Rusand, 1862.

Gowdy, Paul. "Former Toronto Vineyard Pastor Repents." https://www.sermonindex.net/modules/newbb/viewtopic.php?topic_id=13427&forum=35.

Graham, Henry Grey. *Where We Got the Bible: Our Debt to the Catholic Church*. Rockford, IL: Tan, 1977–87. https://archive.org/details/wherewegotbibleooograh/page/n3/mode/2up.

Gregory of Nazianzus. *Oratio 41*. In *PG* 36:449–52.

Grosheide, F. W. *Commentary on the First Epistle to the Corinthians*. NICNT. Grand Rapids: Eerdmans, 1953.

Groves, John. *A Greek and English Dictionary, Comprising All the Words in the Writings of the Most Popular Greek Authors*. Boston: Hilliard, Gray, Little and Wilkins, 1830.

Gundry, R. H. "Ecstatic Utterance." *JTS* 17 (1966) 299–307.

Gutjahr, Paul C. *Charles Hodge: Guardian of American Orthodoxy*. Oxford: Oxford University Press, 2011.

Haarbeck, H. "γλῶσσα." In *NIDNTT* 3:1080–81.

Hagin, Kenneth. "Seven Reasons Why Every Believer Should Speak in Tongues." *Rhema*, November 13, 2019. https://events.rhema.org/seven-reasons-why-every-believer-should-speak-in-tongues/.

Harlan, R. "John Alexander Dowie and the Christian Catholic Apostolic Church in Zion." PhD diss., University of Chicago, 1906.

Hayford, Jack W., and David S. Moore. *The Charismatic Century*. New York: Hachette, 2006.

Healy, Mary. "Answers concerning the Charism of Healing." *Homiletic and Pastoral Review*, December 20, 2018. https://www.hprweb.com/2018/12/answers-concerning-the-charism-of-healing/.

———. *Healing: Bringing the Gift of God's Mercy to the World*. Huntington, IN: Our Sunday Visitor, 2015.

"Heavenly Choir." *AF*, August, 1908.

Henry, Matthew. *An Exposition of the Old and New Testaments*. 6 vols. Philadelphia: Towar & Hogan, 1831.

Herder, Johann Gottfried. *Von Der Gabe Der Sprachen Am Ersten Christlichen Pfingstfest*. Riga: Hartknoch, 1794.

Herodotus. *The Histories*. Translated by A. D. Godley. LCL 1. London: Heinemann, 1920.

Higley, Sarah L. *Hildegard of Bingen's Unknown Language: An Edition, Translation, and Discussion*. New York: Palgrave Macmillan, 2007.

Hobbes, Thomas. *Hobbes's Leviathan*. Oxford: Clarendon, 1909.

Hocken, Peter D. "Charismatic Movement." In *NIDPCM* 477–519.

Hodge, A. A. *A Commentary on The Confession of Faith, with Questions for Theological Students and Bible Classes*. Philadelphia: Presbyterian Board of Publication and Sabbath-School Work, 1869.

Hodge, Charles. *Systematic Theology*. 3 vols. New York: Scribner, 1871–73.

Hoekema, Anthony. *What about Tongue Speaking?* Grand Rapids: Eerdmans, 1966.

Hollenweger, W. J. *The Pentecostals: The Charismatic Movement in the Churches*. Translated by R. A. Wilson. Minneapolis: Augsburg, 1972.

Hopkins, S. F. "Glossolalia: An Outsider's Perspective." In *NIDPCM* 676–77.

Horton, Greg, and Yonat Shimron. "Southern Baptists Change Policy on Speaking in Tongues." *Charisma News*, May 15, 2015. https://www.charismanews.com/us/49661-southern-baptists-change-policy-on-speaking-in-tongues.

Howard, Thomas. *Chance, or the Dance?* San Francisco: Ignatius, 1989.

Howard, Thomas Albert. *Protestant Theology and the Making of the Modern German University*. Oxford: Oxford University Press, 2006.

Howard-Browne, Rodney. *The Touch of God*. Louisville: R.H.B.E.A., 1992.

Hume, David. *An Enquiry concerning the Human Understanding*. Edited by L. Selby-Bigge. London: Oxford University Press, 1894.

Hunter, Harold D. "Beniah at the Apostolic Crossroads: Little Noticed Crosscurrents of B. H. Irwin, Charles Fox Parham, Frank Sandford, A. J. Tomlinson." *CJPCR* 1 (1997). http://www.pctii.org/cyberj/cyberj1/hunter.html.

Hurst, John Fletcher. *History of the Christian Church*. Edited by George R. Crooks and John F. Hurst. 2 vols. Library of Biblical and Theological Literature 7. New York: Eaton and Mains, 1897.

ICCRS. *Baptism in the Holy Spirit*. Jubilee Anniversary ed. Vatican City: International Catholic Charismatic Renewal Services, 2017.

"In Calcutta, India." *AF*, February–March, 1907.

"In Calcutta, India." *AF*, April, 1907.

"Interview with Pastor Paul Gowdy." https://archive.org/details/InterviewWithPastorPaulGowdy.

Irenaeus. *Against Heresies*. https://www.newadvent.org/fathers/0103.htm.

Irving, Edward. *The Collected Writings of Edward Irving in Five Volumes*. Edited by Gavin Carlyle. 5 vols. London: Strahan, 1865.

———. "On Recent Manifestations of Spiritual Gifts: Part 2." *Fraser's Magazine*, March 1832.

———. "On Recent Manifestations of Spiritual Gifts: Part 3." *Fraser's Magazine*, April 1832.

Jackson, Bill. "What in the World Is Happening to Us? Selected Stories and Teachings from the History of Revival." http://www.evanwiggs.com/revival/manifest/holylaff.html.

Jamieson, Robert, et al. *A Commentary, Critical and Explanatory, on the Old and New Testaments*. 2 vols. Hartford, CT: Scranton, 1871.

Jennings, William. *Lexicon to the Syriac New Testament*. Revised by Ulric Gantillon. Oxford: Clarendon, 1926.

Johns, Cheryl Bridges, and Frank Macchia. "Glossolalia." In vol. 2 of *The Encyclopedia of Christianity*, edited by Geoffrey W. Bromiley et al., 413–16. Grand Rapids: Eerdmans, 2001.

Johnson, Bill, and Jennifer Miskov. *Defining Moments: Randy Clark: The Grace of Impartation*. New Kensington, PA: Whitaker, 2019.

Johnson, K. D. *Speaking in Tongues: The History of Glossolalia from Early Christianity to the 21st Century*. Charlotte, NC: Johnson, 2018.

Johnston, Ian. *Aristophanes' Frogs: A Dual Language Edition*. Oxford, OH: Faenum, 2015.

Jones, Charles Edwin. "Holiness Movement." In *NIDPCM* 726–29.

Jones, John. *The Tyro's Greek and English Lexicon: Or a Compendium in English of the Celebrated Lexicons of Damm, Sturze, Schleusner, Schweighaeuser*. London: Longman, Hurst, Rees, Orme, and Green, 1825.

Jones, Kenneth C. *Index of Leading Catholic Indicators*. Fort Collins, CO: Roman Catholic Books, 2003.

Keener, Craig S. *Acts: An Exegetical Commentary: Introduction and 1:1–2:47*. Grand Rapids: Baker Academic, 2012.

Kelsey, Morton. *Tongue Speaking: The History and Meaning of Charismatic Experience*. New York: Crossroad, 1981.

Kildahl, John P. "Psychological Observations." In *The Charismatic Movement*, edited by Michael P. Hamilton, 124–42. Grand Rapids: Eerdmans, 1975.

———. *The Psychology of Speaking in Tongues*. New York: Harper and Row, 1972.

Knox, Ronald A. *Enthusiasm: A Chapter in the History of Religion*. London: Collins, 1987.

Koch, Roy S., and Martha Koch. *My Personal Pentecost*. Scottdale, PA: Herald 1977.

Lampe, G. H., ed. *A Patristic Greek Lexicon*. Oxford: Clarendon, 1978.

Lampman, Jane. "Targeting Cities with 'Spiritual Mapping,' Prayer." *Christian Science Monitor*, September 23, 1999. https://www.csmonitor.com/1999/0923/p15s1.html.

Lapide, Cornelius Cornellii a. *Commentaria in Scripturam Sacram*. 21 vols. Paris: Vives, 1866–74.

———. *The Great Commentary of Cornelius a Lapide: 1 Corinthians*. Translated and edited by W. F. Cobb. London: Hodges, 1890. http://www.catholicapologetics.info/scripture/newtestament/Lapide.htm.

Lawrence, B. F. "The Works of God." *Weekly Evangel*, June 3, 1916.

Lecky, William E. H. *History of the Rise and Influence of the Spirit of Rationalism in Europe*. New York: Appleton, 1919.

Leland, John. *A View of the Principal Deistical Writers*. 3 vols. 3rd ed. New York: Garland, 1978.

Liddell, Henry George, and Robert Scott. *A Greek-English Lexicon*. 8th ed. New York: Harper, 1968.

Lie, Geir. "The Origin of T. B. Barratt's Concept of 'Missionary Tongues.'" *CJPCR* 26 (2019). http://www.pctii.org/cyberj/cyberj26/lie1.html.

Life in the Spirit Team Manual: Catholic Edition. Ann Arbor, MI: Servant, 1979.

Lightfoot, John. *A Commentary on the New Testament from the Talmud and Hebraica*. Vol. 4, *Matthew–1 Corinthians*. Grand Rapids: Baker, 1979.

Lilly, W. S. "Mysticism." In *Religious Systems of the World: A Contribution to the Study of Comparative Religion: A Collection of Addresses*, edited by William Sheowring and Conrad W. Thies, 631–40. 5th ed. London: Sonnenschein, 1901.

Locke, John. *A Discourse on Miracles*. In *The Works of John Locke in Nine Volumes*, 8:256–65. 12th ed. London: C. and J. Rivington, 1824.

———. *An Essay on Toleration*. In *Locke: Political Essays*, edited by Mark Goldie, 134–59. Cambridge: Cambridge University Press, 1997.

Lucan. *The Civil War (Pharsalia)*. Translated by J. D. Duff. LCL 220. Cambridge, MA: Harvard University Press, 1928.

Lum, Kathryn Gin, and Paul Harvey. *The Oxford Handbook of Religion and Race in American History*. Oxford: Oxford University Press, 2018.

Luther, Martin. *Dr. Martin Luther's House-Postil; Or, Sermons on the Gospels for the Sundays and Principal Festivals of the Church-Year*. Columbus, OH: Shulze, 1884.

———. *Festival Sermons of Martin Luther*. Translated by Joel R. Baseley. Dearborn, MI: Mark V, 2005.

Maas, Anthony. "Versions of the Bible." https://www.newadvent.org/cathen /15367a.htm.

MacArthur, John F., Jr. *Charismatic Chaos*. Edited by Leonard G. Goss. Grand Rapids: Zondervan, 1992.

———. *Strange Fire: The Danger of Offending the Holy Spirit with Counterfeit Worship*. Nashville: Nelson, 2013.

Malony, H. Newton, and A. Adams Lovekin. *Glossolalia: Behavioral Science Perspectives*. New York: Oxford University Press, 1985.

Mansfield, Patti Gallagher. *As by a New Pentecost: The Dramatic Beginning of the Catholic Charismatic Renewal*. Golden Jubilee ed. Amor Deus, 2016.

Margerie, Bertrand de. "The Gifts of the Holy Spirit to the Church." *Social Justice Review*, February 1977.

Marin, Antonio Royo. *The Theology of Christian Perfection*. Translated by Jordan Aumann. Eugene, OR: Wipf & Stock, 2012.

Martin, Francis. *Baptism in the Holy Spirit: Reflections on a Contemporary Grace in the Light of Catholic Tradition*. Petersham, MA: St. Bede's, 1998.

Martin, Ralph. "A New Pentecost? Catholic Theology and 'Baptism in the Spirit.'" *Logos: A Journal of Catholic Thought and Culture* 14 (2011) 17–43.

Martindale, Trevor W. "Edward Irving's Incarnational Christology." PhD diss., University of Aberdeen, 2009.

Martínez, Florentino García, and Eibert J. C. Tigchelaar, eds. *The Dead Sea Scrolls: Study Edition*. 2 vols. Leiden: Brill, 1999.

May, L. Carlyle. "A Survey of Glossolalia and Related Phenomena in Non-Christian Religions." *American Anthropologist* 58 (1956) 75–96.

Mayer, Frederick Emanuel, and Arthur Carl Piepkorn. *The Religious Bodies of America.* 7th ed. St. Louis: Concordia, 1961.

McClintock, John, and James Strong. *Cyclopaedia of Biblical, Theological, and Ecclesiastical Literature.* 10 vols. New York: Harper, 1891.

McDermott, John M. "Do Charismatic Healings Promote the New Evangelization? Part I." *Antiphon* 24 (2020) 85–123.

———. "Do Charismatic Healings Promote the New Evangelization? Part II." *Antiphon* 24 (2020) 205–42.

McDermott, Kevin. "A. J. Christ Dowie and the Harmonial Philosophy: A Biography of John Alexander Dowie (1847–1907)." http://www.james-joyce-music.com/extras/dowie_bio.html.

McDonnell, Kilian, and George T. Montague. *Christian Initiation and Baptism in the Holy Spirit: Evidence from the First Eight Centuries.* 2nd ed. Collegeville, MN: Liturgical, 1994.

McGee, Gary B. "Initial Evidence." In *NIDPCM* 784–91.

———. "Shortcut to Language Preparation? Radical Evangelicals, Missions, and the Gift of Tongues." *International Bulletin of Missionary Research* (2001) 118–23.

McHale, Gary, and Michael Haykin. *The Toronto Blessing, a Renewal from God?* Historical Perspectives 1. Ontario: Canadian Christian, 1995.

Mercer, John S. "Speaking in an Unknown Tongue." *Weekly Evangel,* April 22, 1916.

Meyer, Heinrich August. *Critical and Exegetical Handbook to the Epistles to the Corinthians.* Edited by W. P. Dickson. Translated by D. D. Bannerman. Edinburgh: T. & T. Clark, 1887.

M. H. W. "The Gift of Tongues." *The Churchman,* July 6, 1878.

Middleton, Conyers. "An Essay on the Gift of Tongues." In *The Miscellaneous Works of the Late Reverend and Learned Conyers Middleton,* 2:79–103. London: R. Manby and H. S. Cox, 1752.

———. *A Free Inquiry into the Miraculous Powers Which Are Supposed to Have Subsisted in the Christian Church from the Earliest Ages through Several Successive Centuries.* London: R. Manby and H. S. Cox, 1749.

Milne, Garnet Howard. *The Westminster Confession of Faith and the Cessation of Special Revelation: The Majority Puritan Viewpoint on Whether Extra-Biblical Prophecy Is Still Possible.* Milton Keynes: Paternoster, 2007.

Moody Bible Institute. "Sign Gifts of the Holy Spirit." https://www.moodybible.org/beliefs/positional-statements/sign-gifts/.

Montague, George T. *The Holy Spirit: Growth of a Biblical Tradition.* Rev. ed. Eugene, OR: Wipf & Stock, 2006.

Montanari, Franco, et al., eds. *The Brill Dictionary of Ancient Greek.* Leiden: Brill, 2015.

Mormando, Franco. "Introduction: The Making of the Second Jesuit Saint: The Campaign for the Canonization of Francis Xavier, 1555–1622." In *Francis Xavier and the Jesuit Missions in the Far East,* edited by Franco Mormando and Jill G. Thomas, 9–22. Chestnut Hill, MA: Jesuit Institute of Boston College, 2006.

Naumann, Joseph F. "Make 'Missionary Disciples' of All of Us." *The Leaven,* January 5, 2018. http://theleaven.org/holy-spirit-make-missionary-disciples-of-all-of-us/.

Neander, August. *The History of the Christian Religion and Church during the First Three Centuries*. Translated by Henry John Rose. 2nd ed. New York: Stanford and Swords, 1848.

———. *Planting and Training of the Christian Church by the Apostles*. Translated by J. E. Ryland. 2 vols. 3rd ed. London: Bohn, 1851.

"New Kind of Missionaries." *Hawaiian Gazette*, May 31, 1901. https://chroniclingamerica. loc.gov/lccn/sn83025121/1901-05-31/ed-1/seq-8/.

Newman, Joe. *Race and the Assemblies of God Church*. Youngstown, NY: Cambria, 2007.

Newman, John Henry. *Essay on the Development of Christian Doctrine*. London: Longmans, Green, 1920.

———. *Loss and Gain*. Oxford: Oxford University Press, 1986.

Nickell, Joseph. *Looking for a Miracle*. Buffalo: Prometheus, 1993.

Noll, Mark A. *Princeton Theology, 1812–1921: Scripture, Science, and Theological Method from Archbald Alexander to Benjamin Breckinridge Warfield*. Grand Rapids: Baker Academic, 2001.

Oliphant, Margaret. *The Life of Edward Irving, Minister of the National Church*. 2 vols. London: Hurst and Blackett, 1862.

Oppenheimer, Mike. "Prophet: Paul Cain." http://www.letusreason.org/Latrain5.htm.

Origen of Alexandria. *Against Celsus*. In *ANF* 4:395–669.

Overton, John Henry. "Dodwell, William." In *Dictionary of National Biography, 1885–1900*, 15:182–83. https://en.wikisource.org/wiki/Dictionary_of_National_Biography,_1885-1900/Dodwell,_William.

Ozman, Agnes N. "Personal Testimony of Being the First Person to Receive the Holy Ghost at 'Stone's Folly' in Topeka, Kansas (January 1, 1901)." *Apostolic Faith*, April 1951. https://www.apostolicarchives.com/articles/article/8801925/173171.htm.

Pachomius. *Pachomian Koinonia*. Vol. 2, *Chronicles and Rules*. Translated by Arnand Veilleux. Cistercian Studies 46. Kalamazoo: Cistercian, 1981.

———. *Vitae Graecae*. Edited by Francisici Halkin. Subsidia Hagiographica 19. Brussels: Société des Bollandistes, 1932.

Parham, Charles F. *A Voice Crying in the Wilderness*. 2nd ed. Baxter Springs, KS: Apostolic Faith Bible College, 1910.

Parham, Sarah E. *The Life of Charles F. Parham: The Founder of the Apostolic Faith Movement*. New York: Garland, 1985.

Parke, Herbert William, and D. E. W. Wormell. *History of the Delphic Oracle*. 2 vols. Oxford: Blackwell, 1956.

Paul VI. *Lumen gentium*. https://www.vatican.va/archive/hist_councils/ii_vatican_council/documents/vat-ii_const_19641121_lumen-gentium_en.html.

"Pentecost Has Come." *AF*, September, 1906.

"Pentecost in Danville, VA." *AF*, October, 1906.

Perkins, William. *A Discourse of the Damned Art of Witchcraft*. Updated ed. Cambridge: Cantrel Legge, 1618.

Pew Research Center. "Global Christianity—A Report on the Size and Distribution of the World's Christian Population." *Pew Research Center*, December 19, 2011. https://www.pewresearch.org/religion/2011/12/19/global-christianity-exec/.

Pilkington, George. *The Unknown Tongues Discovered to Be English, Spanish, and Latin: and the Rev. Edward Irving Proved to be Erroneous in Attributing Their Utterance to the Influence of the Holy Spirit*. London: Field and Bull, 1831.

Plato. *Plato, Complete in Twelve Volumes*. Translated by Harold Fowler et al. London: Heinemann, 1955.

———. *Platonis Opera*. Edited by John Burnet. Oxford: Oxford University Press, 1903.

Pleins, J. David. *In Praise of Darwin: George Romanes and the Evolution of a Darwinian Believer*. New York: Bloomsbury, 2014.

Plumptre, E. H. "Tongues, Gift of." In *Dictionary of the Bible*, edited by William Smith, 3:1555–62. London: Murray, 1863.

Plutarch. *Moralia, Volume V*. Translated by Frank Cole Babbitt. LCL 306. Cambridge, MA: Harvard University Press, 1936.

Poloma, Margaret M. "Inspecting the Fruit of the 'Toronto Blessing': A Sociological Assessment." *Pneuma: The Journal for the Society for Pentecostal Studies* 20 (1998) 43–70.

———. "Toronto Blessing." In *NIDPCM* 1149–52.

———. "The 'Toronto Blessing': Charisma, Institutionalization, and Revival." *JSSR* 37 (1997) 257–71.

Powell, Baden. "On the Study on the Evidences of Christianity." In *Essays and Reviews*, 94–145. London: John W. Parker and Son, 1860.

"The Power of God Mightily Present." *AFP*, September, 1918.

"The Power of the Blood of Jesus Christ." *AFP*, September, 1911.

"The Promised Latter Rain." *AF*, July–August 1908.

Psellos, Michael. *Michaelis Pselli Theologica*. Edited by Paul Gautier. 2 vols. Bibliotheca Teubneriana. Leipzig: Teubner, 1989.

"Questions and Answers." *Bridegroom's Messenger*, November 2, 1908.

Randles, Bill. *Weighed and Found Wanting: Putting the Toronto Blessing in Context*. Abbots Cambs: St. Matthew, 1995.

Reid, Thomas M. *Carmelite Spirituality and the Catholic Charismatic Renewal*. Detroit: Little Flower, 2009. https://charismataexamined.wordpress.com/2018/01/29/carmelite-spirituality-and-the-catholic-charismatic-renewal/.

Reilly, Thomas à Kempis. "Gift of Tongues." http://www.newadvent.org/cathen/14776c.htm.

Reimers, Adrian J. "Charismatic Covenant Community: A Failed Promise." *CSJ* 3 (1986) 28–42. https://articles1.icsahome.com/articles/charismatic-covenant-community-reimers.

"Revelation: The 'Tongue.'" *Monthly Review* 1 (1832) 21–40.

Rienecker, Fritz, and Cleon Rogers Jr. *Linguistic Key to the New Testament*. Grand Rapids: Zondervan, 1982.

Ripperger, Chad. *Introduction to the Science of Mental Health*. Columbia, SC: Sensus Traditionis, 2013.

———. "Speaking in Tongues, Exorcist Fr. Chad Ripperger, Is it Real?" *YouTube*, April 2, 2018. https://www.youtube.com/watch?v=PcoUwaF6FJQ.

Riss, Richard M. "A History of the Worldwide Awakening of 1992–1995." http://www.deceptioninthechurch.com/history.html.

Robbins, R. G. *Pentecostalism in America*. Santa Barbara, CA: Praeger, 2010.

Robeck, Cecil M., Jr. *The Azusa Street Mission and Revival: The Birth of the Global Pentecostal Movement*. Nashville: Nelson, 2006.

———. "Tongues, Gift of." In *ISBE2* 4:871–74.

Rogers, Cleon L., Jr., and Cleon L. Rogers III. *The New Linguistic and Exegetical Key to the Greek New Testament*. Revised ed. Grand Rapids: Zondervan, 1998.

Rogers, Eddie T. *The Power of Impartation*. Greenwell Springs, LA: McDougal & Associates, 2006.

Rohde, Erwin. *Psyche: The Cult of Souls and the Belief in Immortality among the Greeks*. Translated by W. B. Hillis. London: Routledge & Kegan Paul, 2001.

———. *Seelenkult und Unsterblichkeitsglaube der Griechen*. 2nd ed. Tübingen: Mohr, 1898.

Ronson, Jon. "Catch Me If You Can." *The Guardian*, October 21, 2000. https://www.theguardian.com/theguardian/2000/oct/21/weekend7.weekend.

Roser, Max, and Esteban Ortiz-Ospina. "Literacy." *Our World in Data*, September 20, 2018. https://ourworldindata.org/literacy.

"Russians Hear in Their Own, Tongue." *AF*, September, 1906.

Ruthven, Jon Mark. *On the Cessation of the Charismata: The Protestant Polemic on Post-Biblical Miracles*. Tulsa, OK: Word and Spirit, 2011.

R. Y. "On the New Gift of Tongues, Miracles, Prophecyings—A Dialogue." *The Christian Examiner and Church of Ireland Magazine* 2 (1833) 398–419. https://www.google.com/books/edition/The_Christian_examiner_and_Church_of_Ire/LCwEAAAAQAAJ?hl=en&gbpv=1.

Salas, Elizabeth. "How to Personally Encounter God." *Mosaic Magazine*, April, 2017. https://mosaic.shms.edu/how-to-personally-encounter-god.

———. "Power Evangelization: A Catholic and Carmelite Perspective." *Homiletic and Pastoral Review*, May 31, 2019. https://www.hprweb.com/2019/05/power-evangelization/.

Salas, Victor. "Francisco Suárez and His Sources on the Gift of Tongues." *New Blackfriars* 100.1089 (2019) 554–76.

Samarin, William J. "Sociolinguistic vs. Neurophysiological Explanations for Glossolalia: Comment on Goodman's Paper." *JSSR* 11 (1972) 293–96.

———. *The Tongues of Men and Angels*. New York: Macmillan, 1972.

Sanidopoulos, John. "Contemporary Miracles of St. John Chrysostom." *Mystagogy*, January 27, 2010. https://www.johnsanidopoulos.com/2010/01/contemporary-miracles-of-st-john.html.

Sarles, Ken L. "An Appraisal of the Signs and Wonders Movement." *Bibliotheca Sacra* 145.577 (1988) 57–82.

Saunders, Ernest W. *Searching the Scriptures: A History of the Society of Biblical Literature*. Society of Biblical Literature Centennial Publications. Chico, CA: Scholars, 1982. https://www.sbl-site.org/assets/pdfs/SearchingScriptures.pdf.

Schaff, Philip. *History of the Apostolic Church with a General Introduction to Church History*. Translated by Edward D. Yeomans. New York: Scribner, 1859.

———. *History of the Christian Church*. 8 vols. Grand Rapids: Eerdmans, 1975.

Schrevel, Cornelis, et al., eds. *Lexicon Manuale: Græco Latinum et Latino Græcum*. American ed. Revised and enlarged by Petrus Steele. New York: Collins and Hannay, 1825.

Schulz, David. *Die Geistesgaben der ersten Christen: insbesondere die sogenannte Gage der Sprachen*. Sydney: Wentworth, 2018.

"Shaliach Tzibbur (צבור שליח)." https://hebrew4christians.com/Glossary/Hebrew_Glossary_-_Sh/hebrew_glossary_-_sh.html#loaded.

Shaw, Jane. *Miracles in Enlightenment England*. New Haven: Yale University Press, 2006.

Sherrill, John. *They Speak with Other Tongues*. Grand Rapids: Chosen, 2011.

Smith, J. L. "Glossolalia, Manual." In *NIDPCM* 677–78.

Smith, J. Payne, ed. *A Compendius Syriac Dictionary Founded upon the Thesaurus Syriacus of R. Payne Smith*. Oxford: Clarendon, 1979.

Smith, R. Payne, ed. *Thesaurus Syriacus*. 2 vols. Oxford: Clarendon, 1879–1901.

Smith, William, ed. *Dictionary of the Bible, Comprising Its Antiquities, Biography, Geography, and Natural History*. 3 vols. London: Murray, 1863.

Soal, Alexander D., and Henry Desmond. "The Reversal of Babel: Questioning the Early Church's Understanding of the Gift of the Holy Spirit in Acts as a Reversal of the Curse of Babel." *Verbum et Ecclesia* 39 (2018) 1–10.

Soergel, Philip M. *Protestant Imagination: The Evangelical Wonder Book in Reformation Germany*. Oxford: Oxford University Press, 2012.

Solignac, Aimé. "Jubilation." In *DDS* 8:1472–78.

Sophocles, E. A. *Greek Lexicon of the Roman and Byzantine Periods*. New York: Scribner, 1900.

Soulen, Richard N., and R. Kendall Soulen. *Handbook of Biblical Criticism*. 3rd ed. Louisville: Westminster John Knox, 2001.

Southey, Robert. *The Life of John Wesley: The Rise and Progress of Methodism*. 2 vols. New York: Harper,1847.

Spittler, R. P. "Glossolalia." In *NIDPCM* 670–76.

Steingard, Jerry, with John Arnott. *From Here to the Nations*. Toronto: Catch the Fire, 2014.

"Stone's Folly, Topeka, Kansas." https://www.kansasmemory.org/item/216413.

Storms, Sam. *The Language of Heaven: Crucial Questions about Speaking in Tongues*. Chicago: Charisma House, 2019.

Strabo. *Geography*. Translated by H. L. Jones. LCL 50. London: Heinemann, 1927.

———. *Strabonis Geographica*. Edited by Augustus Meineke. Vol. 2. Leipzig: Teubner, 1899.

Strong, Augustus. *Philosophy and Religion: A Series of Addresses, Essays, and Sermons Designed to Set Forth Great Truths in Popular Form*. New York: Armstrong and Son, 1888.

Suenens, Léon Joseph. *A Controversial Phenomenon: Resting in the Spirit*. Dublin: Veritas, 1987.

———. *Ecumenism and Renewal: Theological and Pastoral Orientations*. Ann Arbor, MI: Servant, 1978.

———. *Malines Documents*. https://www.nsc-chariscenter.org/malines-documents/.

———. *A New Pentecost?* New York: Seabury, 1974. http://webmedia.jcu.edu. s3.amazonaws.com/pdf/Suenens%20Writings/A%20New%20Pentecost%20 by%20Leon%20Joseph%20Suenens.pdf.

———. *Theological and Pastoral Orientations on the Catholic Charismatic Renewal*. Notre Dame: Word of Life, 1974.

Sullivan, Charles A. *Gift of Tongues Project*. https://charlesasullivan.com/gift-tongues-project/.

Sullivan, Francis A. *Charisms and Charismatic Renewal: A Biblical and Theological Study*. Ann Arbor, MI: Servant, 1982.

Synan, Vinson. *The Holiness-Pentecostal Tradition*. Grand Rapids: Eerdmans, 1997.

———. *Pentecostal Tradition: Charismatic Movements in the Twentieth Century*. Grand Rapids: Eerdmans, 1997.

Tertullian. *Against Marcion*. Translated by Peter Holmes. In *ANF* 3:269–475. https:// www.tertullian.org/anf/anf03/anf03-26.htm#TopOfPage.

"The Testament of Job." In *Apocrypha anecdota II*, edited by J. Armitage Robinson, translated by Montague Rhodes James, 103–37. Texts and Studies 5.1. Cambridge: Cambridge University Press, 1897. https://www.scribd.com/document/39565486/Robinson-Texts-and-studies-contributions-to-Biblical-and-Patristic-literature-Volume-5.

Thayer, Joseph Henry, trans. *A Greek-English Lexicon of the New Testament Bing Grimm's Wilke's Clavis Nove Testamenti*. New York: American Book, 1889.

Thelen, Mathias D. "John of the Cross and Exercising Charisms for Evangelization: A Response to Elizabeth Salas." *Homiletic and Pastoral Review*, November 25, 2019. https://www.hprweb.com/2019/11/john-of-the-cross-and-exercising-charisms-for-evangelization/.

Thigpen, T. Paul. "Catholic Charismatic Renewal." In *NIDPCM* 460–67.

Thistlethwaite, Lillian. "The Wonderful History of the Latter Rain." *Apostolic Faith*, April, 1951. https://www.apostolicarchives.com/articles/article/8801925/173173.htm.

Trevor-Roper, Hugh. *The Crisis of the Seventeenth Century: Religion, the Reformation, and Social Change*. New York: Harper & Row, 1967.

The Trial of the Rev. Edward Irving, A.M., before the Presbytery of Annan on Wednesday, March 13, 1833, also Edward Irving's Letter to His Congregation, Taken in Shorthand. London: Harding, 1833.

Tydings, Judith Church. "Shipwrecked in the Spirit." *CSJ* 16 (1999) 83–179. https://www.spiritualabuseresources.com/articles/shipwrecked-in-the-spirit.

Ussher, James. *A Body of Divinity or the Sum and Substance of Christian Religion*. London: J. Robinson, A. and J. Churchill, J. Taylor, and J. Wyatt, 1702.

"Utterance in Tongues." *Confidence*, January, 1913.

Vennari, John. *Close-ups of the Charismatic Movement*. Los Angeles: Tradition in Action, 2002.

Vincent, Marvin R. "Modern Miracles." *The Presbyterian Review* 15 (1883) 473–502.

Virgil. *Eclogues. Georgics. Aeneid: Books 1–6*. Translated by H. Rushton Fairclough. Revised by G. P. Goold. LCL 63. Cambridge, MA: Harvard University Press, 1916.

Voraigne, Jacobus de. *Medieval Sourcebook: The Golden Legend (Aurea Legenda)*. https://sourcebooks.fordham.edu/basis/goldenlegend/.

Wagner, C. Peter. *The Third Wave of the Holy Spirit: Encountering the Power of Signs and Wonders Today*. Ann Arbor, MI: Servant, 1988.

Wainwright, Arthur, ed. *A Paraphrase and Notes on the Epistles of St. Paul to the Galatians, 1 and 2 Corinthians, Romans, Ephesians, as Found in the Clarendon Edition of the Works of John Locke*. Oxford: Clarendon, 1987.

Warfield, B. B. *Counterfeit Miracles*. New York: Scribner's Sons, 1918.

"Weird Babel of Tongues." *Los Angeles Times*, April 18, 1906. https://www.newspapers.com/clip/22155395/1906_april_weird_babel_of_tongues/.

"Weird Travesty of Religion: 'Holy Brothers' Invade Islington." *New Zealand Herald*, May 23, 1908. https://paperspast.natlib.govt.nz/newspapers/new-zealand-herald/1908/5/23/12.

Wesley, John. *An Earnest Appeal to Men of Reason and Religion*. 6th ed. Bristol: Pine, 1765.

———. *Explanatory Notes upon the New Testament*. New York: Lane and Tippett, 1847.

———. "Letter to Dr. Conyers Middleton, January 4, 1749." http://wesley.nnu.edu/john-wesley/the-letters-of-john-wesley/wesleys-letters-1749/.

———. "The More Excellent Way, Sermon 89." https://www.whdl.org/sites/default/files/publications/EN_John_Wesley_089_more_excellent_way.htm.

"What Is the Toronto Blessing?" *Got Questions?*, January 4, 2022. https://www.gotquestions.org/Toronto-blessing.html.

Whitaker, William. *A Disputation on the Holy Scripture against the Papists, Especially Bellarmine and Stapleton.* Cambridge: Cambridge University Press, 1849. https://archive.org/details/adisputationonhoofitzgoog/mode/2up.

Whitehead, Alfred North. *Process and Reality.* Edited by David R. Griffin and Donald W. Sherburne. New York: Free, 1979.

Williams, George H., and Edith Waldvogel. "A History of Speaking in Tongues and Related Gifts." In *The Charismatic Movement*, edited by Michael P. Hamilton, 61–113. Grand Rapids: Eerdmans, 1975.

Wilkerson, David R. *The Cross and the Switchblade.* Grand Rapids: Chosen, 2018.

Wilks, Washington. *Edward Irving: An Ecclesiastical and Literary Biography.* London: Freeman, 1854.

Wimber, John. *Power Evangelism.* Toronto: Hodder & Stoughton, 1985.

Wittgenstein, Ludwig. *Philosophical Investigations.* Translated by G. E. M. Anscombe. Oxford: Blackwell, 1997.

Wordsworth, Christopher. *The New Testament of our Lord and Savior Jesus Christ in the Original Greek with Notes and Introductions. Part 2: The Acts of the Apostles.* London: Rivingtons, 1857.

"The Work in India." *AF*, June–September, 1907.

Yocum, Bruce. "Surviving a Tsunami." *YouTube*, August 3, 2015. https://www.youtube.com/watch?v=WlvwOBA98OI.

Zerwick, Max. *A Grammatical Analysis of the Greek New Testament.* Rome: Editrica Pontificio Instituto Biblico, 1988.

Scripture Index

Name Index

Subject Index

Made in United States
Troutdale, OR
12/22/2023

16341507R00146